WORK

AF396490

Documents of Contemporary Art

Co-published by Whitechapel Gallery
and The MIT Press

First published 2017
© 2017 Whitechapel Gallery Ventures Limited
All texts © the authors or the estates of the authors,
unless otherwise stated

All rights reserved. No part of this publication
may be reproduced, stored in a retrieval system
or transmitted in any form or by any means,
electronic, mechanical, photocopying or otherwise,
without the written permission of the publisher

ISBN 978-0-85488-255-7 (Whitechapel Gallery)
ISBN 978-0-262-53433-8 (The MIT Press)

A catalogue record for this book is available from
the British Library

Library of Congress Cataloging-in-Publication Data

Names: Sigler, Friederike, editor.
Title: Work / edited by Friederike Sigler.
Other titles: Work (M.I.T. Press)
Description: Cambridge, MA : The MIT Press, 2017. |
    Series: Whitechapel : documents of
    contemporary art | Includes bibliographical
    references and index.
Identifiers: LCCN 2017016171 | ISBN
    9780262534338 (pbk. : alk. paper)
Subjects: LCSH: Art--Economic aspects. | Work.
Classification: LCC N8600 .W67 2017 | DDC
    701/.03--dc23 LC record available at https://lccn.
    loc.gov/2017016171

Series Editor: Iwona Blazwick
Commissioning Editor: Ian Farr
Project Editor: Francesca Vinter
Design by SMITH
Allon Kaye, Justine Schuster
Printed and bound in China

Cover, Mierle Laderman Ukeles, *Hartford Wash.
Washing, Tracks, Maintenance (outside)* (1973)
(details). 12 black and white photographs, 2 text
panels, dimensions variable. Courtesy of the artist
and Ronald Feldman Fine Arts, New York.

Whitechapel Gallery Ventures Limited
77–82 Whitechapel High Street
London E1 7QX
whitechapelgallery.org
Distributed to the book trade (UK and Europe only)
by Central Books
centralbooks.com

The MIT Press
Cambridge, MA 02142
mitpress.mit.edu

Whitechapel Gallery   10 9 8 7 6 5 4 3 2 1
The MIT Press   10 9 8 7 6 5 4 3 2 1

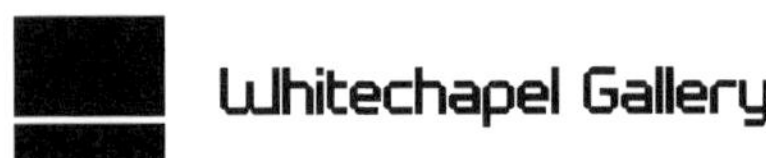
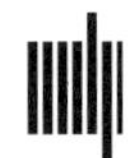

Francis Alÿs//Rasheed Araeen//Marwa Arsanios//
Jonathan Beller//Walter Benjamin//Franco 'Bifo'
Berardi//Claire Bishop//Luc Boltanski//Nicolas
Bourriaud//Julia Bryan-Wilson//Sabeth Buchmann//
Maria Chekhonadskih//Ève Chiapello//Chto Delat//
Alice Creischer//Clémentine Deliss//Jeremy Deller//
Nick Dyer-Witheford//Maria Eichhorn//Kodwo Eshun//
Harun Farocki//Silvia Federici//Fischli & Weiss//Mark
Fisher//Claire Fontaine//Andrea Fraser//Liam Gillick//
Melanie Gilligan//María Teresa Gramuglio//Isabelle
Graw//Gulf Labor Coalition//Haben und Brauchen//
Tehching Hsieh//The Invisible Committee//Marisa
Jahn//Caroline A. Jones//Lamia Joreige//
Anne Teresa de Keersmaeker//Mary Kelly//Jihoon
Kim//Kata Krasznahorkai//Petra Lange-Berndt//
Maurizio Lazzarato//Anthony W. Lee//Sarah Lehrer-
Graiwer//Isabelle Lindermann//Lucy R. Lippard//
Goshka Macuga//Paolo Magagnoli//Karl Marx//
Achille Mbembe//Adrian Melis//Jasmina Metwaly//
Gustav Metzger//Paweł Mościcki//Antonio Negri//
Ahmet Öğüt//Michelangelo Pistoletto//Precarias a la
Deriva//Jacques Rancière//Raqs Media Collective//
Gerald Raunig//Philip Rizk//Irit Rogoff//Nicolás Rosa//
Martha Rosler//Dietmar Rübel//Tino Sehgal//Santiago
Sierra//Robert Smithson//Nick Srnicek//Hito Steyerl//
Mladen Stilinović//Mierle Laderman Ukeles//Paolo
Virno//Joseph Vogl//W.A.G.E.//Anne Wagner//Hamza
Walker//John A. Walker//Peter Weiss//Alex Williams//
Siona Wilson//Giovanna Zapperi//Artur Żmijewski

Work

Whitechapel Gallery
London
The MIT Press
Cambridge, Massachusetts

Edited by Friederike Sigler

Documents of Contemporary Art

In recent decades artists have progressively expanded the boundaries of art as they have sought to engage with an increasingly pluralistic environment. Teaching, curating and understanding of art and visual culture are likewise no longer grounded in traditional aesthetics but centred on significant ideas, topics and themes ranging from the everyday to the uncanny, the psychoanalytical to the political.

The Documents of Contemporary Art series emerges from this context. Each volume focuses on a specific subject or body of writing that has been of key influence in contemporary art internationally. Edited and introduced by a scholar, artist, critic or curator, each of these source books provides access to a plurality of voices and perspectives defining a significant theme or tendency.

For over a century the Whitechapel Gallery has offered a public platform for art and ideas. In the same spirit, each guest editor represents a distinct yet diverse approach – rather than one institutional position or school of thought – and has conceived each volume to address not only a professional audience but all interested readers.

Series Editor: Iwona Blazwick; Commissioning Editor: Ian Farr; Project Editor: Francesca Vinter; Editorial Advisory Board: Roger Conover, Sean Cubitt, Neil Cummings, Sven Spieker, Gilane Tawadros, Sofia Victorino

ART also means WORK, more precisely STRIKE work

Hito Steyerl, 'Politics of Art: Contemporary Art and the Transition to Post-Democracy', 2011

Women were never invited to become a maintenance class, we were just told:
'You are like this. We know what you think. We know what you are.
You take care of us.'

Mierle Laderman Ukeles, In conversation with Tom Finkelpearl, 2000

Friederike Sigler
Introduction//All That Matters is Work

In one of the last rooms of the main pavilion at the 2015 Venice Biennale a large banner hanging from the ceiling, created by British artist Jeremy Deller, greeted visitors with the auspicious words, 'Hello, today you have day off'. If one had a good command of the English language, however, this immediately created a feeling of unease. The missing article 'a' lent the promise of time off a strangely threatening, if not imperative character, and managed to sum up the condition of today's working environment in just six words. The 'day off', once a longstanding workers' dream, has in the neoliberal service economy long since become a nightmare. This applies both to the so-called 'zero-hours workers',[1] who receive the banner's message as a text message when there is no work available and so will not get paid, and to other workers in the post-industrial economies. The new ideal workers do not aspire to a break from work but to even more work – preferably in addition to official working hours. Since the economic paradigm shift from the industrial sector to the service sector that has taken place since the 1970s mainly in Western industrialized countries, work is primarily about turning in the perfect performance. To do this requires the highest standard of communications skills, flexibility, autonomy and creativity and, alongside this, qualities that (and here many theorists agree) have suddenly catapulted the figure of the artist into debates about economic surplus-value production, and at the same time have chosen the artist to be the model of a new class of hyper-workers. As the creative subject par excellence, always alert and always creative, the artist is now considered the avant-garde of an entire society of workers – and even sometimes made responsible for the totalizing condition of work that has not only eliminated all the dividing lines between work and non-work, work and leisure, work and life, but at the same time allowed unemployment to become the major crisis of the twenty-first century.[2]

This alleged blurring of art and work has ignited controversial debates in the arts that have now made the theme of work – long treated as a nostalgic relic of the rebellious 1970s – one of the central questions in contemporary art. Through the economic valorization of artistic work, both artists and theorists find themselves being challenged to have to renegotiate what artistic work actually is. This is the starting point of this collection of texts and of this introduction. Building on the artistic and theoretical positions that follow, my proposition is that work in contemporary art is far more than what was once designated in relation to classic art as 'subject matter'. This intensified artistic engagement

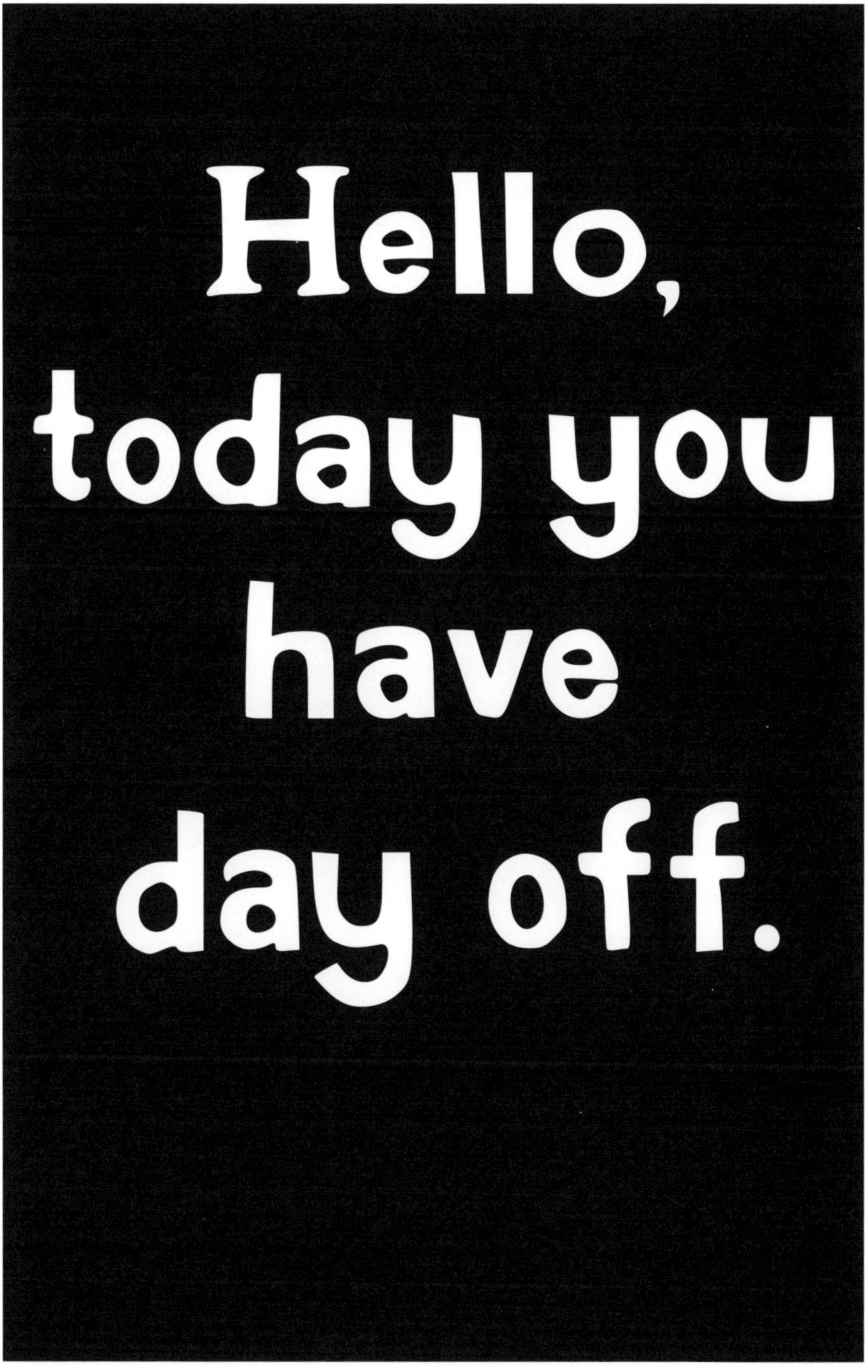

Hello, today you have day off.

Jeremy Deller, text from the work *Hello, today you have day off* (2013)
(wording of a text message sent to a zero hours worker, telling him his
labour was not required on that particular day)

with work, which began in the 1970s and is taken up again today, shows that work, precisely through its totalizing significance in the twentieth and twenty-first centuries, demands an overhaul of artistic strategies. Work is a means of economic production, a setting for social and political conflicts, a technique for constituting the subject, an expression of exploitative and precarious living conditions – and at the same time a category through which the artistic conditions of production can themselves be fundamentally contested. For example, the specificity of contemporary art lies precisely in its shift of focus from the creation of objects to the techniques and mechanisms of production – and thereby to work *within* art and *in the making of* art. During this period, therefore, work has not only been a subject of art but also simultaneously the object of artistic debate, artistic work *and* artistic process.

Despite work's integral, not to say fundamental, significance for art, and intensified interest over the last few years, the topic has hitherto been treated in a relatively marginal way, something this anthology aims to redress.[3] We begin with the debate surrounding artistic work, which has provided a major contribution to the revival of the topic of work in both art and the humanities. The economic and socio-political propositions that are raised here can be seen as the basis of the collection of texts that follows. The second part of this introduction looks at artistic practices whose own techniques and processes have focused on the topic of work since the 1970s. In the final section we look at contemporary crises of art and work, and proposals for overcoming them.

'Bakunin is back in town' or Myths of Work
For a long time 'working in art' was considered a kind of ontological paradox, as the heroes of art were above all those who did not work. Rather it was thought that they wandered about, observing, debating, thinking, drinking, sleeping (or staying up all night) and idling, until at a certain point in time and in some mysterious way, they transformed the sum total of their creative energies into works of art. What exactly happened, and what artists did in their studios, no one exactly knew, but people were agreed on one thing above all else – this was not work. Nevertheless, as the political theorist Hannah Arendt described it in *The Human Condition*, making art was part of the *vita activa*, and belonged to the 'three fundamental human activities'.[4] However, with the emergence of the industrial era, if not earlier, work began to be configured using parameters, most notably economic productivity, which distinguished it almost categorically from 'unproductive' art, thereby almost completely excluding the artist from economic theories of modernity, from Adam Smith to Karl Marx.[5] This dichotomy of art and work (and similarly of artists and workers) was also promoted by traditional historiography, which constantly reproduced the undisputed myth

of the creative artistic subject and located art outside capitalist value processes.[6]

According to the neo-Marxist arguments of the Italian post-operaists[7] and the monumental study by two French sociologists, Luc Boltanski and Ève Chiapello, of the 'New Spirit of Capitalism',[8] with the rise of the service society in the 1970s this system was seriously undermined. As a result of widespread de-industrialization, manufacturing in the West was to a great extent brought to a standstill, mechanized or outsourced, and economic surplus-value production was broadly overtaken by work in the service industries. And this new kind of work itself involves activities that 'are not normally recognized as "work" – in other words, the kinds of activities involved in defining and fixing cultural and artistic standards', according to the post-operaist thinker Maurizio Lazzarato.[9] In the case of 'immaterial work',[10] as the post-operaists call it, the 'creative industries' are becoming the leading industries of today; their workers combine intellectual capabilities, creativity and imagination, and thereby generate precisely those artistic qualities that are now no longer the preserve of the artist but are being elevated to the status of an imperative for an entire society of workers.[11] This is also Boltanski and Chiapello's proposition, with the exception that, after an extensive reading of managerial literature, they locate the origin of 'immaterial work' in the artistic practice of the 1960s. They assert that the new spirit of capitalism can be traced back to an artists' critique that emerged from the political and artistic avant-garde and was expressed, for example, in France's *Socialisme ou barbarie* movement and the Situationist International. Their critique, which was aimed at 'oppression in a capitalist world (the dominance of markets, discipline, the factory), homogenization in a mass society and the transformation of all things into commodities', and which at the same time demanded an 'ideal of individual autonomy and freedom' as well as 'uniqueness and authenticity',[12] was now 'endogenized' by capitalism. In other words, they maintained that the current form of capitalism had consumed the critique of its exploitative and alienating mechanisms and then regurgitated a resistant, artistic practice, which presented itself within this critique as alternative, non-exploitative and non-alienating work, in the form of a list of criteria for the ideal worker of today. Thus Boltanski and Chiapello claim that artistic work or – following the Situationist International's slogan 'Ne travaillez jamais' (Never work) – artistic *non-work*, hitherto broadly excluded from the paradigm of work because of its pursuit of freedom, autonomy and creativity, is now effectively the avant-garde of the new world of work.

The erstwhile dichotomy of art and work now seems shattered. However, the appeal to 'be creative' does not automatically help post-Fordist work become activity carried out in freedom. Even if it seems that the Russian revolutionary anarchist Bakunin 'is back in town' as the sociologist Ulrich Bröckling claims, and that he is now calling for 'a revolution in business [...] wearing a pinstripe suit, with a consultancy contract, Powerpoint presentation, and sometimes with smoke and mirrors',[13] the 'creative imperative' is certainly not to be confused with a call for 'factory sit-ins and collectivization'.[14] Rather, the demand for free and creative action is no more or less than 'a strategy for maintaining a hold on the markets'[15] and thus representative of the condition of the new kind of work (as referred to in Jeremy Deller's banner) as the 'antinomy of the modern age'.[16] The appropriation of artistic, that is autonomous and free kinds of behaviour has been an imperative in the post-Fordist world of work for a long time. It is a governmental technique of self-control,[17] which, as Michel Foucault described it, promises a better life and thereby engenders a new generation of precarious 'creatives' who, between short-term contracts and low pay, achieve burn-out instead of freedom.[18] For many, 'be creative' has long meant 'be precarious' in the creative industries, the rest of the working world and even in the case of those who are here treated as the better workers, namely artists themselves. These sudden opportunities for valorizing artists' work have aroused criticism from some who, like German artist and theorist Marion von Osten, talk about 'propagandist' abuse of the 'flexible biography and considerable self-motivation of cultural workers'. Indeed, von Osten claims, this creates the impression 'that the "resistant", "self-determined" subject, insisting upon their lifestyle, is surrounded by forces it has conjured up, without ever having haggled with these forces for the prize of "self-determination"'[19] – a situation for which there is no art-historical evidence. Rather, the theories have contributed to a re-examination of contemporary art along the lines of such analogies, thereby creating numerous standpoints that demand such self-determination – precisely through the definition of art as work. In the exemplary study *Art Workers: Radical Practice in the Vietnam War Era*, art historian Julia Bryan-Wilson has shown that since the late 1960s and 1970s, in the spirit of the anti-Vietnam and May '68 protests in the USA and other countries, artists began to identify themselves as 'art workers'.[20] They set up alliances modelled on trade unions, stood up collectively against the exploitative and alienating mechanisms of large art institutions, advocating better working conditions – and even, as in the case of Gustav Metzger and Robert Morris, called for strikes as well.[21] However this convergence of art with work is not to be confused with the all-consuming process of the 'new spirit of capitalism'. Rather, artists want to show that their activity is 'socialized', namely that it is an activity as much subject to economic, political and social conditions as is work in general. As in the Soviet avant-garde movements of the early twentieth century, where artists had long been acknowledged as workers, and as art critic Boris Arvatov put it in the 1920s in his proletarian aesthetic of production, the 'gulf between the arts as the monopolists of some sort of "beauty" and society as a whole should be destroyed'.[22] Instead of calling for a position beyond capitalist valorization mechanisms, the aim was rather to advocate better work, or a world beyond work, in the manner of revolutionary workers. Such aspirations have intensified again in recent years, with artists once more organizing in collectives or larger alliances, such as the Precarious Workers Brigade in England, the Revolutionary Artists' Union in Egypt, or Haben und Brauchen (To Have and to Need) in Germany, and publicly declaring their position. In their eponymous manifesto Haben und Brauchen have criticized the 'creative industries' for giving the impression that artists 'possess the same money-making opportunities as other "creative professionals"'. This is of course rarely the case; rather, 'the majority of culture makers' in Berlin live 'at or under the poverty line'.[23]

Bakunin is indeed back in town – however not only in a pinstripe suit but primarily in the shape of the artist tasked with deconstructing the myths of post-Fordist work, and thereby doing what the arts have always been good at doing, namely providing sharp, contemporary critique, or, in Bakunin's words, rendering 'priceless services to the revolutionary movement'.[24]

Working on Work: Artistic Practice and Artist Critique
The potential of artist critique can be seen not only in thinking about artistic work in the age of the service society, but also within artistic practice. 'By the second half of the twentieth century', according to curator Helen Molesworth, 'artists consistently explored the limits of what could be conceived of as art – and, by extension, what could be considered legitimate artistic labour'. And 'they did so in large measure by turning away from traditional media such as painting and sculpture, finding them too static, too commodifiable, too predictable and too emblematic of traditional elite culture'.[25] With the emergence of interest in artistic work, a new kind of practice appeared in opposition to object-based art, one that highlights the artistic process, the techniques, procedures and strategies of creation, and thus also work *within* and *in the making of* art. Despite the status of this role of work in contemporary art, research has until recently been sidelined in a similar way to the discourse surrounding materials and materiality. As art historian Petra Lange-Berndt points out, it becomes 'a political decision to focus on the materials of art: it means to consider the processes of making and their associated power relations, to consider the workers – whether they are in factories, studios or public spaces, whether they are known or anonymous – and their tools and spaces of production'.[26] Theories surrounding the analogy between artistic and 'immaterial' work have contributed to an increased emphasis on this change in artistic focus, thereby highlighting the techniques of production as a central moment in contemporary art. In this context in particular

the 'dematerialization'[27] of art, identified by Lucy Lippard and John Chandler as a benchmark of contemporary practice, has attracted renewed interest, as art historian Sabeth Buchmann notes: 'If the dematerialization discourse is interpreted in the sense of superimposing "material" with "symbolic" production, it can be seen as corresponding to a social process: "the reconfiguration of labour relations in the major industrial nations" that began in the early 1970s'.[28] Exhibitions such as 'Work Ethic' (curated by Helen Molesworth at the Baltimore Museum of Art and other venues in 2003) or 'Playtime' (co-curated by Susanne Ehrenfried and Matthias Mühling at the Lenbachhaus, Munich, in 2014) demonstrate that important aspects of conceptual art, performance, Happenings and Fluxus, as well as Minimalism and Land art have focused, in terms of experiments in de-skilling and post-studio practice, on the topic of work.[29] Artists such as John Baldessari are examined in terms of the division of labour, Allan Kaprow and his Fluxus colleagues in terms of the concepts of 'useless labour', and Yoko Ono and Valie Export in terms of their experiments in taking viewers out of their 'leisure' mode and inciting them to work.[30] Andy Warhol, whose Catholic work ethic made such an impression on Lou Reed and John Cale that they included his Sunday prayer mantra 'It's just work, all that matters is work' in a song, is now examined for his managerial qualities, both at the Factory and when he exchanges his 'proletarian costume'[31] (jeans and workshirt) for bespoke suits before going to the office. The same goes for contemporary manager-artists Olafur Eliasson and Takashi Murakami, whose own factories of ideas and art under their megalomaniac control have long since become part of their artistic practice.

But a focus on the potential of artistic practice does not remain at the level of affirmative take-over strategies, as seen in the artistic worlds created by the Eliassons and Murakamis who act like SME businesspeople, but emphasizes above all art's critical faculties as the central object of a dematerializing art. American artist Mierle Laderman Ukeles, who has been, as it were, rediscovered in this context, plays an important role here. In her *Manifesto for Maintenance Art* and her associated actions, Ukeles takes as her subject her socio-politically marginalized status as a woman artist *and* mother/housewife, seeing her artistic practice as analogous to domestic, reproductive activities that are connoted as female and thus excluded from the paradigm of work. In this case the activities of both 'House Work and Art Work',[32] are performative, affective and ephemeral – and are thus considered to be economically 'unproductive'. For her 'maintenance' actions, Ukeles brings these 'unproductive' activities into the space of art, gives them a physical presence, demonstrates the fundamental importance of this work (as she says in her manifesto, 'After the revolution, who's going to pick up the garbage on Monday morning?'), but also shows the physical strength needed to perform this labour, and at the same time highlights both the potentiality of these activities and the reasons for their marginalization. In other words, she works *within* her art *for* art, and in so doing reveals the negative aspects of a gendered world of work. Ukeles' position could not be more pertinent, with 'female activity', because of its reproductive character, indicating parallels with 'immaterial work'. Theoretically, Toni Negri and Michael Hardt have diagnosed a revalorization of the 'female' in post-Fordism and even discussed a 'feminization of work'[33] – a proposition categorically refuted by philosopher Silvia Federici.[34] In the service society housework and care work have achieved neither an adequate social nor economic status, indeed the care sector has for a long time been considered one of the most precarious areas of work today.[35]

Since the 1990s, work within art, which now ranges from the sex industry via management consultancy to founding a limited company, no longer amounts to the artist's work alone, as critic Claire Bishop describes.[36] Performative practices, she writes, reveal a trend for handing over work. An example of this is the practice of Spanish artist Santiago Sierra, who in his 'delegated performances'[37] has people from the precariat carry out badly paid and physically demanding pieces of work, thereby extending the debate about work to its global dimensions. The transformation into a service society has not reduced the proportion of material manufacturing, but has just largely outsourced it to so-called low-wage countries. Sierra's delegation of precarious work thus corresponds to the economic strategies of outsourcing, whereby in post- or neo-colonial style difficult and legally dubious work is often relocated to an ostensible 'nowhere'. Through the art institutions of the global financial centres, Sierra and other artists such as Steve McQueen and Mika Rottenberg bring the sweatshops back to the locations that promote themselves as puppet-masters of the capitalocene, global winners in the struggle for the best strategies of exploitation. Thus the understanding of the post-Fordist era as one of 'immaterialization' is brought into question, and this issue becomes the object of investigation of an artistic practice that now challenges its own tendency towards dematerialization.

From Precarious Labour to a World beyond Work
These various positions have demonstrated that three modes of work in art – the artist's activity; artistic process; and work as the object of artistic debate – cannot be understood separately from one another. Rather, hybridization, a term identified in connection with contemporary practices of art and work, is in operation here as well. Artistic engagement with work thus leads to a realization that work cannot simply be represented but necessarily presupposes thinking about and involving artistic strategy. In his homage to the first films in cinematic history, the artist Harun Farocki referred expressly to this problem when he

observed that work had been broadly excluded from cinema and that the camera only rolled when the workers leave the factory.[38] Critic Jonathan Beller comes to a similar conclusion when he writes of Mika Rottenberg's work that 'in a sense, [her] videos, which have been called surreal, are more realistic than most Realism'.[39] Likewise, according to art historian Dietmar Rübel, slapstick alone can provide the only credible images of work.[40] By contrast with the visual representations of Gustave Courbet, Rosa Bonheur, Ilya Repin and others in the late nineteenth and early twentieth centuries, today the representability of work is beset by crisis, while at the same time it demands entry to the arts through new strategies and processes. However, not just representation but work too is in crisis, and this is evidenced by the artistic practice of the immediate present, mainly through the fact that work is visualized primarily in its precarious aspects. An example of this, once again, is the 2015 Venice Biennale, which exhibited, alongside Jeremy Deller's paradoxes of work, Chinese women workers producing artificial pearls (Mika Rottenberg); the privatization of an Egyptian factory (Jasmina Metwaly and Philip Rizk); a critique of working conditions at the Guggenheim Museum in Abu Dhabi (Gulf Labor); the scope of finance capital (Isaac Julien); and the consequences of the financial crisis in Greece on retail and manual work (Maria Papadimitriou). In these examples, work is no longer romanticized as it was in the work of Vincent van Gogh or even Richard Serra. Rather, all these projects demonstrate that in critical debates about the present and, in the spirit of the Biennale's title, in negotiations about 'All the World's Futures', work must be of central importance. Work is revealed to be one of *the* fundamental techniques that creates precarious life, produces social exclusion and (re-)produces national and global power relations – and can even decide on matters of life and death, as the philosopher Achille Mbembe, for example, has claimed.[41] He says that history has shown convincingly that modern techniques of government also 'exercise control over mortality',[42] precisely because they are focused on the bio-political reproduction of life. In slavery, but also in the concentration camps of the National Socialists in Germany, Foucault's biopower has long since been transformed into 'necropolitics'[43] – a path that is also being taken today in contemporary labour camps, as shown in McQueen's films about coltan mining in the Congo and in Sierra's reconstructions of sweatshops. Artists and theorists seem to agree that precariousness is a permanent feature of the present. Indeed, post-Fordism has set up a 'generalized subjective insecurity' that is no longer limited to certain social milieus but now extends across the entire world of work.[44] In order to comprehend the implications of this, the philosopher Judith Butler has even suggested that a new 'bodily ontology' be written which posits the body as precarious per se, and which understands all techniques, including work, as 'maximizing' or 'minimizing' this precariousness.[45]

Seen in this light, work is one of today's essential techniques of power, which does not impose precariousness on the body merely retrospectively but controls whether and where it manifests itself – and where it does not.

The totalization of work and precarious living conditions encompasses not only the problem of determining exactly where and how work actually manifests itself, but also how to resist it. Rather, the 'immaterial world of work' emerges as an arsenal of power techniques through which resistance *to* work is immediately suppressed *by* work, and swallowed up as quickly as possible. This also involves rejecting the possibility of imagining alternative forms of work, or even a world beyond work.[46] At first glance, the dystopian worlds of work explored in contemporary art seem inclined towards a similar conclusion. But the diversity of positions that have addressed the shortcomings of the new world of work over the last few years makes it clear that because work is being intensively addressed in art, the possibility of post-work worlds has also become the subject of in-depth enquiry. This anthology is emblematic of the related intention finally to break down the oft-quoted mantra, 'There is No Alternative'. In the following seven sections, organized according to particularly crucial relationships between art and work, a wide variety of approaches are presented, ranging from queer undermining strategies, through occupied Egyptian factories, to museum workers' unexpected holidays. Reading these contributions may create the impression that, as the French writers' collective The Invisible Committee claimed for the 'insurrections' that spread 'from Greece to Chile', 'in the coming years … wherever the fires are lit' the artists too will be there.[47] In this sense the following texts and the diverse artistic practices on which they are based could be seen collectively as 'the beginning of a plan'.[48]

1   In Britain, 'zero-hours worker' is the term for workers with contracts that specify no minimum number of working hours.

2   See Timo Skrandies, 'der/die Arbeitslose' in *What can a Body do? Praktiken und Figurationen des Körpers in den Kulturwissenschaften*, ed. Netzwerk Körper (Frankfurt am Main: Campus, 2012) 19–25.

3   While art periodicals such as e-flux regularly discuss the latest theories, to date art histororical research and curatorial practice have reacted to the notion of 'work' only to a limited extent. The following publications and exhibitions are exceptions to this: Julia Bryan-Wilson, *Art Worker: Radical Practice in the Vietnam War Era* (Berkeley and Los Angeles: University of California Press, 2009); Siona Wilson, *Art Labour, Sex Politics: Feminist Effects in 1970s British Art and Performance* (Minneapolis: University of Minnesota Press, 2015); 'Work Ethic' (The Baltimore Museum of Art et. al., 2003); 'Playtime' (Lenbachhaus Munich, 2014); Manifesta 9 ('The Deep of the Modern' at the Waterschei former coal mine complex in the city of Genk, Belgium, 2012) and Manifesta 11 ('What People Do For Money: Some Joint Ventures', Zurich, 2016).

4   Hannah Arendt, *The Human Condition* (Chicago: University of Chicago Press, 1998)7. In the *vita activa* human activities were divided into labour, work and action. In the modern age, however, this system was discarded: labour, which had hitherto been restricted to activities focusing on human reproduction, was equated with work and subject to 'glorification' in the transformed work society. See Arendt, op. cit., 85.

5   Cf. Arendt, op. cit., 85.

6   Cf. Andreas Reckwitz, *The Invention of Creativity: On the Aestheticization of Society* (Cambridge: Polity Press, 2017).

7   For an overview of post-operaist approaches cf. *Radical Thought in Italy: A Potential Politics*, ed. Paolo Virno and Michael Hardt (Minneapolis: University of Minnesota Press, 2006).

8   Luc Boltanski and Ève Chiapello, *Le nouvel esprit du capitalisme* (Paris: Editions Gallimard, 1999); trans. Gregory Elliott, *The New Spirit of Capitalism* (London and New York: Verso, 2007);

9   See Maurizio Lazzarato in this volume, 30.

10   Ibid.

11   Ibid.

12   See Luc Boltanski and Ève Chiapello in this volume, 44.

13   Ulrich Bröckling, 'Bakunin Consulting, Inc: Anarchismus, Management und die Kunst, nicht regiert zu werden' in *Norm der Abweichung*, ed. Marion von Osten (Zurich: Springer, 2003) 19.

14   Ibid., 22.

15   Ibid.

16   Skrandies, op. cit., 22.

17   Cf. Michel Foucault, *Naissance de la Biopolitique: Cours au Collège de France, 1978–1979* (Paris: Éditions du Seuil / Gallimard, 2004); trans. Graham Burchell, *The Birth of Biopolitics: Lectures at the Collège de France, 1978-1979* (New York: Palgrave Macmillan, 2008).

18   Cf. Angela McRobbie, *Be Creative: Making a Living in the New Culture Industries* (Hoboken, New Jersey: John Wiley & Sons, 2015).

19   Marion von Osten, 'Kulturelle Arbeit im Post-Fordismus', *trend online zeitung*, no. 12 (2001), http://www.trend.infopartisan.net/trd1201/t321201.html

20   Cf. Julia Bryan-Wilson, op. cit.

21   Ibid., 83–126.

22   Boris Arvatov, 'Die Kunst im System der proletarischen Kultur', in *Kunst und Produktion* (Munich: Carl Hanser Verlag, 1972) 22.

23   See Haben und Brauchen in this volume, 181.

24   Mikhail Bakunin, 'Statism and Anarchy' (1873) in Sam Dolgoff, ed. and trans., *Bakunin on Anarchy. Selected Works by the Activist-Founder of World Anarchism* (New York and Toronto: Vintage Books, 1972) 333.

25   Helen Molesworth, 'Introduction' in Molesworth, ed., *Work Ethic* (University Park: Penn State University Press, 2003) 17.

26   Petra Lange-Berndt, 'Introduction: How to Be Complicit with Materials' in Lange-Berndt, ed., *Materiality* (London: Whitechapel Gallery/Cambridge, Massachusetts: The MIT Press, 2015) 12.

27   Lucy R. Lippard and John Chandler, 'The Dematerialization of Art', *Artforum International* (February 1968) 31–6.

28   See Sabeth Buchmann in this volume, 59.

29   Cf. Helen Molesworth, *Work Ethic*, op. cit.

30   Cf. Helen Molesworth, 'Work Ethic' in ibid., 25–51.

31   Caroline A. Jones, *Machine in the Studio: Constructing the Postwar American Artist* (Chicago: University of Chicago Press, 1996) 199.

32   See Helen Molesworth, 'House Work and Art Work', *October*, no. 92 (Spring 2000) 71–97.

33   Antonio Negri and Michael Hardt, *Commonwealth* (Cambridge, Massachusetts: Harvard University Press, 2009) 133.

34   See Silvia Federici in this volume, 186.

35   See ibid., and also Luis L.M. Aguiar and Andrew Herod, eds., *The Dirty Work of Neoliberalism: Cleaners in the Global Economy* (Oxford: Blackwell Publishing, 2006).

36   See Claire Bishop in this volume, 99.

37   See ibid..

38   See Harun Farocki in this volume, 148.

39   See Jonathan Beller in this volume, 40.

40   See Dietmar Rübel in this volume, 161.

41   See Achille Mbembe in this volume, 192.

42   See ibid.

43   See ibid.

44   Cf. Pierre Bourdieu, 'Job Insecurity is Everywhere Now' in *Acts of Resistance: Against the New Myths of our Time* (Cambridge: Polity Press, 1998) 83.

45   Judith Butler, *Frames of War: When Is Life Grievable?* (London and New York: Verso, 2009) 2–3.

46   Cf. Tiqqun, *Theory of Bloom* (Berkeley: LBC Books, 2012).

47   The Invisible Committee in this volume, 94.

48   Ibid.

Translated by Philippa Hurd.

THE ARTISAN SEEMINGLY TRANSACTS HERSELF OUT OF HISTORY, MAKING WAY FOR THE DRONE AND THE GENIUS, FOR THE POLARITIES OF DRUDGERY AND CREATIVITY, WORK AND ART

Raqs Media Collective, 'X Notes on Practice: Stubborn Structures and Insistent Seepage in a Networked World', 2004

ART WORKERS AND THE NEW ECONOMY

Raqs Media Collective
X Notes on Practice: Stubborn Structures and Insistent Seepage in a Networked World//2004

I. The Figure of the Artisan

The artisan stands at the outer threshold of early modernity, fashioning a new age, ushering in a new spirit with movable type, plumb line, chisel, paper, new inks, dyes and lenses, and a sensibility that has room for curiosity, exploration, cooperation, elegance, economy, utility and a respect for the labour of the hand, the eye and the mind. The artisan is the typesetter, seamstress, block-maker, carpenter, weaver, computer, oculist, scribe, baker, dyer, pharmacist, mason, midwife, mechanic and cook – the ancestor of every modern trade. […]

The figure of the artisan anticipates both the worker and the artist, in that it lays the foundations of the transformation of occupations (things that occupy us) into professions (institutionalized, structural locations within an economy). It mediates the transfiguration of people into skills, of lives into working lives, into variable capital. The artisan is the vehicle that carried us all into the contemporary world. She is the patient midwife of our notion of an autonomous creative and reflective self, waiting out the still births, nursing the prematurely born, weighing the infant and cutting the cords that tie it to an older patrimony. The artisan makes us who we are.

Yet the artisan has neither the anonymity of the worker drone, not the hyperindividuated solipsism of the artist genius. […] She belongs neither in the factory, nor in the salon, but functions best in the atelier, the workshop and the street, with apprentices and other artisans, making and trading things and knowledge. The artisan fashions neither the mass-produced inventories of warehouses, nor the precious, unique objects that must only be seen in galleries, museums and auction houses. The objects and services that pass through her hands into the world are neither ubiquitous nor rare, nor do they seek value in ubiquity or rarity. They trade on the basis of their usage, within densely networked communities that the artisan is party to, not on the impetus of rival global speculations based on the volumes and volatility of stocks, or the price of a signature. As warehouses and auction houses proliferate, squeezing out the atelier and the workshop, the artisan loses her way. At the margins of an early industrial capitalism, the artisan seemingly transacts herself out of history, making way for the drone and the genius, for the polarities of drudgery and creativity, work and art. […]

III. The Call Centre Worker and Her World

A call centre worker in the suburb of Delhi, the city where we live, performs a Californian accent as she pursues a loan defaulter in a poor Los Angeles neighbourhood on the telephone. She threatens and cajoles him. She scares him, gets underneath his skin, because she is scared that he won't agree to pay, and that this will translate as a cut in her salary. Latitudes away from him, she has a window open on her computer telling her about the weather in his backyard, his credit history, his employment record, his prison record. Her skin is darker than his, but her voice is trained to be whiter on the phone. Her night is his day. She is a remote agent with a talent for impersonation in the IT enabled industry in India. She never gets paid extra for the long hours she puts in. He was laid off a few months ago, and hasn't been able to sort himself out. Which is why she is calling him for the company she works for. He lives in a third world neighbourhood in a first world city, she works in a free trade zone in a third world country. Neither knows the other as anything other than 'case' and 'agent'. The conversation between them is a denial of their realities and an assertion of many identities, each with their truths, all at once. Central to this kind of work is a process of imagining, understanding and invoking a world, mimesis, projection and verisimilitude as well as the skilful deployment of a combination of reality and representation. Elsewhere, we have written of the critical necessity of this artifice to work (in terms of creating an impression of proximity that elides the actuality of distance) in order for a networked global capitalism to sustain itself on an everyday basis, but here, what we would like to emphasize is the crucial role that a certain amount of 'imaginative' skill, and a combination of knowledge, command over language, articulateness, technological dexterity and performativity plays in making this form of labour productive and efficient on a global scale. [...]

Raqs Media Collective, extracts from 'X Notes on Practice: Stubborn Structures and Insistent Seepage in a Networked World' (2004), in *Data Browser 02*, ed. Geoff Cox and Joasia Krysa (New York: Autonomedia, 2005) 213–31.

Maurizio Lazzarato
Immaterial Labour//1996

A significant amount of empirical research has been conducted concerning the new forms of the organization of work. This, combined with a corresponding wealth of theoretical reflection, has made possible the identification of a new conception of what work is nowadays and what new power relations it implies.

An initial synthesis of these results – framed in terms of an attempt to define the technical and subjective-political composition of the working class – can be expressed in the concept of *immaterial labour*, which is defined as the labour that produces the informational and cultural content of the commodity. The concept of immaterial labour refers to *two different aspects* of labour. On the one hand, as regards the 'informational content' of the commodity, it refers directly to the changes taking place in workers' labour processes in big companies in the industrial and tertiary sectors, where the skills involved in direct labour are increasingly skills involving cybernetics and computer control (and horizontal and vertical communication). On the other hand, as regards the activity that produces the 'cultural content' of the commodity, immaterial labour involves a series of activities that are not normally recognized as 'work' – in other words, the kinds of activities involved in defining and fixing cultural and artistic standards, fashions, tastes, consumer norms, and more strategically, public opinion. Once the privilegeged domain of the bourgeoisie and its children, these activities have since the end of the 1970s become the domain of what we have come to define as 'mass intellectuality'. [...]

The 'great transformation' that began at the start of the 1970s has changed the very terms in which the question is posed. Manual labour is increasingly coming to involve procedures that could be defined as 'intellectual', and the new communications technologies increasingly require subjectivities that are rich in knowledge. It is not simply that intellectual labour has become subjectecl to the norms of capitalist production. What has happened is that a new 'mass intellectuality' has come into being, created out of a combination of the demands of capitalist production and the forms of 'self-valorization' that the struggle against work has produced. The old dichotomy between 'mental and manual labour', or between 'material labour and immaterial labour', risks failing to grasp the new nature of productive activity, which takes this separation on board and transforms it. The split between conception and execution, between labour and creativity, between author and audience, is simultaneously transcended within the 'labour process' and reimposed as political command within the 'process of valorization'.

The Restructured Worker

Twenty years of restructuring of the big factories has led to a curious paradox. [...] In today's large restructured company, a worker's work increasingly involves, at various levels, an ability to choose among different alternatives and thus a degree of responsibility regarding decision making. [...] What modern management techniques are looking for is for 'the worker's soul to become part of the factory'. The worker's personality and subjectivity have to be made susceptible to organization and command. It is around immateriality that the quality and quantity of labour are organized. This transformation of working-class labour into a labour of control, of handling information, into a decision-making capacity that involves the investment of subjectivity, affects workers in varying ways according to their positions within the factory hierarchy, but it is nevertheless present as an irreversible process. [...] Workers are expected to become 'active subjects' in the coordination of the various functions of production, instead of being subjected to it as simple command. We arrive at a point where a collective learning process becomes the heart of productivity, because it is no longer a matter of finding different ways of composing or organizing already existing job functions, but of looking for new ones. [...]

Participative management is a technology of power, a technology for creating and controlling the 'subjective processes'. As it is no longer possible to confine subjectivity merely to tasks of execution, it becomes necessary for the subject's competence in the areas of management, communication and creativity to be made compatible with the conditions of 'production for production's sake'. Thus the slogan 'become subjects', far from eliminating the antagonism between hierarchy and cooperation, between autonomy and command, actually re-poses the antagonism at a higher level, because it both mobilizes and clashes with the very personality of the individual worker. First and foremost, we have here a discourse that is authoritarian: one has to express oneself, one has to speak, communicate, cooperate, and so forth. The 'tone' is that of the people who were in executive command under Taylorization; all that has changed is the content. Second, if it is no longer possible to lay down and specify jobs and responsibilities rigidly [but instead] jobs now require cooperation and collective coordination, then the subjects of that production must be capable of communication – they must be active participants within a work team. The communicational relationship (both vertically and horizontally) is thus completely predetermined in both form and content; it is subordinated to the 'circulation of information' and is not expected to be anything other. The subject becomes a simple relayer of codification and decodification, whose transmitted messages must be 'clear and free of ambiguity', within a communications context that has been completely normalized by management. [...]

The management mandate to 'become subjects of communication' threatens to be even more totalitarian than the earlier rigid division between mental and manual labour (ideas and execution), because capitalism seeks to involve even the worker's personality and subjectivity within the production of value. [...]

Maurizio Lazzarato, extracts from 'Immaterial Labour'', in *Radical Thought in Italy: A Potential Politics*, ed. Michael Hardt and Paolo Virno (Minneapolis: University of Minnesota Press, 1996) 132–5.

Isabelle Graw
When Life Goes to Work: Andy Warhol//2010

[W]hy does Andy Warhol's production still seem so topical, so up to date? What is it that allows for this particular past to reach into our present with such insistence? I will begin with the premise that the border between his 'work' and what could be called his public display of an 'attitude towards life' is fundamentally unstable and blurred. [...]

Let me give you an example. According to eyewitness Bob Colacello, Warhol could not relax and hated vacations.[1] Even having fun meant working, since he used every social occasion (such as parties) in order to 'get more portraits' or 'more ideas' or to 'sell more ads for *Interview*'. [...] This anecdote also sheds light on a pose that Warhol actually did cultivate, one in which *life becomes work*. His diaries not only record all these networking activities, they present going out as a way to meet rich people who would eventually – when they had enough to drink – buy his art.[2] What was formerly called 'fun' or 'leisure time' is quite explicitly represented as work. Even intimate relationships sooner or later turned into working relationships, as Billy Name recalled.[3]

This instrumentalization of formerly private activities and friendships resonates with how the Italian philosopher Paolo Virno has defined our 'post-Fordist condition', in which 'life' and 'work' become indistinguishable.[4] But Warhol's merging of the professional and private spheres is also in line with how all 'legendary' artists have been depicted at least since Giorgio Vasari's famous lives of Renaissance artists. They are represented as rather exceptional beings – celebrities *avant la lettre*, if you will – who are supposed to have dedicated their entire lives to their work.[5] There is nothing 'new' about this condition, and I am far from claiming a radical break. What I would argue, though, is that this condition has intensified and expanded its reach since the 1960s due to the successful implantation of a media culture busily producing affects by focusing on people's lives. [...]

[One of the conditions of neoliberalism is] that the market reaches into areas that were formerly considered 'private' and sheltered from its evaluative logic, such as the body, health, social relationships, one's looks, one's friendships, etc. These areas are now exposed to the constant pressure of economic optimization: we are interpellated to make the best of ourselves [...]. Warhol's diary is a case in point, demonstrating how these normative ideals keep us in check and exert a strong impact on our subjectivities. Nothing escaped his scrutinizing and classifying gaze – whether someone had gained weight, had more wrinkles, or was wearing a Halston dress on two occasions. How people looked was measured against the beauty standards set by the fashion world, standards whose enforcement has only become more emphatic since Warhol's days. But it is crucial to note that Warhol did not only submit his social environment to these standards, he also analysed their appeal in his work. An obvious example would be *Before and After* (1960) – a work that is based on a low-tech advertisement propagating the obvious virtues of a nose job. The work establishes a visible distance from these norms of beauty, if only by virtue of the way the image is cropped and the presence of Ben-Day dots. But the image also captures the hopes for personal improvement bound up in such an advertisement. Warhol himself desperately tried to keep up with these norms, for instance by undergoing a nose operation, logging regular visits to his dermatologist, and working out with his fitness trainer in the 1980s. [His] diaries are a testimony to how this internalization works, for instance when he explained his 'early appointment with Dr Li' (his dermatologist) as follows: 'This is all to make myself beautiful for business.'[6] What is openly acknowledged (and subscribed to, albeit in a slightly resigned manner) is that the importance of one's looks only increases in a labour market that wants all of you. [...]

Warhol's work certainly communicates with the laws of 'celebrity culture', but it also deviates from and even conflicts with them. There are two main ideological functions operating in 'celebrity culture'. It individualizes and promotes the neoliberal belief that you can make it if you work really hard on yourself. Through arbitrary selection and brutal exclusion, it makes people resigned to the idea that only a few will hit the jackpot and if they fail, it will be their own responsibility (and not what is, in reality, a structural inevitability).

I believe that Warhol's commissioned portraits essentially contradict these ideological messages. Celebrity status is *not* presented as a place you either deserve or were lucky enough to get. It is presented as something money can buy. You do not have to work hard on yourself, let alone on your looks – Warhol does it for you. [...]

While his early portraits certainly testify to a certain fixation on mainstream stars (such as Marilyn Monroe, Liz Taylor or Elvis) we should never forget that Warhol was soon to produce his own underground 'superstars' (a term invented by Jack Smith) – even organizing his own casting with the *Screen Tests*, which established new criteria. By providing a 'litmus test of the subject's response to an unblinking camera',[7] the *Screen Tests* constituted an enquiry into his or her celebrity potential. Warhol's legendary 'superstars', such as Ingrid Superstar, Viva, Baby Jane Holzer, International Velvet and Edie Sedgwick, all had celebrity potential but also deviated from the image of a typical mainstream star. […] Many of Warhol's superstars were drag queens, which similarly radically challenged Hollywood's heterosexist norms and assumptions.

Consider his *Philosophy*, which could be described as a kind of *dictionnaire des idées reçues* of 'celebrity culture' – full of gossip, self-help advice, and commonplaces. It is here, for instance, that an awareness of the dangers of overexposure is expressed. Like a true theorist of celebrity culture, Warhol noticed that too much media presence can cause harm, 'because … they use you up and it's scary'.[8] The dangers resulting from the production of one's self as a public appearance are subject to ongoing reflection, giving rise to a piece of advice that is my favourite line from Warhol's *Philosophy*: 'You should always have a product that's not you.'[9] What is acknowledged here is that the 'person' and the 'product' should not collapse into one another, and this precisely because they are so interconnected. […]

Warhol's work is a vivid demonstration of how product and person reach into one another, especially when circulating in the neoliberal and biopolitical context of celebrity culture, while potentially also leading separate existences. Despite his willingness to surrender to these conditions, Warhol did not allow his work to be governed by them.

1   See Bob Colacello, *Holy Terror: Andy Warhol Close Up* (New York: Cooper Square Press, 1990) 167.

2   See Pat Hackett, ed., *The Andy Warhol Diaries* (New York: Grand Central Publishing, 1989) 646.

3   See Steven Watson, *Factory Made: Warhol and the Sixties* (New York: Pantheon, 1990) 128.

4   See Paolo Virno, *A Grammar of the Multitude* (New York: Semiotext[e], 2004).

5   See Giorgio Vasari, *Lives of the Most Eminent Painters, Sculptors and Architects* (1550); trans. Gaston du C. de Vere (New York: General Books L.L.C., 1979).

6   [footnote 18 in source] Pat Hackett, ed., *The Andy Warhol Diaries*, op. cit., 560.

7   [footnote 37 in source] Steven Watson, *Factory Made*, op. cit., 131.

8   [38] Pat Hackett, ed., *The Andy Warhol Diaries*, op. cit., 272.

9   [39] Andy Warhol, *The Philosophy of Andy Warhol* (San Diego: Harvest Books, 1975) 86.

Isabelle Graw, extracts from 'When Life Goes to Work: Andy Warhol', *October*, no. 132 (Spring 2010) 99–100, 103–4, 110–11, 113.

Julia Bryan-Wilson
Dirty Commerce: Art Work and Sex Work since the 1970s//2012

In 1974, artist Carlos Ginzburg wandered around the port of Antwerp, Belgium, looking for a prostitute. He wanted to hire a woman for the afternoon – not for a sexual encounter, but as a prop for a performance. The artist negotiated with a local pimp who, when he learned that Ginzburg was from Argentina, offered up a recent transplant from Buenos Aires. The woman was paid somewhat less than her usual fee for an afternoon's work, work that consisted of sitting in a gallery holding a sign emblazoned with a quote from Charles Baudelaire: 'Qu'est ce l'Art? Prostitution ...' [...]

In Ginzburg's 1974 performance, sex acts performed for money are associated with artistic exchange. Note that the prostitute is gendered female as a default, while the client is assumed to be male, reflecting the pervasive heterosexualization of scenes of prostitution within the cultural imagination regardless of the self-identified sexual preference of the woman. [I]n its simplest gloss, *Latin American Prostitute* crystallizes how the long-held associations between the circulation of art, artistic personalities and commerce are persistently gendered, as well as consistently yoked to the idea of prostitution, with women peddling and men purchasing. It is worth asking what might be at stake for feminism in this formulation, especially as contemporary artists continue to mine the conjunction between selling sex and trafficking in art. In what follows, I look at artistic engagements with prostitution in a range of critical and artistic contexts since the 1970s to consider how they might be seen as a response to anxieties about gender, labour and artistic value. [...] I assert that the ongoing connections between art and prostitution, when understood as practices that visibly register shifts in labour, help us rethink the complex affective efforts involved in producing critical feminist work within a late capitalist market economy. [...]

Ginzburg's photograph of a light-haired young woman holding up a sign [the documentation of *Latin American Prostitute*] recalls another that also dates from the 1970s. In this image, a woman is seated outside with a sheaf of leaflets, her bags at her feet and a flower in one hand. Her hand-lettered protest poster reads: 'Art Workers Won't Kiss Ass'. Though the woman depicted in this image has not been identified, the approximate time and place of its taking are clear; it is New York sometime around 1970. Against Ginzburg's staged performance in which a woman serves as a living illustration for another's scripted question, here a woman holds a declarative statement presumably of her own making, one that places obsequiousness on a continuum with sexual licentiousness. The statement asserts that she will not bend to the viewer's (or the institution's, or the art world's) bidding, and she will not shape her will to any external desire; in this, she refuses Ginzburg's parallel between art and prostitution. While Ginzburg's performance piece and the 'art worker' photo differ in tone and kind, the two images are instructive to place in relation to each other, for both underscore another crucial factor in the conjunction between prostitution and art-making in the 1970s: the explicit reframing of these activities as labour.

It is important to note, then, that the late 1960s and early 1970s were marked by an international mobilization of artists seeking to validate their efforts *as work*; that is, as effortful, productive, and managed by economic constraints imposed by subjugating ruling-class interests. In countries such as England and Argentina, artists asserted that their practices were governed by the power differentials (and exploitation) inherent to the rules of wage labour within the capitalist West.[1] This redefinition of art as work was made most clear in the US context with the 1969 formation of the Art Workers' Coalition, a group that organized in New York to agitate for artists' rights and to protest against the Vietnam War, among other leftist concerns. Its members were artists and critics, including many conceptual artists who did not make traditionally salable objects, aiming to publicly redefine themselves as workers – even, some would insist, proletarians.[2] [...]

The Art Workers' Coalition managed in its brief existence (it faded in 1971) to bring into focus the art worker as an identity to rally around within the art industry. The term gave collective voice to artists seeking to validate their forms of production within a shifting economy and lent momentum to their organizational efforts within the era's social upheavals. A shared sense of financial uncertainty, and an urge to assert that what they did was politically relevant, motivated many artists to redefine their often non-remunerative work as a form of honest labour.

Emerging from a similar impetus to organize a previously under-recognized sector of labour and agitate for collective recognition as workers, Margo St. James, a feminist sex activist based in San Francisco, formed COYOTE (Call Off Your Old Tired Ethics) in 1973. This rights group aimed at decriminalizing and destigmatizing prostitution. According to one historian, 'Since the 1970s prostitutes have been organizing in the United States, Britain and Australia [...]. In short, prostitutes are endeavouring to be acknowledged as workers in an occupation that lacks trade union safeguards or protection.'[3] Throughout the 1970s, trade unions for sex workers began to take hold throughout Europe and the struggles of prostitutes became part of a wider feminist agenda regarding unpaid labour. Drafting off this momentum, in 1978 activist Carole Leigh popularized the term 'sex worker' to describe the full range of those who engaged in sex (broadly conceived) for money: burlesque performers, escorts, exotic dancers, and so on. [...]

The emergence of these two identifications in this decade is indicative of shifting values about what constitutes 'work'. [...] Elizabeth Bernstein, in her sociological study of sexual commerce *Temporarily Yours*, postulates that the 1970s economic restructuring also signalled a larger shift in attitudes towards intimacy, given the ever-eroding lines between public and private, home and workplace. Bernstein discusses how the political frame of sex work as work that developed in the 1970s resulted in sex workers' placing their labour within 'a conceptual template which explicitly situates prostitution in terms of the likely array of other available working-class jobs'.[4] What is more, prostitution began to overlap with the kind of service work historically understood to be part of affective labour, in particular, as it was increasingly geared towards providing intimacy. Affective labour such as kin work, care and nursing is not new, of course, and has long been feminized, but as Michael Hardt has noted, since the early 1970s it has 'become generalized through wider sectors of the economy'.[5] Within this model, clients are offering not just rote sexual release but a complete 'girlfriend experience' that includes the production of a perceived genuine affective connection. This is what has been referred to as the 'emotional labour' of prostitution.[6]

The prostitute, like the performance artist who generates no salable object, is a figure of ambiguous exchange who encapsulates the instability of the commodity object and the uncertainty of forms of worthwhile labour, ones that have been converted (or evaporated) into pure exchange value. One might speculate that in the 1970s, women artists – particularly those who were making artwork with their bodies – identified with prostitutes because performance and sex work are analogously affective and precarious practices. This dynamic has the potential to cross the gender divide, for though artists conventionally make highly valued objects, many art workers (male and female alike) of the early 1970s vigilantly attempted to decommodify their work via conceptual and performance art. Along with the production of affect and the commercialization of intimacy, then, art workers and sex workers of the 1970s had in common their lack of reproductive labour.[7] In other words, in this decade traditional artistic objects were undergoing a transition to dematerialized practices, changing the very nature of the salable commodity; inevitably, this mutating of commodities – their reorganization or dissolution – had gendered consequences. [...]

The Baudelaire quotation 'What is art? Prostitution' is certainly the pithiest, and arguably the most famous, assertion of a sexualized convergence between art and the market. [...] Literary critics such as Leo Bersani and Maria Scott have offered readings of this enigmatic text. [...] Baudelaire equates prostitution with the infinite capacity for destabilizing empathic pleasure across or beyond gender, a far cry from the Marxist and feminist questions regarding dispossession, waged work or feminized labour. As Scott comments, across Baudelaire's oeuvre, 'the role of penury in a woman's decision to become a prostitute is strangely occluded'.[8] The unanchored loss of self implicit in the prostitute is both orgiastic and terrifying, as it pivots, finally, on a kind of openness to shared sensations, that is to say, affective intimacies that cannot be confined to a purely mechanistic understanding of the market.

For many artists since the 1970s, art-as-prostitution offers an opportunity to reflect on the gendered commodification of social relations, the consumability of critique, and the anxiety of autonomy. However, expanding on the original Baudelaire metaphor presents quite a different picture of the art work/sex work equivalence, for it alludes neither to the taint of art by capitalism nor to a shock to bourgeois moralism, but to an unruly libidinal aesthetic exchange that is not necessarily financial or physical. Released from normal constraints of gender and sexuality, it even becomes a bit queer – that is, it does not imply a heterosexual frame or possession in the sense of property.

This kind of Baudelarian perspective was taken up by a group of queer women artists in the 2007 exhibit 'Shared Women', curated by Eve Fowler, Emily Roysdon and A.L. Steiner at Los Angeles Contemporary Exhibitions (LACE). [...] 'Shared Women' embraced the affective connections forged between artists, critics, and curators. The curatorial statement explains: '"Shared Women" is an exhibition that is dependent on cronyism, feminism and nepotism. [...] This is a gay feminist show that picks up the tools of our mothers and refashions them to seduce and influence each other. [...] Welcome to our dirty commerce.'[9] 'Shared Women' took up the sexualized language elsewhere shunned and turned it into something to be celebrated, particularly vis-à-vis queer community formation. In the exhibit's promotional image, designed by dyke artist Carrie Moyer, schematized nude female bodies intertwine, their limbs exuberantly and suggestively overlapping as they form a triangular pattern. Each identical, faceless woman holds her hands behind her head and has her legs spread – typically passive postures. But rather than have them lie prone, Moyer has oriented them upright and upside down around a vertical axis, with feet playfully plunging into crotches, harking back to Baudelaire's 'sensuous bliss in the multiplication of numbers'. Contrary to art-world murmurings that take a disapproving, even conspiratorial tone toward interpersonal connections, the curators of 'Shared Women' argued that they can be generative and sustaining. [...]

With this in mind, we might venture to envision what it would look like if sex workers and artists organized together for a more just economy.[10] If this vision of solidarity across disparate class positions and variously valued forms of feminized labour seems remote, perhaps the art-as-sex work comparison, with all its ambivalence, offers us a new way to think about the limits and promises of cross-class identifications as it beckons us to reconceive the way categories of affective labour are organized and policed.

1   [footnote 5 in source] Some members of the British Artists Union, founded in 1972, demanded wages and governmental benefits for all artists. And as Andrea Giunta chronicles, Argentine artists in the 1970s actively sought connections with workers and activists as they attempted to move from artistic object making to political agitation.

2   See Julia Bryan-Wilson, *Art Workers: Radical Practice in the Vietnam War Era* (Berkeley and Los Angeles: University of California Press, 2009)

3   [footnote 2 in source] Jessica Spector, *Prostitution and Pornography: Philosophical Debate about the Sex Industry* (Palo Alto: Stanford University Press, 2006) 62.

4   [3] Elizabeth Bernstein, *Temporarily Yours: Intimacy, Authenticity and the Commerce of Sex* (Chicago: University of Chicago Press, 2007) 48.

5   [4] Michael Hardt, 'Affective Labour', *boundary 2*, vol. 26, no. 2 (1999) 97.

6   [5] Wendy Chapkis, *Live Sex Acts: Women Performing Erotic Labour* (London: Cassell, 1997) 69–82.

7   [9] Aspects of non-reproductive labour, including housework and prostitution, have been understood within feminist terms (see Silvia Federici, 'Precarious Labour: A Feminist Viewpoint', *Journal of Aesthetics and Protest* (2008); Leopoldina Fortunati, *The Arcane of Reproduction: Housework, Prostitution, Labour and Capital*, trans. Hilary Creek, ed. Jim Fleming (New York: Autonomedia, 1995).

8   Maria C. Scott, *Baudelaire's 'Le spleen de Paris': Shifting Perspectives* (London: Ashgate, 2005) 74.

9   Eve Fowler, Emily Roysdon and A.L. Steiner, curators, 'Shared Women', Los Angeles Contemporary Exhibitions, 28 February to 8 April 2007.

10 [19] During the 2000 strike of the union for Museum of Modern Art staff, the Professional and Affiliated Staff Association (PASTA MoMA), one of the small handful of artists who refused to cross the picket line was Julia Query, the maker of *Live Nude Girls Unite!*, a documentary film about the unionization of strippers at San Francisco's Lusty Lady strip club. Query had been invited to screen her movie as part of MoMA's film series, but in solidarity with the strikers, she honoured the picket line and declined the museum's invitation. Instead, she held a screening at New York University as a benefit for Local 3882–AFT, NYU's clerical worker's union. The evening included reports from United Students Against Sweatshops, the NYU graduate student union, and the PASTA MoMA campaign. With this gesture, Query's status as a worker trumped her status as sex worker and as artist. [...]

Julia Bryan-Wilson, extracts from 'Dirty Commerce: Art Work and Sex Work since the 1970s', *differences: A Journal of Feminist Cultural Studies*, vol. 23, no. 2 (August 2012) 71–112.

Jonathan Beller
Rottenberg Pearls//2016

[W]hat is central for Mika Rottenberg is the role of women – a concern that some might erroneously consider specialized when in actuality every business depends upon the work of women in one way or another. In thematizing the fact, variety, worldwide distribution, unevenness of circumstance and specialization of labour done by women, Rottenberg's video and installation work represents what Hsuan L. Hsu has described as 'the global art factory'. It also raises the complex question of product valorization in financial, political and aesthetic terms. Rottenberg understands that the art factory is not a stand-alone entity but rather intersects with and depends upon what autonomist Marxism calls 'the social factory', in which society is subsumed by capital and everyday activities take on a virtuosic character, as increasingly specialized accommodations by ordinary individuals to the extraordinary protocols of capitalist production. The life-world itself becomes a factory, and the metabolism of the social is reconfigured by capital as labour. In targeting aesthetic production and creating her own money shots from the relations therein, the artist at once enters into the generic space of the commodification of globalized post-Fordist labour, and endeavors, through her own sensate acts, poetically to redeploy its terms. […]

Rottenberg's video installations depict rigorously designed and rigorously absurd machines that manufacture impossible products via the unique capacities of mostly women, whose appearances do not fit into the iconic templates offered by those other sense machines known as Hollywood and the advertising industry. New products demand new production regimes demand new sensations and thus new senses; the artist too, if she wants to stave off the falling rate of profit, must decode and provide. Under the new regime, sense and sensibility no longer function the way they used to (or were thought to), as natural, human faculties relatively autonomous from market forces. Rather, as Rottenberg's work demonstrates on multiple levels, our sense-making faculties are restructured by markets and intimately incorporated in production networks – they are, in fact, senses of global market forces. No wonder *NONOSEKNOWS* (2015) seems to follow loosely from 'No Nose Knows', an episode of the highly attuned cultural indicator and cutting-edge disseminator of cultural scripts SpongeBob SquarePants.

Rottenberg's work self-reflexively embodies the conditions of contemporary aesthetic production in its ineluctable relation to capital, gender, globalization and post-Fordist empire. It is aware of attention economies (the production of value through the extraction of attention) along with a generalized proletarianization of the senses (the putting of the senses to work for capital, as well as their alienation and dispossession from other mental activities). At the start of *NONOSEKNOWS*, a middle-aged white lady drives an electric cart through deserted streets, enters a building, and moves through a series of rooms full of magnificent, seemingly sentient, floating bubbles. She goes to her office and, pushing aside a large restaurant dish cart full of haphazardly stacked plates of pasta, vermicelli, udon and the like, sits at her desk to smell plastic-wrapped potted flowers. She smells them thanks to a breeze generated by a rickety fan connected by a drive belt coming through the floor from a room below, powered by an Asian woman turning a crank while seated at a table with approximately twenty other Asian women, who we slowly realize are inserting micro-slices of foreign oyster bits into small live oysters to force them to grow cultured pearls. With remarkable skill, these women are cutting and splicing oyster with oyster to create future aesthetic appeal; basically, they are editing life in what turns out to be a pearl factory in Zhuji, China.

We figure out that this process is pearl culture, and glean its analogy to video and art-making: Rottenberg's own method is analogous. While upstairs in her modern office the white lady – an imported actor and the only Caucasian in the video – sniffs flowers with her steadily growing, highly specialized schnozz, we see also that in a wet kill room somewhere below her, the big oysters are being harvested in a series of (machete) cuts that slash their flesh in half, allowing a working woman in gloves and hat (we never see her face) to use her fingers to hungrily grab the pearls from the muck of gonads. The structure of relations that organizes diverse activities – spanning the gamut of scripted interactions from gonad to pearly aesthetic – is revealed gradually and understood retroactively. As we see another group of about twenty women, each using all ten fingers to sort huge piles of pearls into burlap sacks with incredible dexterity and speed, we realize that those big bags of what we might have thought was rice, previously seen randomly lying around the multiple rooms (or were they offices?) inhabited by those various bubbles, were actually full of pearls. [...]

NONOSEKNOWS depict[s] Rottenberg's ingenious machines for the making of new types of outlandish and ostensibly useless products, but these are now combined with documentary footage of actually existing labour processes engaged in by women in the global South. [T]he Chinese pearl factory workers are not only shown to underpin the work of the white lady artist in all of her grotesque specialization but are literally incorporated into the product: their work becomes part of the artwork. This literal incorporation of feminized labour into the artwork makes visible the generalized incorporation of specialized and feminized labour in the rest of commodity culture: from pearls to beauty products, to nearly every commonplace item.

In a sense, Rottenberg's videos, which have been called surreal, are more realistic than most Realism. [...] Thus, as commodities produced under conditions of globalization, Rottenberg's own works partake of the same disturbing incorporation and sublation of the labour of global South women as does your iPhone, and indeed nearly all commodities today; but they also render that incorporation legible and somehow perverse rather than invisible and unremarkable. At least Rottenberg's pearls are not deracinated and ideologically sanforized, shearing off the history of the production process. Rather, they retain the temporality and signature of their mode of production to the point that the strange imperatives imposed on life and labour by the exigencies of universal commodification are apprehended as at once obscene and amazing. In this, the images are, to use an increasingly unpopular word, dialectical – the product of the entire process is grasped as at once a useless bauble that is part of the flotsam of lurid refinement and rarefied taste of the global bourgeoisie and its art world, and a lucid indicator of the conditions of inequality presupposed and indeed enjoyed by that very same world. In fact, the skill of these workers, like the skill of the artist, extends the very idea of what (post) humans, cybernetically intertwined with capitalized technologies, are capable of embodying, enduring and/or enjoying. Exceeding the dominant ideals governing the normative forms of human beings and humanism, the worker-actors – in their singularity within a world committed to imposing standards, and their seemingly excessive presence within a world committed to effacing the visibility of labour – transmit the kind of fortitude, creativity, everydayness and dignity with which those facing the conditions of so-called feminized labour (labour that redounds to women or that disempowers workers of any sex/gender conformation) confront the imperatives of the market.

Rottenberg's pearls show us first hand how capitalist production intensifies its processes of alienation. Having separated people from the land and from one another, it now ramifies bodies by isolating, separating and specializing human capacities and senses and putting them to work. Wagging tongues stick out of holes in sheetrock, butts from walls, feet from buckets of pearls. But strangely, all of these separated faculties require watering with a spray bottle. These little acts of attention and care for fragmented human beings are part of the work necessary for a new distribution of corporeal organization and sense under a production regime that fragments organisms and utilizes their pieces as its own organs. [...] Rottenberg shows that the labour of caring is also part of the labour of labour; her work is also an extension of this care. These are forms of recognition and valorization that to some extent invert the relations of commodification.

Nonetheless, the condition for the emergence of Rottenberg's work is not only third-world labour and non-normative female bodies, organized by the exigencies of work and the production of new needs, but the moneyed, glamorous, well-heeled and indeed well-pearled world of the rich man's art market. As pearl culture indicates, by standing as analogous to art culture through its elaborate process and seemingly sheer uselessness of the product, the entire art market and its world rests atop this sea of invisibilized labour – labour whose form and function, it is imperative to remark, is part of the history not only of hetero-patriarchy but of racism and imperialism. This labour, devalued and erased through patriarchy and racialization, is also the source of much of the world's wealth, including that of art patrons. This is no doubt why, when working on top of all those women of colour, the white lady's nose gradually but inexorably grows erect beyond all proportion: to attain representation in the apex of the phallocratic white supremacist capitalist spectacle (aka the art world), and to produce to its taste, it is imperative to go the way of Pinocchio. As even SpongeBob's starfish friend Patrick sensed when he longed for a nose like the rest of the gang, if you want to be acknowledged among the real boys, you have to grow a dick. Or, at least, get a strap-on.

Jonathan Beller, extracts from 'Rottenberg Pearls', *Parkett*, vol. 98 (2016) 150–57 [footnotes not included].

W.A.G.E.
wo/manifesto//2008

W.A.G.E. (WORKING ARTISTS AND THE GREATER ECONOMY) WORKS TO DRAW ATTENTION TO ECONOMIC INEQUALITIES THAT EXIST IN THE ARTS, AND TO RESOLVE THEM.

W.A.G.E. HAS BEEN FORMED BECAUSE WE, AS VISUAL + PERFORMANCE ARTISTS AND INDEPENDENT CURATORS, PROVIDE A WORK FORCE.

W.A.G.E. RECOGNIZES THE ORGANIZED IRRESPONSIBILITY OF THE ART MARKET AND ITS SUPPORTING INSTITUTIONS, AND DEMANDS AN END OF THE REFUSAL TO PAY FEES FOR THE WORK WE'RE ASKED TO PROVIDE: PREPARATION, INSTALLATION, PRESENTATION, CONSULTATION, EXHIBITION AND REPRODUCTION.

W.A.G.E. REFUTES THE POSITIONING OF THE ARTIST AS A SPECULATOR AND CALLS FOR THE REMUNERATION OF CULTURAL VALUE IN CAPITAL VALUE. W.A.G.E. BELIEVES THAT THE PROMISE OF EXPOSURE IS A LIABILITY IN A SYSTEM THAT DENIES THE VALUE OF OUR LABOUR.

AS AN UNPAID LABOUR FORCE WITHIN A ROBUST ART MARKET FROM WHICH OTHERS PROFIT GREATLY, W.A.G.E. RECOGNIZES AN INHERENT EXPLOITATION AND DEMANDS COMPENSATION.

W.A.G.E. CALLS FOR AN ADDRESS OF THE ECONOMIC INEQUALITIES THAT ARE PREVALENT AND PROACTIVELY PREVENTING THE ART WORKER'S ABILITY TO SURVIVE WITHIN THE GREATER ECONOMY.

W.A.G.E. ADVOCATES FOR DEVELOPING AN ENVIRONMENT OF MUTUAL RESPECT BETWEEN ARTIST AND INSTITUTION.

W.A.G.E. DEMANDS PAYMENT FOR MAKING THE WORLD MORE INTERESTING.

W.A.G.E., *wo/manifesto* (http://www.wageforwork.com/about/1/womanifesto, 2008).

Luc Boltanski and Ève Chiapello
The Work of Critique and Normative Change//2001

We define capitalism in its most minimal form as an amoral process of unrestricted capital accumulation by formally peaceful means. It is the continually repeated supply of capital into the economic cycle with the aim of thereby making a profit. In other words, increasing the capital so that it can be reinvested is capitalism's primary characteristic. The characteristic that gives capitalism this dynamic and this power of transformation has fascinated its observers – even its most hostile. [...]

Capitalist accumulation requires [...] the mobilization of a large number of people whose profit-making opportunities are very weak, and of whom it is unrealistic to think that they were hired by force (that they work in order to survive). Accordingly, modern economic systems demand from more senior employees, above all, but also from all salaried workers, a high level of engagement and a close involvement in the work. One of the essential aspects of this involvement is the idea of being able to give one's activities a 'meaning' that goes beyond the single idea of increasing profit. We call this idea – borrowing Max Weber's concept – the 'spirit of capitalism'. [...]

In *The New Spirit of Capitalism* we discussed the development of the spirit of capitalism between the 1960s and 1990s. [In this] we [based] our discussion on management texts [...] from the 1960s and 1990s. These texts [...] were largely [...] written by consultants. The passages we selected are those that broadly try to describe the nature of the 'new' world we live in and the characteristics of the new business hero, the 'manager'.[1] [...]

Beyond that, the study attempts to understand the origins of the historically unique crisis of anti-capitalist critique. [...] Anti-capitalist critique is as old as capitalism itself. 'Without courting the slightest paradox, it may be argued that anti-capitalism is the most significant expression of capitalism in the eyes of history'.[2] And it is precisely [as] an object of critique [...] that capitalism is forced to justify itself again and again. In order to survive it must equip itself with a capitalist spirit. Without critique this justification is meaningless. We can distinguish between two types of anti-capitalist critique that have been important since the nineteenth century. The first is social criticism: this emphasizes the inequalities, the poverty, the exploitation and the egotism of a world that promotes individualism over solidarity. Its principle driving force was the labour movement. The second type is what we call artist critique. It developed initially in small circles of artists and intellectuals and emphasized other traits of capitalism: it criticizes oppression in a capitalist world (the dominance of markets, discipline, the factory), homogenization in a mass society and the transformation of all things into commodities. Against this, it cultivates the ideal of individual autonomy and freedom, and appreciates uniqueness and authenticity.

In general the form accumulation takes at a particular point in time appears to a very large extent to depend on the type and viciousness of the critique ranged against it. This is why we can see some of the changes in capitalism since May 1968 as a particular appropriation of 'artist critique' and its demands for more autonomy and creativity, for more authentic relationships between people, etc. [...] For artist critique the events of May 1968 represented an opportunity to have its voice heard on the streets.

Without rehearsing the history of employers' reactions to this situation [...], we believe that capitalism could only get back to work because it agreed to capitulate to some of the demands of artist critique. Some of these demands were actually taken into account by new corporate strategies. Without such a process, the resulting changes would never have elicited such reformist enthusiasm. The demand for autonomy was integrated into the new corporate strategies. For example, it was possible to involve the workers into the production process again and reduce the costs of supervision by replacing the latter with processes of self-supervision and by linking autonomy and a sense of responsibility directly to customer demand. When it became clear that an increasing proportion of the profits came about through the exploitation of innovative and imaginative resources – above all in the expanding area of services and cultural production, the question of more creativity found a degree of recognition that would have been inconceivable thirty years previously. The question of authenticity that concerned criticism of the industrialized world, mass production, the homogenization of lifestyles and standardization was defused over time through the multiplication and diversification of merchandise. This was made possible by more flexible short-series production. The question of liberation, which was expressed primarily in the realm of ethics and attacks on bourgeois morality, and which was linked to anti-capitalist critique by referring to a pre-capitalist state without economizing, family virtues and prudery, lost its substance as a protest when, with the advent of new ways of making a profit, the budgeting side of capitalism [...] became less and less important. [...]

Capitalism's recognition of the validity of a number of themes in artist critique robbed the latter of its sharpness. A majority of the spokespeople for this kind of critique were happy with the changes in the world of work and [...] society, even though they too were subject to the new power strategies.

Let us briefly summarize the situation as it appeared in the second half of the 1980s and the beginning of the 1990s. Capitalism fundamentally changed the organizational method and personnel management of its workforce. [...] The predetermined development is clear. [...] The model of the hierarchical, integrated large-scale company is broken down in favour of an idea of society based on the metaphor of a network. The strategies that corresponded to the forms of justice inherent to the second spirit of capitalism (trade unions, collective bargaining, personnel management according to professional status, career trajectories, etc.) lost their influence. New strategies are applied without the critique taking seriously the new forms of selection within the world of work. Ultimately the two critical varieties of capitalism that have been coexisting for a century partly together, [...] separately [or] even in conflict with and alongside each other, enter into a serious crisis simultaneously. Although the reasons for the crisis were various, both varieties turned out to be incapable of preventing the deterioration in working conditions [...]. However the deterioration in social conditions gave rise to a few attempts to reformulate anti-capitalist critique, as the latter took up the objections of both social criticism (poverty, egotism of the ruling class) and those of artist critique (lack of freedom, inauthenticity of the modern world). [...]

The New Spirit of Capitalism [...] offers a reading of the movement that stretched from the events of May 1968 in France when anti-capitalist critique was at its height, via the 1980s when, as critique fell silent, the organizational forms on which capitalism was based changed fundamentally, to the second half of the 1990s when new footholds in critique were tentatively sought. The concept of the 'spirit of capitalism' is of central importance in this work since, as we have seen, this concept can dynamically articulate the two other central concepts of our analyses – capitalism and critique.

But the aim of our investigation is not just a plausible, new description of this time period. With this historical example we are also offering a more general theoretical framework that will help us understand the way ideologies associated with economic activities change. This framework has a) the characteristic of emphasizing the activities of people in insecure and often conflict-ridden circumstances instead of tracing change back to the impersonal forces that have a major influence. It is b) oriented towards the changeover of two different regimes of evaluation: the [...] regime of categorization describes performance records which are recognized [...], institutionalized and regulated as such, and to which the critique can relate; [...] the regime of displacement is distinguished by a series of distances to the institutionalized evaluations, which enable the selection procedures and means of making a profit to change [and] avoid a high level of reflexivity and categorization in order to obviate critique. Finally this model is c) not goal-oriented. It does not rely on a timeline that is geared towards a messianic horizon – whether it be development and progress, revolution or the end of history. The work of critique never ends. It must continually be undertaken anew.

1   'Manager' is a term that has only entered into the French language in recent times, used on those occasions when in the 1960s one spoke of a *cadre* [of management] or a director.
2   Jean Baechler, *Le Capitalisme*, 2 vols. (Paris: Folio, 1995) 268; quoted in Luc Boltanski and Eve Chiapello, *The New Spirit of Capitalism*, trans. Gregory Elliott (London and New York: Verso, 2005) 36.

Luc Boltanski and Ève Chiapello, extracts from 'Die Arbeit der Kritik und der normative Wandel', *Berliner Journal für Soziologie*, vol. 11, no. 4 (December 2001) 459–77. Translated by Philippa Hurd, 2017.

Goshka Macuga
In Conversation with Nicolaus Schafhausen//2016

Nicolaus Schafhausen In a society where creativity and individuality have become general requirements, has the role of the artist also changed?

Goshka Macuga In the same way we are expected to be individual and creative, we can also choose not to be so, and, strangely, no one would care. It's important to identify where the pressure to be an individual or to be creative is coming from. Is it really coming from some external imperative, or is it coming from us trying to follow the standards of the social group we associate ourselves with? Our context projects only to the standards that we define or accept as our context.

Schafhausen And if anyone can, in principle, make the claim to be an artist, do you believe there is still something like the profession of 'artist' in the context of the art world?

Macuga Art requires a certain level of professionalism if it is to be related to the Institution of Art and the economy it generates. We – artists – happily perform this professionalism. We are proud to go to the studio in the morning and work until late, often with longer hours than office workers and often at weekends. We are free to regulate our working hours, or so we think. We don't charge by the hour because we are 'the artists' and our work is rarely accounted for by the hour. Some seem to think that we should not be paid at all and that the other people affiliated with the Institution of Art, such as directors of art institutions, curators, critics or dealers, should be financially rewarded instead of us. But we define ourselves as professional artists, we pay taxes on our professional work, and we affiliate ourselves with dealers, collectors and other artists who share this outlook. We certainly do not exist on the peripheries of society, where some thinkers in the past have placed us.

Schafhausen How does this relate to your own personal experience?

Macuga A few years ago I was invited, along with some other artists based in the UK, to 10 Downing Street for an event celebrating the importance of the role of the arts in the regeneration of the country. In 2015 I was asked to donate a work to the Government Art Collection as a 'charitable gesture'; this gesture was indirectly responded to with a massive tax bill to pay from my artist's earnings.

The British government is collecting art as well as taxes, it seems. As with other professions, artists are expected to pay taxes on their professional income. There is no flexibility in this or in the amount that is requested, no concession made, as if artists somehow occupy a different role or place.

Further to this, our value is such that not only do we have to pay our taxes, we also have to donate our work in recognition of the benefits or value that we create for the state. I must therefore be an 'artist', and my profession seems to have a recognized purpose and a value. This profession, of course, does not come without complications, and these complications are only partly related to the actual practicalities of being an artist. These practicalities are over-shadowed by a larger ethical question of what art generates in a broader sense. I look up to people who call themselves artists but actually who do not choose to be included in the context I belong to. This does not relate to people who call themselves artists from the creative fields, such as music, fashion or design, but rather to people who make art without any expectations to be recognized or even remembered as artists. Of course, many of these people have other professions and other networks and support systems. In the majority of European cities, and especially in London, living on the edge of society and being creative is almost impossible. [...]

Goshka Macuga and Nicolaus Schafhausen, extracts from 'Taxonomies of Knowledge: Goshka Macuga' (interview), *Mousse*, vol. 53 (April/May 2016) 56–64.

Lamia Joreige
Real Encounters//2013

It is often said today that artists of every stripe are more nomadic than ever. One can react to this reality in a number of ways. On the one hand, it could be said that nomadism has caused a homogenization of the global community; for example, even though one may travel all the way from New York to Beijing, it is still common to encounter people who are very similar to each other – despite their cultural diversity. On the other hand, one might emphasize the diversification of identities encouraged by nomadism; for example, since artists are constantly engaged in encountering other artists, they are thus pushed to reflect on their own practices and on their identities in order to recreate them constantly. [...] I want to question the value that such nomadisrn (or what is commonly called nomadism) has in relation to the specific question of what I call a *real encounter*; in what ways does itinerancy shape the kind of encounters artists have today? Is what lies beneath a nomadic lifestyle the hope for an encounter?

In *A Thousand Plateaus*, Deleuze and Guattari oppose the nomad to the figure of the migrant: whereas the former is understood to be rootless, in a state of vital displacement and is only properly understood in terms of trajectories, the migrant becomes a sort of tourist, a visitor of locations with often only the practical on his or her mind. I am tempted to say that the circuitous nomadism of today's artists resembles the migrant more than the nomad on Deleuze and Guattari's terms. The migrant, like any traveller, is easily categorized; he poses no problem of recognition upon arrival or departure. As for the nomad, however, there seems to be a breakdown in such mechanisms of recognition: he fails to demonstrate the correct knowledge at certain circumstances and, in fact, appears to be totally ignorant of customs and obligations. How can such a figure become a transmitter of another culture? This touches on the possible uses of language in such circumstances; what if an artist is ignorant of linguistic conventions or norms that dictate expression? What if an artist employs terms and concepts idiosyncratically and thus distorts the preconceptions of others? I believe that something like this contributes toward a *real encounter*, and that it may exist, although not exclusively, in a kind of figure of artist that does not travel. I don't mean to idealize this figure in any way – or suggest that artists should follow that example – but I want to emphasize that *there was something originally valuable about nomadism which seems to have been diminished in being transposed to another concept like migration: we lose the possibility of real encounter.* [...]

Taken together, the presence of the artist and the efficiency of a homogenized international language give rise to the obvious conclusion that a community has been birthed; a community, in this sense, is a group in which all interests and beliefs are adequately reflected so that particular differences are recognized by others. Today, we speak of a Global Community as if it were a fact, but it is beginning to dawn on many that perhaps this is just a slogan that covers over essential inequalities and misunderstandings. Admittedly, the art community is far more open to diversity than most other organizations; in this respect, it actually seems that the art community, if it exists, succeeds in acting as a community in so far as particular differences are not ignored and are in fact celebrated. There is therefore belief in an ideal circumstance in which artists, while maintaining what is specific to their identities, can come together and share something in common. This is definitely a positive thing, but do we not risk a dilution of the specificity of the artists and their work in all this mutual recognition in the other? [...]

So how does a *real encounter* occur? From my experience, it can take place when a displacement of methods and practices is experienced by those who take part in the encounter – when something feels awkward, but is nevertheless pursued by both (or all) parties. [...]

Although language remains one of the central means by which artists can come to express the meaning of their works, an important feature of Displacement is when participants in an encounter accept the impossibility of a common language that is adequate to both and see that this is a crucial part of the encounter in question – not an obstacle for it. Making the work itself becomes the ground for that encounter.

Finally, it is important not to confuse the possibility of making a real encounter with the time spent in a particular location; in a manner reminiscent of love, *encounters* can occur in a moment's breath, leaving much that is either ungraspable or irreducible beyond that moment. [...] I believe that there is no direct relationship between today's itinerant lifestyles and the sort of encounter artists deeply value between each other; such engagement is the product of something else.

Deleuze and Guattari importantly emphasize that the nomad does not move, if motion is understood in terms of migration from one point to another or across a circuit. In this way, taken metaphorically, the artist who does not travel can be a lesson for other artists. There might be something to be admired about this artist who stays put, who refuses to learn and speak an international language, who refuses to be reduced to one's identity. Would not such an approach perhaps enhance the capacity of an encounter?

Lamia Joreige (with Muhammad Hariri), extracts from 'Real Encounters', in *Life Between Borders: The Nomadic Life of Curators and Artists*, ed. Steven Rand and Heather Felty (New York: apexart, 2013) 31–8.

Mark Fisher
Capitalist Realism: Is There No Alternative?//2009

Mike Judge's unjustly undercelebrated film *Office Space* (1999) is as acute an account of the 1990s/00s workplace as Schrader's *Blue Collar* (1978) was of 1970s labour relations. Instead of the confrontation between trade union officials and management in a factory, Judge's film shows a corporation sclerotized by administrative 'anti-production': workers receive multiple memos from different managers saying the exact same thing. Naturally, the memo concerns a bureaucratic practice: it aims to induce compliance with a new procedure of putting 'cover sheets' on reports. In keeping with the 'being smart' ethos, the management style in *Office Space* is a mixture of shirtsleeves-informality and quiet authoritarianism. Judge shows that this same managerialism presides in the corporate coffee chains where the office workers go to relax. Here, staff are required to decorate their uniforms with 'seven pieces of flair', (i.e. badges or other personal tokens) to express their 'individuality and creativity': a handy illustration of the way in which 'creativity' and 'self-expression' have become intrinsic to labour in Control societies; which, as Paolo Virno, Yann Moulier Boutang and others have pointed out, now makes affective, as well as productive demands, on workers. Furthermore, the attempt crudely to quantify these affective contributions also tells us a great deal about the new arrangements. The flair example also points to another phenomenon: hidden expectations behind official standards. Joanna, a waitress at the coffee chain, wears exactly seven pieces of flair, but it is made clear to her that, even though seven is *officially* enough, it is *actually* inadequate – the manager asks if she wants to look the sort of person 'who only does the bare minimum'.

'You know what, Stan, if you want me to wear 37 pieces of flair', Joanna complains, 'why don't you just make the minimum 37 pieces of flair?'

'Well' the manager replies, 'I thought I remembered you saying that you wanted to express yourself.' Enough is no longer enough. This syndrome will be familiar to many workers who may find that a 'satisfactory' grading in a performance evaluation is no longer satisfactory. In many educational institutions, for instance, if after a classroom observation a teacher is graded as 'satisfactory', they will be required to undertake training prior to a reassessment.

Initially, it might appear to be a mystery that bureaucratic measures should have *intensified* under neoliberal governments that have presented themselves as anti-bureaucratic and anti-Stalinist. Yet new kinds of bureaucracy – 'aims and objectives', 'outcomes', 'mission statements' – have proliferated, even as neoliberal rhetoric about the end of top-down, centralized control has gained pre-eminence. It might seem that bureaucracy is a kind of return of the repressed, ironically re-emerging at the heart of a system which has professed to destroy it. But the resurgence of bureaucracy in neoliberalism is more than an atavism or an anomaly.

As I have already indicated, there is no contradiction between 'being smart' and the increase of administration and regulation: they are two sides of labour in Control societies. Richard Sennett has argued that the flattening of pyramidal hierarchies has actually led to more surveillance of workers. 'One of the claims made for the new organization of work is that it decentralizes power, that is, gives people in the lower ranks of organization more control over their own activities', Sennett writes. 'Certainly this claim is false in terms of the techniques employed for taking apart the old bureaucratic behemoths. The new information systems provide a comprehensive picture of the organization to top managers in ways which give individuals anywhere in the network little room to hide.' [...]

The idealized market was supposed to deliver 'friction free' exchanges, in which the desires of consumers would be met directly, without the need for intervention or mediation by regulatory agencies. Yet the drive to assess the performance of workers and to measure forms of labour which, by their nature, are resistant to quantification, has inevitably required additional layers of management and bureaucracy. What we have is not a direct comparison of workers' performance or output, but a comparison between the audited *representation* of that performance and output. Inevitably, a shortcircuiting occurs, and work becomes geared towards the generation and massaging of representations rather than to the official goals of the work itself. [...] This reversal of priorities is one of the hallmarks of a system which can be characterized without hyperbole as 'market Stalinism'. What late capitalism repeats from Stalinism is just this valuing of symbols of achievement over actual achievement. [...]

It would be a mistake to regard this market Stalinism as some deviation from the 'true spirit' of capitalism. On the contrary, it would be better to say that an essential dimension of Stalinism was inhibited by its association with a social project like socialism and can *only* emerge in a late capitalist culture in which images acquire an autonomous force. The way value is generated on the stock exchange depends of course less on what a company 'really does', and more on perceptions of, and beliefs about, its (future) performance. In capitalism, that is to say, all that is solid melts into PR, and late capitalism is defined at least as much by this ubiquitous tendency towards PR-production as it is by the imposition of market mechanisms.

Mark Fisher, extracts from *Capitalist Realism: Is There No Alternative?* (Winchester, England, and Washington, D.C: Zero Books, 2009) 39–41, 42–3, 44.

What we might earlier have called production, in many respects today bears the characteristics of consumption. One consumes one's job

Tino Sehgal, In conversation with Christiane Fricke, Petra Schwarz, Bernd Ziesemer, 2005

POSTPRODUCTION

Tino Sehgal
In Conversation with Christine Fricke, Petra Schwarz and Bernd Ziesemer//2005

Handelsblatt (Fricke, Schwarz, Ziesemer) You studied political economy and dance. Which came first?

Tino Sehgal I started both in the same week and for the same reason. I was interested in the question of whether there are forms of production other than converting natural resources into consumer goods. Political economy seemed to me to be the place where I could acquire a tool to deal with such a question. By contrast, dance is a kind of solution or answer to this question as dance itself pursues another mode of production: simultaneously dance builds up then breaks down, but it is there nevertheless and produces effects.

Handelsblatt How does that work? Economics is considered one of the most material subjects one can imagine. Dance is immaterial.

Sehgal I certainly took pleasure in the conceptual nature of the combination. But of course that is the heart of my work – bringing these two levels together.

Handelsblatt Is there an anti-capitalist motive behind your work?

Sehgal No. We live within a particular distribution system that we might call the 'market'. It is based on a mode of production that has propelled the process of civilization, namely the transformation of natural resources. These are two different things.

Handelsblatt What does that mean for your work?

Sehgal I'm looking for another form of production, another mode of production. Not looking for whether another distribution system is available. Or even whether another mode of production can be realized within our current distribution system. My works try to introduce another such mode of production into the market and give it a higher status in society.

Handelsblatt Is what you are doing a critique of the economic?

Sehgal Today a critique of the economic is usually aimed at the increasing economization of life. In my opinion this is unstoppable. To the extent to which basic needs can be satisfied with less and less effort, other areas of life are being targeted by offers, as the workforce liberated by increases in efficiency still needs an income. My question concerns how this process can be constructed, rather than saying from the start that it is bad.

Handelsblatt But aren't you withdrawing from the art market with your immaterial art?

Sehgal No. Like every market the art market is fundamentally open: it will offer what is valued culturally, for which there is a demand. I am merely altering the nature of what is exchanged there. Some people mistakenly see this as a critique of the form of distribution, as unfortunately this seems to be the only form of economic critique that our contemporary discourse can envisage.

Handelsblatt You say that the transformation of actions must replace the transformation of natural materials. Do you think that can function in terms of political economy?

Sehgal Today we have our basic essentials. We can't eat a hot meal four times a day. In my view today we are in a transitional phase. We sell things, but we no longer necessarily sell their use value, but rather a form of identity. There is a need for this. We have to and want to differentiate our subjectivity more and more. We have a demand for this, and that is what the latest mobile phone, for example, offers a young person.

Handelsblatt So today what is important is not the shoes but their brand?

Sehgal A brand wants to be a particular view of the world, a particular subjectivity. On the question of whether my principle can function in terms of political economy, I don't know, but on the other hand there's the question of whether our present model is sustainable. I doubt it.

Handelsblatt What does that mean in relation to your objects?

Sehgal What I am attempting is not only to say something, but also to implement something. This is why I am ultimately more interested in art than in economic theories. I produce works that no longer attach subjectivity to a material object. [...]

Handelsblatt Are you interested in debates about capitalism?

Sehgal Fundamentally this is a debate that is oriented towards short-term problems, a debate about the totally relevant question of how the regulatory policy framework should be structured. In my opinion, what is more important is that, unprecedentedly in the history of civilization, there are entire societies that have a surplus of basic necessities. What does economics really mean under such circumstances? Today we still operate according to the premises of a previous era, that is, more growth equals more employment equals more welfare. [...]

Handelsblatt You mean basic necessities in the original sense: food, drink, shelter …

Sehgal Yes. I think that this changes the absolute parameters within which we must look at culture or economics, if we take employment, for example. At the moment when the process of civilization reached its goal, that is, being able to guarantee basic essentials, the question arises of why should there be further growth at all, or the production of new things. The main reason why people today are employed, in my opinion, is no longer because what they produce is of great benefit to the whole of society. The benefit lies rather in lots of people being employed. That they have an income that, of course, they can consume again, and that they derive status from this employment. What we might earlier have called production, in many respects today bears the characteristics of consumption. One consumes one's job. The direct increase in welfare that may be created by the very thing that is produced is minimal. [...]

Handelsblatt What is the benefit of your art?

Sehgal What is interesting about art in general is that it is a model for how products will look in the future if they no longer claim any immediate use value. The products that today in actual fact sell something like subjectivity still think that rhetorically they have to claim a use value. Since art hangs in the museum and is autonomous, art already no longer claims this. I think that in future more and more other products will no longer want to claim a primary use value. [...]

Handelsblatt Are you optimistic that a growth sector could perhaps emerge from what you do?

Sehgal I don't really know. But your question already sounds like 'this might create jobs, this might create employment'. This whole model – I must be employed – or only by having employment can I achieve social status, they are questions that culture must address more intensely. Of course I am in favour of the market. But the market is only a tool. Things also exist that we can resolve outside the market. That's also a strange force in our society today – almost the only way I can achieve status is through employment. We should ask ourselves: are there other ways? Or can we outsource that at least in part? For me this is primarily a conceptual problem. At any rate I am trying to find this out through my works, as examples.

Handelsblatt Of course we always think as employed workers.

Sehgal My questions are: what do we produce in each case? What are the effects on welfare? Why do we produce?

Tino Sehgal, Christiane Fricke, Petra Schwarz and Bernd Ziesemer, extracts from 'Sehgal: "Ich suche eine andere Art der Produktion"', *Handelsblatt* (6 June 2005). Translated by Philippa Hurd, 2017.

Sabeth Buchmann
Under the Sign of Labour//2006

With its interest in linguistics and information theory, Anglo-American conceptual art as it emerged in the mid to late 1960s marked a break with the industrially coded production aesthetics of Pop art and Minimal art. Linked to this was the notion that the replacement of author-centred object production by linguistic or information-based propositions represented a challenge not only to any traditional 'material-object paradigm' (Art & Language) but also to those aspects of craft-based 'production values' which are crucial to claims concerning authorship and the 'work'. Which helps to explain how and why the history of conceptual art has been written (misleadingly) as the history of a 'dematerialization of the object'.[1] [...] Although this goal was not achieved, conceptual art was successful in establishing the idea that instead of being measurable only in terms of the fact of material production, the form of art's symbolic value should be equally open to calibration using scales of social productivity: what traditionally was identified with art in categories of object-based works was put forward here as an avant-garde demand for art as a form of communication that generates publicness. [...]

If the dematerialization discourse is interpreted in the sense of superimposing 'material' with 'symbolic' production, it can be seen as corresponding to a social process: 'the reconfiguration of labour relations in the major industrial nations' that began in the early 1970s.[2] In their book *The Labour of Dionysus*, Toni Negri and Michael Hardt write: 'The most important general phenomenon of the transformation of labour that we have witnessed in recent years is the passage toward what we call the factory society … All of society is now permeated through and through with the regime of the factory, that is, with the rules of specifically capitalist relations of production.'[3] The authors conclude that 'the traditional conceptual distinction between productive and unproductive labour and between production and reproduction … should today be considered completely defunct.'[4] Negri and Hardt thus broaden prevailing concepts of value to such an extent that 'immaterial' or self-utilizing forms of labour can be included.

Although these discourses were not yet public in the 1980s – at least not in the art context – comparable revisions of the traditional concept of labour and production can be detected, albeit in an entirely different theoretical realm. These included, above all, Jean Baudrillard's proposition put forward as early as the 1970s – that 'production' (homologous with the industrial age) had been replaced by 'simulation' (homologous with the information age).[5] Backed up by discourses on the 'immaterial' (Lyotard),[6] postmodern media theory was increasingly to take on the role of a social theory[7] and as such be able to find its way into those (neo-)conceptual forms of thought and praxis that overlapped with the approaches of poststructuralism, deconstruction and cultural studies that were emerging at the time. In contrast to the focus on linguistics that still determined the discourse on the dematerializarion of the object, here semiotics enhanced by cultural criticism came onto the scene, no longer measuring the 'real' as a fact of material production, but rather as an effect of a process of 'de-realization' driven forward by media technology. Concepts often used at the time, such as the 'simulacrum', the 'surrogate' and 'fake', as well as the founding of fictional 'corporate identities', provide a sense of how references to ideas like 'labour' and 'production' have undergone a form of virtualization, and, even if only 'simulated', a form of corporate privatization.

The fact that the playful analogy of artistic self-organization and fictional 'corporate identities' was to turn into economic reality in the 1990s could be one of the reasons why postmodernist media theory slowly went out of fashion. So-called reality had returned to the art world, and not as a result of the crisis in the art market that took place in the interim. Political and economic discourses around post-Fordism, service culture and neoliberalism, including the concepts they used for capital, labour and production such as 'flexibilization', 'deregulation' and 'mobilization', became key terms within those post-conceptual developments that took recourse to approaches from the 1970s (such as site-specificity, identity and institutional critique) and thereby positioned themselves against the ongoing demand of the art market for 'good craftsmanship' and quantifiable 'production values'. Parallel to this, the economic situation of those institutions and artists dependent on public funding became more drastic, as the cultural sphere was increasingly hit by cuts, meaning that budgets for production formats not adequate to the art market became scarcer and new forms of 'aggressive sponsoring' found their way into museums and art associations. Thus, any talk of 'fictional corporate identities' became hopelessly obsolete when, due to a mix of voluntary and forced self-determination, artists saw themselves confronted with the necessity of organizing their own financial means for production, work spaces, exhibition sites, contacts, possibilities of distribution and publics. Hence, the discourse on the 'mobilized relation between capital and labour'[8] became increasingly obsolete with the increasing entanglement of self-organized, institutional, corporate and state economics. This was a process that became a major issue and also a subject in their work for artists who sought to integrate into their works the changing conditions of labour and production and the discourse on the public and the private that these conditions engendered. [...]

1   Lucy R. Lippard and John Chandler, 'The Dematerialization of Art', *Art International*, vol. 12, no. 2 (1968) 31–6.

2   [footnote 6 in source] Michael Willenbücher, *Migration–Illegalisierung–Ausnahmezustände: Der Illegalisierte als Homo Sacer des Postfordismus*, unpublished Magister thesis (Heidelberg: Ruprecht-Karls-Universität, 2005).

3   [7] Antonio Negri and Michael Hardt, *The Labour of Dionysus: A Critique of the State Form* (Minneapolis: University of Minnesota Press) 9–10.

4   [8] Ibid., 10.

5   [10] Jean Baudrillard, *Symbolic Exchange and Death* (London: Sage Publications: 1993).

6   [11] Consider in this context the 1985 exhibition 'Les Immatériaux' at the Centre Pompidou, Paris.

7   [12] Katja Diefenbach, *Theorien der neuen Technologien: Zur Bedeutung der Informations- und Kommunikationstechnologien im Spätkapitalismus*, unpublished Magister thesis (Munich: Ludwig-Maximilian-Universität, 1992).

8   [15] See Willenbücher, op. cit.

Sabeth Buchmann, extracts from 'Under the Sign of Labour', in *Art after Conceptual Art*, ed. Alexander Alberro and Sabeth Buchmann (Cambridge, Massachusetts: The MIT Press, 2006) 179, 180–81.

Isabelle Lindermann
Bodies in Use//2016

In May 1968 Louis Ricardo Rodriguez took a few days' break from his work in the factory, and swapped it for something different: he and his family sat on a podium in the middle of the 'Experiencias '68' exhibition at the Instituto Torcuato Di Tella in Buenos Aires, and allowed themselves to be inspected by the visitors. Accompanied by recordings of everyday noises from an ordinary household, they could be observed carrying out activities such as reading, writing, smoking and eating. It was planned that Elena Quiroga, Luis Rodriguez and their son Máximo Rodriguez Quiroga should spend eight hours a day on the podium throughout the duration of the exhibition. A wall panel explained that they were remunerated for their work, in an amount equivalent to the income that the father would normally receive for his work in the factory.[1] Oscar Bony had hired the family[2] and together with them, under the title of *La Familia Obrera* (*The Working Class Family*), he had set in train in the exhibition hall a critical process that raises questions about the categories of work and the working class. For although paradoxically what the family performs here does not appear to be work itself, they are on the contrary evidently pursuing activities to pass the time, activities which in Fordist theories of labour belong more to the world of leisure, a specific system of work and its primary setting – bodies – seems to be made visible by Bony's strategy. How does work actually happen here and what is produced? What is the manner of this work? And why are these particular bodies of the working-class family under negotiation in this enquiry?

The structure in which Bony locates his actors is characterized by the activities and soundtrack as the private sphere. It is precisely not work in a factory that is being exhibited here, but rather the intimate space of the family's everyday activity, which makes visible a traditional classification of work and its hierarchy: the dichotomizing division according to capitalist logic between paid and thus official work, and the sphere of supposed non-work – the private household (*oikos*) and unpaid, more inferior reproductive work. However, through *La Familia Obrera*'s remuneration, based on the main wage-earner and its embedding in an eight-hour shift, the family's otherwise unpaid activity is now not only designated as work, but in addition the engagement of the whole family means that the hidden actors operating beyond the sphere of work are included and revealed – namely the bodies of the mother and son. It is significant that in the case of *La Familia Obrera* Oscar Bony specifically takes the mode of reproductive work into account. His contribution to 'Experiencias '68' should be seen against the backdrop of radicalizing and politicizing artistic approaches, which formed practices of resistance provoked by the increasing social and political repression of the ruling powers of Onganía's dictatorship following the coup of 1966. By turning to activist strategies it was no longer a question of the production of aesthetic, traditional objects and entities, but of the creation of critical situations that eliminated the division between 'the people who propose situations and those who create them'.[3] Bony himself said that in this case the family was not installed as a work of art but rather, as he argued at a later date, is to be understood 'in lieu of the work of art and not the art itself'.[4] What Bony was thus urging in his own artistic practice is also demonstrated with and through the working-class family on the podium: the work being performed here is no longer considered a production of things for the capitalist system of exploitation. Rather the work creates the presence of bodies being exhibited. The mode of work lies in the use of their bodies and thus – following Giorgio Agamben's understanding of work – neither in the production nor in the practice itself.[5] Equally, this use cannot be integrated into the sphere of modern work, so that here perhaps there arises a situation in which they work for or with art. This work for art, the exhibiting and being exhibited, moves the bodies into the mode of the visible. In addition they are ascribed a certain status – as they are the bodies of the working class to which the family is ascribed merely by virtue of the work's title. Moved into the arena of a bourgeois cultural establishment – the institution of the exhibition – they suddenly become visible to the 'people in power' as agents of an oppressed and exploited class. And through the use of their 'actual bodies' they transcend the gulf separating them from the bodies of others.

1   Previously it was assumed to be double the income, which is questioned by Daniel R. Quiles. See Daniel R. Quiles, 'Between Organism and Sky. Oscar Bony, 1965–1976', *Caiana*, no. 4 (2014) 1–14.

2   According to Claire Bishop the family responded to an advert in the local newspaper. Cf. Claire Bishop, *Artificial Hells. Participatory Art and the Politics of Spectatorship* (London and New York: Verso, 2012) 113.

3   See lecture by Jorge Romero Brest, curator of 'Experiencias '68', in Inés Katzenstein, ed., *Listen! Here! Now! Argentine Art of the 1960s: Writings of the Avant-Garde* (New York: The Museum of Modern Art, 2004) 130–31.

4   Oscar Bony, in Luis Camnitzer, *Conceptualism in Latin American Art: Didactics of Liberation* (Austin, Texas: University of Texas Press, 2007) 178.

5   Giorgio Agamben, *The Use of Bodies*, trans. Adam Kotsko (Stanford: Stanford University Press, 2015) 23.

Isabelle Lindermann, 'Bodies in Use: Oscar Bony's *La Familia Obrera*'. Commissioned for this volume, 2016. Translated by Philippa Hurd, 2017.

Mierle Laderman Ukeles
In Conversation with Tom Finkelpearl//2000

Mierle Laderman Ukeles [The 1969 *Manifesto for Maintenance Art*] proposed an exhibition, called 'CARE', where I would move into a museum with my husband and my baby, and I would do my family things, and also take care of the museum, maintain it, as well as taking care of, servicing, the visitors who came to the museum. The museum would be home. And that would be the artwork. In other words, I would clean it, I would change the lightbulbs, whatever was necessary to keep this place operating. The museum's life-processes would become visible. Second, the *Manifesto*'s exhibition proposed to ask all different kinds of people in society, 'What do you have to do to keep alive? How do you get from minute to minute?' There would be many tables where people would be interviewed about what they did to stay alive. In Western culture, you're not supposed to talk about this stuff in polite company. Certainly in 1969, there were very few ways to talk about ongoing sustenance. The third part of the exhibition was constructing an image of the earth (outside) as a needy and finite place. Every day, containers of ravaged earth, air and water would be delivered to the museum. Each day, scientists and pseudo-scientists (artists) would process and purify these elements in the museum, and then return the elements to the city in a healthy mode. […]

Tom Finkelpearl After the *Manifesto*, what sorts of project did you undertake?

Ukeles In 1973, I was invited to be in 'c. 7,500', a show that Lucy Lippard organized of women artists. I sent several photo-series documenting maintenance tasks such as Jack [Ukeles' husband] diapering the baby, me dressing the children to go out in the winter and undressing them to come in, doing the laundry washing the dishes, other workers in my neighbourhood doing repetitive tasks. The exhibition travelled, and I got jealous. I thought, if my work can travel, how about me? So I started contacting these locations where the show was going, asking them if I could come and do a maintenance art performance work. I ended up doing about 17 different maintenance art performance works. I dealt with maintenance of continuity in nature, personal maintenance, institutional maintenance, maintenance of ethnic traditions. In these art institutions, I'd take over the persona of The Maintenance Worker, who is supposed to be unseen, and cleans behind the scenes, after hours. Or the guard, who keeps the keys silently. I was trying to bring maintenance out in public.

In 1976 I was invited to be in a group show called 'ART <--> WORLD', at the Whitney's branch at 55 Water Street. I went to check out the site and said, 'Oh my God, a skyscraper!' I had been waiting for years to get my hands on a skyscraper. Why? Because a skyscraper needs tremendous maintenance. In this sort of high-end commercial building, the maintenance people are supposed to be completely invisible. There's an Apollonian ethos in a skyscraper. Its maintenance mission is to create, during the property owners' and their clients' prime action hours, an appearance of stasis, beyond time. The goal is to look publicly as if nothing has happened and everything is always clean, always quiet. Which is actually shocking if you think about it. In other words, everything is secret. At 55 Water Street, for example, the maintenance workers were supposed to wear ties, and keep their long-sleeved shirts buttoned while cleaning, because that was the proper presentation for the real estate interests that owned the building – that one could do this maintenance work without even sweating. Of course, at night, when the office workers went home, when no 'one' (important) was watching, people would wash the floors in their undershirts.

The branch-museum concept was actually a utopian idea of the Whitney: a branch in an office building, so that people could have art right in the middle of their work day. I loved that idea. You didn't have to leave your life to go to the art museum, the art museum would come to your life. Except that the 300 maintenance workers in the building never, ever came into the museum, except to change a lightbulb and wash the floor. So I tried to turn the tables, make a piece with all the workers that kept this building operational 24 hours a day. The Whitney got me connected up with the owners, who said they would allow me to do this. I wrote a letter to 300 workers in this building. I invited them to do an artwork with me. The piece was called *I Make Maintenance Art One Hour Every Day*. I asked them to select one hour of their regular work, and think of that work, that one hour, as art. It was completely up to them if they wanted to do this or not. Opening up the power to choose and power to name was critical.

I went around with a Polaroid camera documenting their work. There's an inch of white space at the bottom of each picture, which always intrigued me, so I made labels that fit that space. One label said 'Maintenance Work', and the other said 'Maintenance Art'. I would approach a worker, and I would say, ''Can I take your picture?' If they said yes (and they all said yes), I would show the picture to them when it came out of the camera and said, 'Is this art or work?' In other words, have I crossed your path during that hour that you picked? Some people would say, 'This is art.' Sometimes, when people were working together, one person would be making art, and one person would be making work. I also gave everyone a button that said 'I Make Maintenance Art One Hour Every Day', which, shockingly, most people wore for the seven weeks of this exhibition. […]

Every day I mounted the photographs I had taken in the museum. When I started the show, 'my space' was empty. Over the seven weeks, there was a gradual accumulation of photographs that recorded the choices of the people: this is art, this is not art. [...]

When I wrote the *Manifesto*, I had come to understand that, as a woman, as a mother, I was connected to most people in the world – the whole entire world of maintenance workers. Women were never invited to become a maintenance class, we were just told: 'You are like this. We know what you think. We know what you are. You take care of us.' Women have been defined like that within the domestic sphere, while service workers, of either gender, do this stuff outside, to make a living. That's most of the people in the country, and most of the people in the world. [...]

Mierle Laderman Ukeles and Tom Finkelpearl, extracts from 'Interview: Mierle Laderman Ukeles on Maintenance and Sanitation Art', in *Dialogues in Public Art* (Cambridge, Massachusetts: The MIT Press, 2000) 295–322.

Clémentine Deliss
Brothers in Arms: Laboratoire AGIT'Art//2014

[...] Artists' collectives often acquire mythical status despite the fact that they rarely remain intact over time. Misunderstandings and arguments together with purely circumstantial conditions can lead to bifurcations within what was once a shared ideal. The reason why one disavows a collective can be as banal as the wish to move on. It can also result from the mix of passion and enmity that constitutes any dynamic, experimental practice. Similarly, the narrative about a collective is likely to be recast according to whose participation is vocal at whichever moment in time. The following account is therefore subjective and inevitably partisan. It is rooted in my personal contact with artists, philosophers, writers and politicians-in-the-wings who lived and worked in Dakar in the 1990s. This includes the Laboratoire AGIT'art, of which I have been a member since 1995 and also the manifestations of Tenq and Huit Facettes, both important artist-run initiatives that, like the Laboratoire AGIT'art, were driven in great part by the curatorial work of Senegalese artist El Sy. At the time, my engagement with these collectives constituted a form of extended practice, beyond producing exhibitions. Indeed, exhibiting these artists and their group projects was perhaps the least productive curatorial channel through which to mediate their practice. Instead, performances, workshops, think tanks and the publishing organ *Metronome*, first produced in Dakar in 1996, helped to convey both the specificity of our collaborations and the differentiated models of documentation that represented and communicated this work. [...].

In London in September 1995, after working together for three years, El Sy and Issa Samb informed me that I had been co-opted into the Laboratoire AGIT'art. [...] Over the following years, El Sy and Issa Samb introduced me to numerous collaborators of the Laboratoire AGIT'art. As I understood it, the main quality of the group was its methodology: there were no exhibitions of the Laboratoire AGIT'Art; instead the heterogeneity and the complementary character of its members were reflected in the performances that they initiated together over the years. In the 1990s these had become sporadic, even though daily discussions in the courtyard with impromptu visitors and members were a central part of the collective's activities. During my visits to Dakar I met and spent time with: the philosopher and critic As M'Bengue; the actors Magaye Niang and Pap Oumar Diop dit Makéna; the latter's brother, the theatre director and actor Ablaye Dani Diop; the filmmaker Djibril Diop Mambéty; the fashion designer Oumou Sy; the feminist and politician Marie-Angélique Savané; the architect Pierre Goudiaby; the arts organiser Mor Lyssa Bâ; the itinerant poet Thierno Seydou Sall; the sculptor Babacar Sadikh Traoré; the photographer Bouna Médoune Seye; the trader Abdou Bâ; the banker and collector Libasse Thiaw; and Mamadou Traoré Diop, author and advisor to the president. Each person in the Laboratoire AGIT'Art held a particular role and responsibility, so that everyone's individual competence would always find its position within the group. The dramaturge Yussufa John, who later emigrated from Senegal to Martinique, was, until his untimely death in 1995, the 'Chef de l'atelier de théâtre' ('Head of the theatre studio'). His role appears to have been central to the creation of the collective in the mid 1970s, when performance and painting were first experimented with. When Issa Samb arrived at Heathrow Airport in the summer of 1995, unexpectedly dragging a two-metre-long bundle of rags through customs, he was effectively re-enacting Yussufa John's interment. This corpse-like sculpture subsequently became part of the installation curated by El Sy for 'Seven Stories from Africa' [at the Whitechapel Gallery], which included, together with four paintings by Souleymane Keita, numerous 'objects of performance' recuperated from the courtyard in Dakar and sent to London via more conventional routes.

In the Laboratoire AGIT'art, El Sy was 'Chef de l'atelier de peinture et de costume' ('Head of the painting and costume studio'), responsible for the *mise en espace*, or visual dramaturgy, of the projects the group was involved in. He created the visible parameters of the stage area, designed the costumes, engineered the lighting and also acted certain parts. Additional members took care of noise (*bruitage*), some wrote (like myself) and others were responsible for film and photography. The artist and filmmaker Bouna Médoune Seye documented the courtyard, and shot an important photographic series in 1994 titled *Les Trottoirs de Dakar* (Dakar's Pavements): startling black-and-white portraits of madmen and misfits who populated the city's streets. Another key figure at the time was the poet Thierno Seydou Sall, who travelled to villages reciting biting parodies of contemporary politics, the pharmaceutical industry and the role of non-governmental organizations in Africa, and who was also involved in the Laboratoire AGIT'art's investigations into anti-psychiatry. [...]

After a performance or a meeting took place, the group appeared to dissolve, leaving little trace of a physical communal presence beyond Issa Samb's courtyard, which acted as a depot for various objects left over from performances. What remained powerful was the act of verbal reiteration, a mnemonic referencing that recalled absent members. When I visited Dakar during the 1990s, several members were visible, even if many were no longer actively engaged in producing collective situations. Nevertheless, the former contributions of those who were absent, departed or deceased would invariably be called to mind by their colleagues through a process of repeated vocal referencing. [...]

Restive and controversial during its time, the Laboratoire AGIT'art's numerous collaborators were always cautious about divulging too many details about the way it operated. Instead the collective was founded on an ethos of initiate and interdisciplinary experimentation that was performed and exchanged through the different roles played by each of its protagonists. To break down this cryptic methodology into an art-historical analysis for the benefit of today's global audience throws up many questions about the accelerated commodification of alternative theories of knowledge production and art practice. However legitimate it may seem to disseminate information on former artistic methodologies, this procedure raises many questions about the language employed to do so, the status of the document produced, the ownership of this material and, with it, the cannibalistic urge to accumulate the codes of other cultures as one's own. Before his death, filmmaker Djibril Diop Mambéty warned El Sy and me of the dangers of vulgarizing the Laboratoire AGIT'art and betraying the ethos behind its autonomy. El Sy's recent comment that the group no longer functions with the collective identity it once had reminds one of the dangers that exist today in romanticizing former moments of creative conjunction between artists: 'The mummy has been buried. You can't exhume it now!'

Clémentine Deliss, extracts from 'Brothers in Arms: Laboratoire AGIT'Art and Tenq in Dakar in the 1990s', *Afterall*, no. 36 (Summer 2014) 5–6, 12, 13–14, 15, 19 [footnotes not included].

Maria Chekhonadskih
Museum of Proletarian Culture. The Industrialization of Bohemia//2012

[...] Arseny Zhilyaev's project *Museum of Proletarian Culture. The Industrialization of Bohemia* has appeared amidst a new round of public debates on the destiny and role of old cultural institutions, a round marked by the emergence of an alternative political and ethical attitude to the Soviet project that is bereft of 'hysterical sighing' and emotional reactions. Breaking the taboo on all things Soviet and trying to pull it out of the ghetto-cum-zoo of tourist 'creativity', Zhilyaev attempts to analyse the past's institutional vicissitudes and understand what our new future might be like if we examine the Soviet project in all its multidimensionality and complexity. Opening up new areas of potentiality in the avant-garde objectives of sixties-era Soviet modernism, on the one hand, and the complex dialectic of the struggle amongst various tendencies within institutions, on the other, Zhilyaev enters an old museum in order to present his research in the shape of a fictional museum of the future.

The exhibition of *Museum of Proletarian Culture. The Industrialization of Bohemia* was held at the branch of the Tretyakov State Gallery specializing in twentieth-century art. In creating his own museum within the museum, Zhilyaev turns to its archive in order to research exhibition practices in the 1930s and the history of Soviet modernist architecture in the 1960s. Zhilyaev enters the museum through the back door, paying attention to the design of the Soviet museum and exposing its architectonics, which were meant to support specific mechanisms of knowledge production. [...]

Zhilyaev's objective coincides with the line of critiquing outmoded forms of museum work, while his research of displaced and marginal types of creativity suggests an alternative viewpoint on art practices. [...]

In addition, the *Museum* forms a conceptual response to Alexei Fedorov-Davydov's 'Experimental Marxist Exhibition', which opened at the Tretyakov State Gallery in 1931. For the first time, viewers were shown the art of oppressed classes. [...] In the didactic exhibition model, items are presented not as free-standing objects or autonomous artworks, but as phenomenon from a single chain of causes and effects. [...]

Indeed, viewers [in the *Museum*] find themselves as it were in the era of didactic exhibitions. First, the late Soviet period unfolds before them: its protagonists are workers, engineers and amateur artists. This then gives way to the history of the creative class during the almost-futuristic 1990s and 2000s. [...] [Zhilyaev] 'conceptualizes' phenomena of Soviet self-made design, the various late-Soviet craft items made by workers, and artefacts of today's media culture in order to tell an alternative history of art. Assuming that the rejection of autonomous art, which was imbricated in the logic of the Soviet avant-garde and expressed in the utopian appeal to fuse art and life, was continued in the leisure activities of workers and the technical intelligentsia, Zhilyaev revisits species of spontaneous creativity, giving them the status of an avant-garde that evolved in parallel with official art. [...]

Ultimately, his exhibition is a total installation of anonymous works, reconstructed artefacts and found objects. He finds the material he needs on the Internet, in trash dumps and old buildings, and some of the objects he makes himself. [...]

In his project Zhilyaev contrasts two eras – the late Soviet period of work/leisure, at whose dawn independent, anonymous forms of creativity were born, and the post-Soviet era, which professionalized them and raised the 'ploughboy artists' to the level of commercial culture. [...].

Here we are confronted with the anonymous creators of the late Soviet era – for example, railroad worker Ilya Dondurenko, who dreamed of an era of new high speed trains and spaceships that would enable people to move around the globe easily and quickly. He laid kilometre after kilometre of railroad sleepers, and in his leisure time crafted architectural models from matches. His *Model No. 14* is built in the shape of a sickle and hammer crowned with a five-domed church. The maniacal love for fashioning tiny houses from matchboxes, burning portraits and landscapes onto wood, and building shelves and tables amidst the scarcity of Soviet daily life, had only one face, and that was the face of a Soviet worker escaping from factory discipline into the realm of 'creative leisure', where the dogmas of Soviet ideology passed through the filters of his social experience.

Zhilyaev attempts to show us the features of that face, and that is why there is something Kabakovian about the exposition: the protagonists of this exhibition are partly fictitious, have partly been turned into characters, and have partly themselves become artefacts of Soviet and post-Soviet culture as such. They give way to the cacophony of the experiments of the 1990s, when workers' clubs and houses of cultures generated a new pop culture, and creative time, which had been liberated from work, demanded that it be recognized as work. Former workers, engineers and female vocational school students became musicians, artists and talk-show hosts, such that new forms of cultural politics and show business emerged in which the culture of the future was forged, and the model of alternative cultural production turned into entrepreneurship. This grassroots culture was privatized by business. [...] While the creative professions have become the basis of the post-Fordist economy, their scope and idealist fervour have been reduced to working to order. This is exactly what has happened to grassroots forms of spontaneous creativity, which have gradually been transformed into the machine of the culture industry, a process that Andrew Ross has termed the 'industrialization of Bohemia'.[1]

Zhilyaev's creative class has found new ways of resisting creativity's usurpation by capital. He believes that today the poetry of the multitudes, who are fashioning the idiom of contemporary visual culture in the social networks, might be deemed an incarnation of the folk avant-garde. [T]he folklore of demotivators, Internet memes, graffiti, texts, photos and posts has generated a space of free exchange and co-operation among millions of people around the world both inside and outside the Web. [...]

[I]nstead of constituted power (the rule of institutions, with their attendant hierarchies and canonical forms of representation) we are faced with the constituent power of the multitudes and the anonymous, who despite everything continue to resist the machinery of power. The *Museum* gives no final answers but rather leaves questions open. Who is an artist at this point in history, and what should we call art? What are its functions, and can we speak of the emergence of a new subject who does not conform to the rhythms of the institutional assembly line?

1   Andrew Ross, *No-Collar: The Humane Workplace and Its Hidden Costs* (Philadelphia: Temple University Press, 2004) 123–60.

Maria Chekhonadskih, extracts from 'The Museum of Proletarian Culture. The Industrialization of Bohemia', in Arseniy Zhilyaev, *Museum of Proletarian Culture. The Industrialization of Bohemia* (Moscow: Tretyakov State Gallery, 2012) 17–23.

Caroline A. Jones
The Server/User Mode: On Olafur Eliasson//2007

Few artists have had Picasso's arrogant confidence: 'I do not seek. I find.' Far more typical of modernity was the desire to align one's work with *research* [...]. Materialization could sometimes seem incidental – yet materialization was exactly what the artist could bring: a way to make research come alive as experience in the body of the viewer. Robert Irwin's collaborations with scientists from Bell Labs began to mean something when he materialized those laboratory set-ups of the *ganzfeld* in public art museums. The theatricality of such manoeuvres was rhetorically minimized by reading the work as *de*materialized – feeding tensions between theory and materiality, research and production, that are more present than ever in contemporary art.

The case of Olafur Eliasson sharpens such debates. The artist insists on physical materialization, but in the service of *experience* (perhaps in the French sense of the word, as 'experiment'). The built-in tension between research and production is fuelled by Eliasson's insistence that his studio is 'like a laboratory', while it also functions pretty effectively as a factory for contemporary art. The artist cultivates this dynamic – 'the translation from thinking into doing is the radical thing' – but it forces the question: Just *what* is being researched and produced? In the art of Eliasson (and, I would argue, much of his generation), the objects being produced, and the socio-material technologies they imply, are only part of the story. Seen in a broader context, the physical works are nodes in the ongoing activity of *knowledge production.* [...]

In much contemporary knowledge production, what counts is non-universalist, localized and embodied. The subjectivities generated by contemporary art can be performative, relational, networked or (in Eliasson's case) restlessly phenomenological.

The historical impetus for all this can be traced to the postwar shift from information to informatics, affecting economics, science and art. These epistemic shifts were portended by factory models of aggregative labour (physicists scaled up from desktop experiments to the industrial assemblages of big science; artists shopped out work or set up basic assembly lines). [...] The machine was more than a metaphor. It retooled the producer *and* the receiver. The concept of knowledge production is thus useful only if it can capture these discursive dynamics, by which the 'object' of art or science is nothing less than the local 'subject' making meaning: of experience, of data, of sensory phenomena, of the broader social field. [...]

With the fundamentally decentring tools of the Internet and the Web, there emerged a new logic of multiple, interacting servers and users. [...] The old economy of maker/receiver shifted ineluctably around 2000, toward a 'hive mind' of users and servers. In place of the studio as final site of authentication, we were forced to accept knowledge production as inevitably hybrid, mediated, deferred and diffuse. [...]

Fullfilling the artist's self-professed 'desperate' need to engage with the world, Studio Eliasson is many things. As of 2007, it was: roughly thirty employees; a two-and-a-half-floor, 15,000-square-foot former train depot behind Berlin's Hamburger Bahnhof; a corporation, a factory and a dynamic knowledge-production machine [...]. (From 2009 to 2014, it was also a functioning branch of the Berlin University of the Arts.) Eliasson's studio emphasis strategically underlines the increasingly marketable physical objects with their shadow in research. Allowing the artist to be manifestly generous, self-deprecating and collaborative, Studio Eliasson also leaves him intact as the central point through which all information must pass, proclaiming, *We are producers of knowledge, not (just) objects.* [...]

The studio is central to this dynamic, defying standard fantasies of solitary creation with the complexities of production one might have seen during the baroque: master geometers projecting coordinates for a ceiling painting, woodworkers crafting mouldings, sculptural technicians producing casts of putti, lowly assistants grinding pigment, and patrons putting in their two cents about emblems and iconography. The baroque artist was only as good as the team he had assembled, but effective in the given economy only if an 'Andrea Pozzo' (for example) could still be the contractual result.

Studio Eliasson is both less and more than that baroque model might suggest. Less, because once a prototype is produced or a design completed, outside fabrication can be used to extend operations to steelworkers in southern Germany or carpenters in Switzerland. More, because the studio itself incorporates wildly disparate forms of expertise: digital parametric draughtsmen, lighting technicians, architects, an archivist, a documentarian, cooks, babysitters. [...] Studio Eliasson is thus more than a stage for propelling objects into the world; it is a world, providing all the artist needs to complete himself. He has remarked of his employees, 'They represent me and all of not-me.' Of this group (its ranks increased by temporary workers as needed), roughly a third are skilled fabricators (carpenters, welders, electricians), a third are architects and designers, and a third are discourse workers (trained art historians, an archivist, a secretary). The knowledge factory is clearly productive, yet the 'laboratory' function insulates and buffers it from the booms and busts of the art market. [...]
Knowledge is thus resource *and* product, sustaining the collective's belief that theirs is a 'flat' organization, anti-hierarchical in its distribution of labour, and permeable to restless streams of intelligence from all its players. (When I mentioned to one assistant that her reading material was cropping up in Eliasson's discussions, she said gravely, 'It goes both ways.') [...]

Eliasson describes the community of workers he has gathered as a 'psychographic anatomy' – a body whose various desires need to be negotiated. 'I profit from their uncertainty', he says of his skilled design team: 'Everybody is slightly hesitant about whether the consequences of the choice I'm about to make are foreseeable. That can be very productive … in the artistic context of having acknowledged that what we work on are prototypes and models, constructions of reality. Which essentially are *real*.' Commerce requires invariance and replication; Eliasson's practice aims to locate a given effect more unpredictably, in the monad of the percipient. [...]

Like the communities of servers and users being established in contemporary scientific practice, these artistic experiments are dispersed social-technical-spatial entities in which no single author holds priority on the production of knowledge or power over its distribution. We can see in all this the harbinger of larger shifts, in which the dispersal of contemporary knowledge production offers considerable freedom to form local subjects and volitional collectives. Makers become nodes in a net; takers are just other nodes generating further meanings. The studio is a model, but of a larger world of servers and users. Its imagined dominance cedes to the ones who imagine, and the 'user function' may be what we need to think about next.

Caroline A. Jones, extracts [slightly updated] from 'The Server/User Mode: Caroline A. Jones on the Art of Olafur Eliasson', *Artforum* (October 2007) 316–25.

Nicolas Bourriaud
Postproduction//2002

[...] When Daniel Pflumm works with the logos of large companies like AT&T, he performs the same tasks as a communications agency. He alienates and disfigures these acronyms by 'liberating their forms' in animated films for which he produces soundtracks. And his work is similar to that of a graphic design firm when he exhibits the still identifiable forms of a brand of mineral water or a food product in the form of abstract light boxes that evoke the history of pictorial modernism, 'Everything in advertising', Pflumm explains, 'from planning to production via all the conceivable middle-men, is a compromise and an absolutely incomprehensible complex of working steps.'[1] According to him, the 'actual evil' is the client who makes advertising a subservient and alienated activity, allowing for no innovation. By 'doubling' the work of advertising agencies with his pirate videos and abstract signs, Pflumm produces objects that appear cut out of their context, in a floating space that has to do at once with art, design and marketing. His production is inscribed within the world of work, whose system he doubles without caring about its results or depending on its methods. He is the artist as phantom employee.

In 1999, Swetlana Heger and Plamen Dejanov decided to devote their exhibitions for one year to a contractual relationship with BMW: they rented out their workforce as well as their potential for visibility (the exhibitions to which they were invited), creating a 'pirate' medium for the car company. Pamphlets, posters, booklets, new vehicles and accessories: Heger and Dejanov used all the objects and materials produced by the German manufacturer in the context of group exhibitions. Pages of group exhibition catalogues that were reserved for them were occupied by advertisements for BMW. Can an artist deliberately pledge his work to a brand name? Maurizio Cattelan was content to work as a middleman when he rented his exhibition space to a cosmetics manufacturer during the Aperto at the Venice Biennale. The resulting piece was called *Lavorare e un brutto mestiere* (Working is a Dirty Job, 1993). For their first exhibition in Vienna, Heger and Dejanov made a symmetrical gesture by closing the gallery for the duration of their show, allowing the staff to go on vacation. The subject of their work is work itself: how one person's leisure time produces another's employment, how work can be financed by means other than those of traditional capitalism. With the BMW project, they showed how work itself can be remixed, superimposing suspect images – as they are obviously freed from all market imperatives – on a brand's official image. In both cases, the world of work, whose forms Heger and Dejanov reorganize, is made the object of a postproduction. [...]

Pflumm's images are the products of an analogous micro-utopia, in which supply and demand are disturbed by individual initiatives, a world where free time generates work, and vice versa, a world where work meets computer hacking. We know that some hackers make their way into hard drives and decode the systems of companies or institutions for the sake of subversion, but sometimes also in the hopes of being hired to improve the security system: first they show evidence of their capacity to be a nuisance, then they offer their services to the organism they have just attacked. The treatment to which Pflumm subjects the public image of multinationals proceeds from the same spirit: work is no longer remunerated by a client, contrary to advertising, but distributed in a parallel circuit that offers financial resources and a completely different visibility. Where Heger and Dejanov position themselves as false providers of a service for the real economy, Pflumm visually blackmails the economy that he parasites. Logos are taken hostage, then placed in semi-freedom, as freeware that users are asked to improve on themselves. Heger and Dejanov sold a bugged application program to the company whose image they propagated; Pflumm circulates images along with the 'pilot', the source code that allows them to be duplicated.

When Pflumm makes a video using images taken from CNN (*CNN, Questions and Answers*, 1999), he switches jobs and becomes a programmer – a mode of production with which he is familiar through his activity as a DJ and musician.

The service industry aesthetic involves a reprocessing of cultural production, the construction of a path through existing flows; producing a service, an itinerary, within cultural protocols. Pflumm devotes himself to supporting chaos productively. While he uses this expression to describe his video projects in techno clubs, it may also be applied to the whole of his work, which seizes on the formal scraps and bits of code issued from everyday life in its mass media form, to construct a formal universe in which the modernist grid joins excerpts from CNN on a coherent level, that of the general pirating of signs. [...]

As practised by Pflumm, the mix is an attitude, an ethical stance more than a recipe. The postproduction of work allows the artist to escape the posture of interpretation. Instead of engaging in critical commentary, we have to experiment, as Gilles Deleuze asked of psychoanalysis: to stop interpreting symptoms and try more suitable arrangements.

1   Daniel Pflumm, 'Art as Innovative Advertising', interview by Wolf-Gunter Thiel, *Flash Art* (November/December 1999) 78–81.

Nicolas Bourriaud, extracts from *Postproduction* (Berlin and New York: Lukas & Sternberg, 2002) 77–81.

Joseph Vogl
The Spectre of Capital//2014

It happened in New York on an April day in the year 2000. The Twin Towers of the World Trade Center were still standing. The American economy had been growing non-stop for more than a hundred months; the Dow Jones Industrial Index had just climbed above 11,000 points to reach an all-time high, while electronic trace on the NASDAQ was rallying steadily. [...] After a sleepless night, a twenty-eight-year-old billionaire fund manager decides to leave his apartment on Manhattan's East Side to go to a hairdresser on the shabby West Side [...]. He rides down in one of the private elevators and climbs into his white armour-plated stretch limousine, fitted out with cork sound-proofing, surveillance cameras and numerous screens relaying world news and stock exchange prices. His chiefs of security and technology are already waiting for him [...]. The vehicle turns into Forty-seventh Street on its way west, passing one high-rise apartment building after another. As the night wears on, it gets caught up in a series of adventures and complications that may rightly be called an odyssey.

On the way, the fund manager meets his wife and one or other of his mistresses. There is a report that the IMF director has been murdered, and likewise a Russian oligarch, a media entrepreneur, who had been a friend of this young billionaire. Crawling through the traffic, the limousine crosses Park and Madison Avenues, drives through the old Jewish neighbourhood and reaches the Broadway theatre district, only to be trapped in the chaos of an anti-globalization protest. A bomb explodes at the entrance to an investment bank; as a young man sets himself on fire, our speculator looks on, unaware that he himself will soon fall victim to a pie attack. Suddenly, and for no particular reason, he kills his chief of security and reaches his childhood hairdresser's near the docks. Then, equally inexplicably and abruptly, he leaves the hairdresser, gets involved with three hundred extras in a late-night film shoot, and coincidentally runs into his wife for the last time. An ex-colleague is waiting for him in a deserted ruin, and this man, he must finally understand, will be his murderer.

With this strange story, Don DeLillo's novel [*Cosmopolis*] takes us right into the arena of the modern financial market, touches on the question of whether the market lends itself to narrative treatment and offers a series of narrative and rhetorical figures to represent the riddle of the finance economy, its protagonists and their operations. [...]

DeLillo's protagonist, sporting the vigorous-sounding name of Eric Packer, enters the scene in disguise, as a character mask – or rather, a dream figure, an apparition – personifying the most recent form of finance capitalism. He is not only hyper-alert and sleep-deprived, manic and prone to excess, he is at home everywhere and nowhere, an Odysseus of globalization and citizen of a monetary cosmopolis. He is marked, above all, by his longing to leave behind the ponderous heaviness of the material world, where physical conditions of ownership still prevail. He dreams that use value will die out and that the referential dimension of reality will vanish; he dreams, too, of the dissolution of the world into streams of data and the absolute tyranny of the binary code, and he places his faith in the spiritual appeal of cyber-capital, transposed into eternal light via the shimmering and flickering of charts on countless screens.

It is the dream of ultimate, radical transubstantiation. Émile Zola's novel about financial speculation, *Money*, had already referred to poets of sublime sums of money. This novel deals with a more recent mutation: Verlaine's *poète maudit* returns in a new generation of professional symbolists. Obsessive and extravagant, they devote themselves to making money 'talk to itself'[1] in a free, artificial and self-referential play of signs [...]. What is finally accomplished here is nothing less than a raid by the future on the rest of time. [...]

Faced with the mysteries of the most modern form of finance capitalism, DeLillo responds in his novel by combining elements of the old and the new capitalist mentality. On the one hand, this allows him to portray the addiction to change and the continual revolutionizing of global and economic structures in the name of capitalist free enterprise as a process of 'creative destruction', to borrow Joseph Schumpeter's famous phrase: 'Destroy the past, make the future'.[2] [...] On the other hand, it enables him to show how these forces have freed themselves from the sphere of production. Thanks to the alliance of 'technology and capital', the culture of the market has become as insubstantial as it is from the material manifestations of wealth, it has installed itself in 'a time beyond geography and touchable money'.[3] It dictates its own dynamics and standards of mobility, abandoning all local, social and political constraints. [...]

1   Don DeLillo, *Cosmopolis* (London: Picador, 2004) 77.

2   Ibid., 93.

3   Ibid., 36.

Joseph Vogl, extracts from *The Spectre of Capital* (Stanford: Stanford University Press, 2014) 1–2, 3, 4.

Melanie Gilligan
In Conversation with Tom Holert//2012

Tom Holert Your films *Crisis in the Credit System* (2008) and *Popular Unrest* (2010) could both be considered in terms of how their narratives, including the 'futuristic' language and the cinematographic codes deployed, treat temporality with regard to capitalism's regimes of time. In *Crisis in the Credit System*, the arcadian setting where the investment banking firm holds a role-playing seminar (the scenes were filmed at Pergola and Hill Garden, Hampstead Heath, London) seems systematically to negate or disavow the contemporariness of the credit crunch in order to put the protagonists in a pedagogical non-place, in a-history – a delusional vantage point from which they can indulge in the fantasy of being able to engage freely with the roles they play in a system that is both gone and going on. The narrative of *Popular Unrest* is set in the present-futurity of (post) apocalyptic science fiction à la David Cronenberg or J.G. Ballard. Should the films be seen as responding to the financial system's manipulations of historical but also individual/biographical time, perhaps following Italian sociologist Elena Esposito's musings about capitalism's present futures and future presents?[1]

Melanie Gilligan Yes, both films look at capital's relation to time. You're right that in *Crisis in the Credit System* the idyllic garden setting for the brainstorming session gives a metaphorical distance from the losses of the crisis. The consensus belief before the crisis was that financial markets had become invulnerable, and so I was depicting a denial that was endemic. But temporality becomes an even clearer theme later in the work when the role-playing session develops into an imagined financial TV news feature about a trader at the fictitious Delphi Capital Management, who in a trance-like state connects with the financial markets and predicts future market behaviour. In finance, investor activity is always oriented towards anticipating market shifts, whether through mathematical models, research or insider information. The assumed invulnerability was supposedly achieved through finance's ability to anticipate, outmanoeuvre and ultimately capture future outcomes through a variety of financial instruments. If the future-telling trader and other moments in the film imply a certain mysticism, this is because while researching the film I was struck by mystical overtones in the way many people in finance spoke of the behaviour of financial markets.

Holert Maybe this discovery of various levels of the speculative – from future-oriented speculation on falling or rising prices and quotations to almost out-of-body experiences of meditative speculation –can be linked to the ways in which capital has developed an uncanny ability to tap the noncognitive and affective. [...] Financial capital seems to be speculating on futures that reside in intuition, in tacit knowledge and forethought – as a potential to be explored in an anticipatory mode.

Gilligan That's completely right, and without having come across any particular writing dealing with this I wrote these scenes to intimate how capital's grasping to capture the future leads it to mine the deepest recesses of 'human capital', subjectivities that in turn attune themselves ever more closely to the market's own subjectivity. Not until my next films – *Self-Capital* and *Popular Unrest* – did I bring the affective and physical focus of contemporary capitalism to the fore. For instance, *Popular Unrest* looks at how capital manages and captures the future behaviour and physical health of populations. [...] The logic of pre-emption, the calculation and modelling of probabilities, drives capitalist biopolitics increasingly to incorporate the affective and biophysical dimensions of people's lives. You could say that capital's orientation towards the future is due to the basic fact that capital can expand (and it needs constantly to expand) only when value produced at one point in the circuit of capital is valorized through an exchange at some later point in that circuit. Capital is therefore forward-looking and trying to control future outcomes to ensure the valorization of value [...].

Holert As much as contemporary capitalism is marked by an overwhelming (and awe-inspiring) ideology of the complexity of the cyberneticized financial markets, of seemingly incomprehensible and eventually uncontrollable feedback dynamics of speculation, betting, risk calculation, stochastics and probability, it appears to find impossible the creation of an appropriate, comprehensible visualization and narration of the virtual processes that led to the recent crunch and crisis.

Gilligan Yes, and *Crisis in the Credit System* doesn't attempt to represent the causes of the crisis in their totality (as this totality involves capital as a whole) but focuses on communicating important aspects of the financial crisis [...].

Capital as a whole is inexpressible. I wrote *Popular Unrest* from the understanding that capital as a totality can't be represented, but I still wanted to try to get across what this totality – in Marx's phrase, the 'total social capital' – means today.[2] In capitalism the abstract equivalence of exchange links all of our activity, and you could say that the total social capital is the sum of all these exchange relations. Towards the end of *Popular Unrest* the group confronts and does final battle with the Spirit. As this segment ends, they encounter a vision of capital in its totality and see it for what it is – the totality of human relations touched by capital. They realize that the Spirit is not the totality but that we are and that capital's mediation of our actions both unites us and puts all our activity into abstract relation. This point in the film is meant to suggest that perhaps this totality itself – or its contact through abstraction, if this characteristic could somehow exist without the value form – could be the ground for a new movement out of capital.

Earlier in the film we are given glimpses of how the contemporary biopolitical agglomeration of capital/state today tries to picture something similar to the total social capital through computational and statistical analyses of populations' behaviour, oriented around huge amounts of digital data (from the data we produce when shopping or browsing the Internet to our contact with governments). And the calculus of this population view dovetails with the new data character of scientific information. The data nature of all this information across the biopolitical spectrum of biological, commercial and social systems furnishes new comparisons, new kinds of equivalences across systems, making it easier to apply the logic of one – for example, finance – to another, such as human biology or human social behaviour. [...]

Holert Whereas *Crisis in the Credit System* dwells on the social milieu of those atomized professionals who are commonly blamed for having caused the crisis through their irresponsible and often somewhat surreal behaviour, *Popular*

Unrest maps the effects of biopolitical capitalism on the subject formation (and transformation) of individuals coming from a variety of social and professional backgrounds who are drawn together by an unknown force to form the so-called groupings which are almost Sartrean, 'apocalyptic' collectives that fuse in the face of terror and the impossible and which, if only temporarily, seem to escape the powerful reach of the Spirit (of capitalism). In both cases the protagonists lack any agency that is not imbued by an external, even metaphysical authority that remains as invisible as Adam Smith's notorious hand. […].

Gilligan Crisis in the Credit System tries to unpack what's happening in the financial system, and the film never really contemplates the subjective position of those investment bank employees and the high-flying hedge fund managers and private equity executives that they mime in their role-playing. The characters operate as agents of systemic economic forces and tendencies in the finance world. The fictions they frantically produce to keep their jobs mirror the fiction that finance has been telling itself and the world. The employees' fictions fall apart in the same way that finance's fiction has. But the work looks at how shifts on the systemic level shape lived experience. For instance, at the end of episode three, the catastrophic effects of the crisis on the real economy violently break through the corporate brainstorming reveries. But if any agent is operating here, it's the one the private equity boss intimates: capital itself. […]

1   [footnote 2 in source] See Elena Esposito, *The Future of Futures: The Time of Money in Financing and Society* (Northampton, Massachusetts: Edward Elgar, 2011).

2   [4] See Karl Marx, *Capital: A Critique of Political Economy*, vol. 2, ed. Friedrich Engels (Moscow: Progress Publishers, 1956) pt. 3, ch. 18, sec. 1.

Melanie Gilligan and Tom Holert, extracts from 'Subjects of Finance: Melanie Gilligan Interviewed by Tom Holert', *Grey Room*, no. 46 (Winter 2012) 85–8, 91–2.

Anne Wagner
Mechanics of Meaning, or the Painting Machine//2003

Rosemarie Trockel's *Untitled (Painting Machine)* had been made and used and first shown by June 1990. The piece was put on view alongside its ostensible painterly products, the wall piece called *56 Brushstrokes*, in Cologne. This context needs looking at, yet title and date alone already offer information enough, from an art-world perspective, to put us in immediate touch with the work's main issues and themes. Here is a piece that addresses both authorship and artistic identity as 'mechanical' constructs: it draws its fuel straight from a high-octane postmodern tank. Or so it seems, until we take a second look. For once a single run of images had been made – a set of seven sheets of straggling parallel lines – and its uniqueness guaranteed (each is numbered 1/1), the artist herself pulled and cut its plug, as if in anticipation of the fact that soon enough the motor of this particular object would strike its viewers as outmoded – all too difficult, even impossible, to fire up. It was belated from the beginning, in other words: assertively so. Belated, yet not quite obsolescent. When I look at the machine's now quiet carcass, I cannot imagine that the scrap heap calls. Remember that appliances are often delivered without their plugs; it's the work of a moment to get wired, and be off and away. Away towards an account of authorship that aims both to admit, as well as to question, its endless mystique. […]

Trockel's characteristic objects are formally at odds: they take explicit and material exception to the appropriationist's main rules and concerns. She quite literally stretches and embroiders the commodity and readymade: her knitted stockings would fit a long-legged fairy-tale giantess; her dresses place trademarks strategically, where else other than atop each breast as if to target and disauthenticate what lies below. […] Alongside such ironies, the *Painting Machine* seems right at home. In all these contexts expression is objectified and made physical, even mechanical; it is pushed and pulled, made rote and repetitive, in pursuit of a particular interest in sites and systems of meaning, and how they might be given a literal, even lexical form in objects, and so be revalued or laid to rest. Hence the *Painting Machine*. One way of stating the aims of this essay is to say that what follows tracks the odd intersection of the literal and the expressive in Trockel's art: they meet in her physical objects, and they are likewise to be found in what is potentially the most expressive and objective element in the artistic lexicon, as well as the most disembodied – I mean the brushed-in line. 'What's in a line?' My query echoes an echo: this is the same question that Briony Fer posed – again the year was 1990 – as a means to speak of gender within modernist abstraction, when it is women who produce the lines. In particular she considered Liubov Popova, that archetypal 'producer', Soviet-style, who herself aimed to turn her art to the machine and factory, albeit with limited success.1 It might be helpful in this context to cite Walter Benjamin, tersely predicting in 1936 that transformed conditions of production would impact the superstructure so as to 'brush aside a number of outmoded concepts such as creativity and genius, eternal values and mystery'.[2] In 1990 that day had still not yet securely arrived. For line we might once again read name, so as to summon the pervasive 1980s reassertion, rather than refusal, of 'signature style'. Trockel's machine may be mechanical but it is also feminist and critical, above all about lines and names.

The first exhibition of *Untitled (Painting Machine)* was strategic. Trockel's work was on view in A.R. Penck's gallery, while he showed in hers. A simple tactic: it aims to point to gender and artistic identity, and to mine viewers' expectations of both. In the words of Isabelle Graw, who reviewed the show, 'to make this one-time switch of dealers can only imply a different series of conditions of production, different techniques for the selling of the work, a different mode of advertising, and different mechanisms of mediation with respect to a different public'.[3] Different, indeed: together the two artists posed kissing for a poster, wearing costumes – for her a mac and kerchief, for him denim and soft felt hat – that suggests a performance of class. Here is a labouring couple: Benjamin's producers, perhaps, in a performance that would have made him squirm.

Yet the main illusion of the *Painting Machine* concerns its products, the seven panels that are shown with it as a kind of evidence or proof. Fifty-six brushstrokes, eight per panel: eight tracks of India ink that skitter across Japan paper that was then laid down on a canvas support.[4] If this is a painting machine, then it has given us 'painting' in a large or liberal – or perhaps just modernist – reading of the term. For it seems that much that matters in the work hangs directly on the nature of the brushstroke and what we might be tempted to conclude from the look of the many drawn (yet hardly calligraphic) lines. [...] There are eight of them hanging from each of seven cross bars; these, we are meant to think, have generated the slew of skittish lines. None of the brushes is an off-the shelf item; each was made to order - the manufacturer was a Japanese firm called, as luck or art would have it, Da Vinci (I kid you not) – each was made to order from a lock of artists' hair. Hence the difference among the various brush-heads – soft, curly, blonde, bristly – and hence the differences among the marks they (apparently) make.

Not, however, that while looking we have any easy way to tie marks back to brushes, even though the brushes themselves are keyed by gold-lettered names to the cast of characters who proved willing to snip the hair from their heads. We have to read the fine print: Sophie Calle, Vito Acconci, Georg Baselitz, Sigmar

Polke, Barbara Kruger – the list acts like an up-to-date art index to a 1990s Who's Who. These are artist's artists, in an almost literal sense of that familiar term: they stand close enough to Trockel to have sent her a bodily talisman at the drop of a hat. [...] Yet there is also something Victorian and morbid about this process: the brushes are oddly like memorials, as if in making them, Trockel has killed off a whole generation, at one fell swoop. All that remains is the array of bristles; it is as if the locks of hair pour or spurt out from the brushes like marks themselves. [...]

No one needs reminding that Trockel is also the designer – not the 'producer' – of painting-like objects that were entirely and declaratively machined. These are her knitted 'paintings', in quotes, works that do quote the heroic dimensions of postwar painting, and dominate the wall. And they are unique images – very much one of a kind. But the likeness stops here: where paint should be, find yards and yards of industrially knitted wool. Anyone who has worn a sweater, however it was made, knows that such tight regularity and unvaried tension can only be due to absolute insentience: they must be machined. Here then are works that doubly trope the work of the hand, which in this group of objects, neither knits nor paints. On the one hand, so Trockel claims, she was concerned with 'the signifiers of the feminine – culturally inferior materials and skills such as wool and knitting', and wanted to find out 'whether it is possible to overcome the negative cliché by eliminating the handicraft aspect from the whole complex'.[5] On the other hand – it now seems clear that this second hand is rhetorically male – the handmade aspect of painting, as customarily practiced, is likewise excluded by these same means.

The neither-nor comes together almost effortlessly in one particular object, the knitted painting (*Untitled (Speckled)*, 1988) that apes a group of Pollock-derived paint splatters, over and over again. Splatter as logo, then: what measure of authenticity does it now guarantee? Whose practice does it name? Trockel's or Pollock's or both? The work finds a partner and parallel conundrum in another of the knitted objects from 1988, across which wanders a time-honoured assertion of subjective being, its script now ventriloquised by a machine: *Cogito ergo sum*. Below the borrowed proposal broods a black square. No, the Black Square. Another negation knit large. Trockel's *Cogito* clearly asks us to think of identity – even her own artistic identity – in terms that embrace and take their distance from this founding declaration of the independent western self.

1   [footnote 2 in source] Briony Fer, 'What's in a line? Gender and Modernity', *Oxford Art Journal*, vol. 13, no. 1 (1990) 77–88.

2   [3] Walter Benjamin, 'The Work of Art in the Age of Mechanical Reproduction', in *Illuminations*, ed. Hannah Arendt, trans. Harry Zohn (New York: Schocken Books, 1969) 218.

3   [4] Isabelle Graw, 'Rosemarie Trockel A.R. Penck Space Switch', *Flash Art* (November/December
     1990) 150.

4   [5] The most extensive treatment of the *Painting Machine* is that offered by Wilfried Dickhoff in
     Sidra Stich, ed., *Rosemarie Trockel* (Boston: Institute of Contemporary Art, 1991) 106–9.

5   [14] Rosemarie Trockel, 'Endlich ahnen, nicht nur wissen. Ein Gespräch mit Doris von Drateln',
     Kunstforum International, no. 93 (February 1988) 212–13, as quoted by Uwe M. Schneede in
     'Wool, Knitting, and Thinking About Art in Knitted Pictures', *Rosemarie Trockel: Bodies of Work
     1986–1998* (London: Whitechapel Art Gallery, 1998).

Anne Wagner, extracts from 'Mechanics of Meaning, or the Painting Machine', *Afterall* (Autumn/
Winter 2003) 78–81, 83.

Nick Srnicek and Alex Williams
Inventing the Future: Postcapitalism and a World without Work//2015

A twenty-first-century left must seek to combat the centrality of work to contemporary life. In the end, our choice is between glorifying work and the working class or abolishing them both. The former position finds its expression in the folk-political tendency to place value upon work, concrete labour and craftwork. Yet the latter is the only true postcapitalist position. Work must be refused and reduced, building our synthetic freedom in the process. […]

We have argued that the most promising way forward lies in reclaiming modernity and attacking the neoliberal common sense that conditions everything from the most esoteric policy discussions to the most vivid emotional states. This counter-hegemonic project can only be achieved by imagining better worlds – and in moving beyond defensive struggles. We have outlined one possible project, in the form of a post-work politics that frees us to create our own lives and communities. Triumph in the political battles to achieve it will require organizing a broadly populist left, building the organizational ecosystem necessary for a full-spectrum politics on multiple fronts, and leveraging key points of power wherever possible.

Yet the end of work would not be the end of history. Building a platform for a post-work society would be an immense accomplishment, but it would still only be a beginning. […] To be satisfied with post-work would risk leaving intact the racial, gendered, colonial and ecological divisions that continue to structure our world. While such asymmetries of power would hopefully be unsettled by a post-work world, the efforts to eliminate them would undoubtedly need to continue. Further, we would still be seeking a systemic replacement for markets and facing the task of building new political institutions. We would still not know what a sociotechnical body can do, and we would still have to unfetter technological development and unleash new freedoms. Transcending our reliance on waged labour is important, but we would still be faced with the immense tasks of undoing other political, economic, social, physical and biological constraints. A project towards a post-work world is necessary but insufficient.

Yet a post-work platform does provide us with a new equilibrium to aim at, completing the shift from social democracy to neoliberalism to a new post-work hegemony. We believe it focuses the tasks of the present and provides a stable point from which to seek out further emancipatory gains. As with any platform, those who create it cannot fully predict how it will be used. While certain constraints and opportunities are built into a platform, they do not exhaustively determine the ways of life it will enable. A platform leaves the future open, rather than presuming to close it. When it is designed correctly, it succeeds precisely by allowing people to build further developments on top of it. With a post-work platform, people may begin to participate more in political processes, or perhaps they will retreat into individualized worlds formed by media spectacles. But there are reasons for hope, given the shift in work ethic required for a post-work society. Such a project demands a subjective transformation in the process – it potentiates the conditions for a broader transformation from the selfish individuals formed by capitalism to communal and creative forms of social expression liberated by the end of work. Humanity has for too long been shaped by capitalist impulses, and a post-work world portends a future in which these constraints have been significantly loosened. This does not mean that a post-work society would simply be a realm of play. Rather, in such a society, the labour that remains will no longer be imposed upon us by an external force – by an employer or by the imperatives of survival. Work will become driven by our own desires, instead of by demands from outside. Against the austerity of conservative forces, and the austere life promised by anti-modernists, the demand for a post-work world revels in the liberation of desire, abundance and freedom.

Such a future is undoubtedly risky, but so is any project to build a better world. There are no guarantees that things will work out as expected: a post-work world may generate immanent dynamics towards the rapid dissolution of capitalism, or the forces of reaction may co-opt the liberated desires under a new system of control. Concerns about the risks of political action have led parts of the contemporary left into a situation where they desire novelty, but a novelty without risk. [...] The best utopias are always riven by discord.

This imperative runs in opposition to the kind of precautionary principle that seeks to eliminate the contingency and risk involved in making decisions. […] In seeking to err always on the side of caution, and hence of eliminating risk, it contains a blindness to the dangers of inaction and omission. While risks need to be reasonably hedged, a fuller appreciation of the travails of contingency implies that we are usually not better off taking the precautionary path. The precautionary principle is designed to close off the future and eliminate contingency, when in fact the contingency of high-risk adventures is precisely what leads to a more open future – in the words of conceptual artist Jenny Holzer, 'you live the surprise results of old plans' (*Survival* series, 1983–85). Building the future means accepting the risk of unintended consequences and imperfect solutions. We may always be trapped, but at least we can escape into better traps.

Nick Srnicek and Alex Williams, extracts from *Inventing the Future: Postcapitalism and a World Without Work* (London and New York: Verso, 2015) 126, 175, 176–7, 177–8 [footnotes not included].

If we are always already serving, artistic freedom can only consist in determining for ourselves – to the extent that we can – who and how we serve

Andrea Fraser, 'How to Provide an Artistic Service: An Introduction', 1994

WORKING TOGETHER

Ahmet Öğüt
CCC: Currency of Collective Consciousness//2015

I grew up in a place where civil war was part of daily life, where safety in public space was divided into day and night, into wide roads and back streets, mountains with cages or fields with burned trees. [...] Growing up in circumstances of radically militarized everyday life with very limited resources, I am not coming from a place where world views of 'Western moralism' or ethics as 'conventional wisdom' were taken for granted. I am coming from a place where I learned the importance of consciousness – more importantly, collective consciousness – when one is isolated both culturally and politically.

Already during the early years of my artistic practice, I had to face a number of polarizing challenges. I remember participating in two significant meetings on the second and ninth of April 2005, in Istanbul with other artists, writers, critics and students to discuss the notion of a national exhibition, with reference to several exhibitions that had been organized since 2000. Exhibitions about Istanbul, Turkey and the Balkans, and more specifically the exhibition 'Urban Realities: Focus Istanbul', which was planned to open at Martin-Gropius-Bau (2005) in Berlin, were discussed at these meetings. At the end of them, ten artists – myself, Can Altay, Hüseyin Alptekin, Halil Altındere, Memed Erdener, Gülsün Karamustafa, Neriman Polat, Canan Senol, Hale Tenger and Vahit Tuna – decided to withdraw from this exhibition. The show went on, but it became an exhibition about Istanbul without the participation of artists from Istanbul (with a few exceptions). Through this withdrawal we expressed our fatigue over exhibitions based on national identity, over the utilization of artists as illustrations of politics between nations, and the categorization of artists according to geographical, national or regional specifications. [...]

When we look back at history, what comes into focus is the collective consciousness that emerges during what Ute Meta Bauer has called 'magnetic moments in time.'[1] [...] Starting in 1950, the Irascibles, a group of American abstract artists, including most of the leading figures of the New York School such as Louise Bourgeois, Robert Motherwell, Willem de Kooning and Ad Reinhardt, signed an open letter to Roland J. McKinney, the president of the Metropolitan Museum of Art, demanding an improvement in the presentation of abstract art in the museum.[2] The Irascibles' protest eventually brought change to the museum's plans for upcoming exhibitions. [...]

I was one of the invited artists who took part in a conditional withdrawal from the 19th Biennale of Sydney in 2014. The biennial experienced weeks of controversy over links between the event and its founding sponsor, Transfield, an Australian multinational corporation that had secured a $1.22 billion contract in January 2014 to work on Manus Island and the Nauru Mandatory Detention Centres. Under Australian law, any asylum seeker arriving in the country without a visa can be detained indefinitely, which contradicts the UN Refugee Convention of 1951. On 19 February, 46 participating artists issued an open letter calling for the board to 'act in the interests of asylum-seekers' and 'withdraw from the current sponsorship arrangements with Transfield'. The board's response was intransigent: 'Without Transfield', it explained, 'the Biennale of Sydney would cease to exist.' On 26 February, five artists – Libia Castro, Ólafur Ólafsson, Charlie Sofo, Gabrielle de Vietri, and myself – withdrew from the biennial. We were joined by four more artists on 5 March: Agnieszka Polska, Sara van der Heide, Nicoline van Harskamp and Nathan Gray. [...]

In the meantime, other major sponsors of the 19th Biennale of Sydney, such as the city of Sydney, began to question the event's relationship with Transfield. On 4 March, the issue was raised in the Australian parliament, with Green Party senator Lee Rhiannon bringing a motion in support of the artists. The motion was defeated by the major parties. Perhaps in response to the ongoing controversy, Transfield shares dropped 9 per cent over this week, after an initial 21 per cent rise when the contracts were first announced. On 7 March, just fourteen days before the opening, Luca Belgiorno-Nettis made the decision to step down as chair of the biennial (a position he had held for over fourteen years) and the board announced that it was severing it 44-year-old ties with Transfield, the company that founded the biennial in 1973. After our demand was met, seven of the nine artists who had withdrawn from the biennial re-entered.[3] [...]

Artists and other cultural workers are fragile when acting alone, facing more personal consequences. After every radical and transformative act, heavy aftershocks might resonate for a long time, which might puzzle us. Finding a strategy is not only about choosing which method is to be used. The lost or not-yet-discovered blueprint is hidden somewhere between a joint action with clever timing and masterminding a long-term campaign.

1   Interview with Ute Meta Bauer, 'Magnetic Moments in Time', *Echo Gone Wrong* (20 December 2013).

2   'The Irascibles', *Life* (15 January 1951). Open letter: *The New York Times* (22 May 1950).

3   Ahmet Öğüt and Zanny Begg, 'The Biennale of Sydney: A Question of Ethics and the Arts', *Broadsheet Magazine* (2014).

Ahmet Öğüt, extracts from 'CCC: Currency of Collective Consciousness', *e-flux journal*, no. 62 (February 2015).

María Teresa Gramuglio, Nicolás Rosa, et al.
Tucumán is Burning//1968

[...] The collective work is based on the current situation in Argentina, radicalized in one of its poorest provinces, Tucumán, which has been subjected to a long tradition of underdevelopment and economic oppression. The current Argentine government, insistent upon a disastrous colonial policy, closed most of the Tucumán sugar refineries, a vital force in the province's economy. The result has been widespread hunger and unemployment, with all its attendant social consequences.

'Operation Tucumán', devised by government economists, aims to disguise this blatant aggression against the working class with the fiction of economic development based on the creation of new or hypothetical industries financed by US capital. The truth hiding behind this operation is the following: by dissolving worker groups, they intend to destroy a substantial, explosive, union movement that has taken root throughout north east Argentina. They plan to break up the workers into small industrial installations or force them to emigrate to other areas in search of temporary work that is badly paid and lacks stability. One of the serious consequences of this event is the dissolution of the nucleus of the working family left to improvisation and chance for their subsistence. The economic policy pursued by the government in the province of Tucumán is on the order of a pilot program for testing the working population's level of resistance. After neutralizing labour union opposition, the government plans to transfer this programme to other provinces that have similar economic and social features.

'Operation Tucumán' is reinforced by an 'operation silence', organized by government institutions to confuse, distort and silence the serious situation in Tucumán. For reasons of common class interests, the so-called 'free press' is going along with the government. Regarding this situation, assuming their responsibility as artists committed to the social reality that includes them, the avant-garde artists are responding to 'operation silence' by performing the work *Tucumán Arde* [Tucumán is Burning].

The work consists of creating an information super-circuit to point out the surreptitious distortion of the events that have taken place in Tucumán through the media that disseminates information and is controlled by government authorities and the bourgeoisie. The media is a powerful mediating force, susceptible of being loaded with various content; its positive influence on society depends on its adherence to the truth and reality. The information flowing from the government and the official media on the events that unfolded in Tucumán has tended to remain silent on the serious social problem unleashed by the closing of the refineries. The false picture given of the province's economic recovery is refuted by the actual data to a scandalous degree. In order to gather this data and display the deceptive contradiction of the government and the class that supports it, a group of avant-garde artists travelled to Tucumán. Accompanied by technicians and specialists, the artists sought to verify the social situation that the province is now living through. Their activities culminated in a press conference that publicly and vehemently repudiated the government's performance. They also pointed out the complicity of the cultural media, which collaborated to maintain a shameful and degrading social situation for the working population of Tucumán. The artists' activities were carried out in co-operation with groups of students and workers, who thus became involved in implementing the work.

The artists travelled to Tucumán with extensive documentation of the province's economic and social woes and a detailed knowledge of all the information produced by the media on the problems in Tucumán. This report had previously been subjected to a critical analysis to measure the degree of manipulation and distortion applied to the data. In a second round, the information gathered by the artists and technicians was prepared for use in the exhibition currently installed in the Centrales Obreras [Workers' Halls]. Finally, the information produced by the media on the performance of the artists in Tucumán will be added to the first phase of the information circuit.

The second part of the work is the presentation of all the information gathered on the situation and on the artists' actions in Tucumán, a part of which will be disseminated in labour unions and student/cultural centres, as well as the exhibition of audiovisual materials and performance going on at the Confederación General de Trabajo (CG1) de los Argentinos [General Confederation of Labour of the Argentines] in the Rosario region and later taken to Buenos Aires. The basic purpose of the information super-circuit is to start dismantling the picture of the Tucumán situation drawn by the mass media. This will culminate in the third and last phase, when the action stimulates gathering and formal publication of a third round of information. This document will record the process of conceiving and performing the work and all documentation produced along with a final evaluation.

The position adopted by the avant-garde artists requires them to decline inclusion of their works in the official institutions of the cultural bourgeoisie, and postulates the need for artists to take their works into another context. Thus this exhibition is presented at the CGT de los Argentinos because this body forms the nucleus of the class leading the struggle whose objectives are ultimately shared by the authors of this work.

María Teresa Gramuglio and Nicolás Rosa, in collaboration with the 28 other participants, extracts from 'Tucumán is Burning: Statement of the Exhibition in Rosario' (1968), in *Listen! Here! Now! Argentine Art of the 1960s: Writings of the Avant-garde*, ed. Inés Katzenstein (New York: The Museum of Modern Art, 2004) 319–23.

The Invisible Committee
To Our Friends//2014

[…] The falsity of the entire Western apocalyptic consists in projecting onto the world the mourning we're not able to do in regard to it. It's not the world that is lost, it's *we* who have lost the world and go on losing it. It's not the world that is going to end *soon*, it's *we* who *are finished*, amputated, cut-off, we who refuse vital contact with the real in a hallucinatory way. The crisis is not economic, ecological or political, *the crisis is above all that of presence.* […]

A man dies, a country rises up. The one is not the cause of the other, just the detonator. Alexandros Grigoropoulos, Mark Duggan, Mohamed Bouazizi, Massinissa Guesma – the name of a dead person became, during those days, those weeks, the proper name of the general anonymity, of the shared dispossession. And at its beginning, insurrection is the doing of those who are nothing, of those who hang out in the cafés, in the streets, in life, at the university, on the Internet. It coalesces the whole floating element, plebeian and petty bourgeois, that is secreted in excess by the continuous disintegration of the social. Everything regarded as marginal, obsolete or without prospects returns to the centre. At Sidi Bouzid, Kasserine, Thala, it was the 'crazies', the 'lost souls', the 'good-for-nothings', the 'freaks' who first spread the news of the death of their companion in misery. They climbed onto chairs, tables, monuments, in all the public places all over town. Their tirades stirred everyone willing to listen. Right behind them, there were the high school students who swung into action, those without any remaining hope of a career.

The uprising lasts a few days or a few months, and brings about the fall of the regime or the exposing of every illusion of social peace. It is itself anonymous: no leader, no organization, no demands, no programme. The slogans, when there are any, seem to reach no further than the negation of the existing order, and they are abrupt: 'Clear out!', 'The people want the system to fall!', 'We don't care about your shit.' 'Tayyip, winter is coming.' On TV, on the airwaves, the authorities pound out their same old rhetoric: 'they're gangs of *çapulcu* [looters], smashers, terrorists out of nowhere, most likely in the pay of foreign interests.' Those who've risen up have no one to put on the throne as a replacement, perhaps just a question mark instead. It's not the bottom dogs, or the working class, or the petty bourgeoisie, or the multitudes who are rebelling. They don't form anything homogenous enough to have a representative. There's no new revolutionary subject whose emergence had eluded observers. So if it's said that the 'people' are in the streets it's not a people that existed previously, but rather the people that previously *were lacking*. It's not the people that produce an uprising, it's the uprising that produces its people, by re-engendering the shared experience and understanding, the human fabric and the real-life language that had disappeared. Revolutions of the past promised a new life. Contemporary insurrections deliver the keys to it. [...]

Yet it's true that there was something going beyond that feeling in these occupations, and it was precisely those things that had no place in the theatrical moment of the assembly, everything having to do with the miraculous ability of living beings to *inhabit*, to inhabit even the uninhabitable: the heart of the metropolis. In the occupied squares, all that politics since classical Greece has basically held in contempt, and relegated to the sphere of 'economy', of domestic management, 'survival', 'reproduction', 'daily routine' and 'labour', was affirmed instead as a dimension of collective political potential, escaping in this way from the subordination of the private. The organizational ability that was routinely demonstrated every day and that managed to feed 3,000 persons at every meal, construct a village in a few days, or take care of wounded rioters, can be seen as marking the real political victory of the 'movement of the squares'. [...]

Everyday life has not always been *organized*. For that to be accomplished, it was necessary first to dismantle life, starting with the city. Life and the city have been broken down into *functions*, corresponding to 'social needs'. The office district, the factory district, the residential district, the spaces for relaxation, the entertainment district, the place where one eats, the place where one works, the place where one cruises, and the car or bus for tying all that together are the result of a prolonged reconfiguration of life that devastated every form of life. It was carried out methodically, for more than a century, by a whole caste of *organizers*, a whole grey armada of managers. Life and humanity were dissected into a set of needs; then a synthesis of these elements was organized. It doesn't really matter whether this synthesis was given the name of "socialist planning" or "market planning." It doesn't really matter that it resulted in the failure of new towns or the success of trendy districts. The outcome is the same: a desert and existential anemia. Nothing is left of a form of life once it has been partitioned into organs. Conversely, this explains the palpable joy that overflowed the occupied squares of the Puerta del Sol, Tahrir, Gezi, or the attraction exerted, despite the infernal muds of the Nantes countryside, by the land occupation at Notre-Dame-des-Landes. It is the joy that attaches to every commune. Suddenly, life ceases being sliced up into connected segments. Sleeping, fighting, eating, taking care of oneself, partying, conspiring, discussing all belong to the same vital movement. Not everything is *organized*, everything *organizes itself*. The difference is meaningful. One requires management, the other attention – dispositions that are incompatible in every respect. [...]

In the coming years, we'll be wherever the fires are lit.
During the periods of respite, we're not that hard to find.
We'll continue the effort of clarification we've begun here.
There will be dates and places where we can mass our forces against logical targets.
There will be dates and places for meeting up and debating.
We don't know if the insurrection will have the look of a heroic assault, or if it will be
    a planetary fit of crying, a sudden expression of feeling after decades of
    anaesthesia, misery and stupidity.
Nothing guarantees that the fascist option won't be preferred to revolution.
We'll do what there is to be done.
Thinking, attacking, building – such is our fabulous agenda.
This text is the beginning of a plan.
See you soon,
Invisible Committee

The Invisible Committee, extracts from *To Our Friends* (October 2014); reprinted in *To Our Friends* (Los Angeles and New York: Semiotext[e], 2015).

Lucy R. Lippard
The Art Workers' Coalition: Not a History//1970

On 10 April 1969, some 300 New York artists and observers thereof filled the amphitheatre of the School of Visual Arts for an 'Open Public Hearing on the Subject: What Should Be the Programme of the Art Workers Regarding Museum Reform, and to Establish the Programme of an Open Art Workers' Coalition.' [...] The hearing was preceded by a list of thirteen demands to The Museum of Modern Art, and demonstrations supporting them which emphasized artists' rights: legal, legislative and loosely political; they were the product of the newly named Art Workers' Coalition (temporarily and simultaneously the Artists' Coalition). The AWC was conceived on 3 January 1969, when the kinetic artist Takis (Vassilakis) made a symbolic attempt to remove a work of art, made by him but owned by The Museum of Modern Art, from the museum's 'Machine' show, on the grounds that an artist had the right to control the exhibition and treatment of his work whether or not he had sold it. Not a revolutionary proposition, except in the art world.

Despite the specific subjects announced for the open hearing, taped and later published verbatim by the AWC, the real content of the night was the airing of general complaints about The System, epitomized by Richard Artschwager's use of his two minutes to set off firecrackers instead of talk. The picture of frustrated violence that emerged from this motley cross section of the art community (the speakers were 70 artists, architects, filmmakers and critics, a number of them black) surprised the establishment at which it was aimed. [...]

The extent to which each 'member' agrees with each 'demand' fluctuates to the point where structural fluidity of the organization itself is unavoidable. The AWC has as many identities as it has participants at any one time (there are no members or officers and its main manner of fundraising is a 'Frisco circle' at meetings; the number of participants varies as radically as does their radicality, according to the degree of excitement, rage, guilt, generated by any given issue). It has functioned best as an umbrella, as a conscience and complaint bureau incorporating, not without almost blowing inside out, groups and goals that are not only different, but often conflicting. [...].

Despite the heterogeneous composition, during the winter and spring of 1969 the AWC became a community of artists within the larger art community. The honeymoon period centred on plans for the open hearing and publication of its record, and later on the 'alternatives committee', whose search for alternative structures ran the gamut between a trade union complete with dental care, a massive take-over of the city's abandoned Hudson River piers for studio and exhibition space (that is now being done by the establishment itself), and an information centre complete with Xerox machine, ending comfortably, if a little wearily, as a discussion group covering the highest tides of idealism [...] The weekly general meetings consisted of about 60 people, sometimes 100; the committees were much smaller. Both were characterized by reversals and arguments and endless bullshit (usually defined as somebody else talking), naïveté, commitment and lack of knowledge about how to implement it, [...] all backed up by an excited realization that MoMA was, for some inexplicable reason, afraid of us. [...]

The AWC did not begin as a political group, but its models were clearly the black and student movements of the 1960s, and by the time of the open hearing it was obvious that non-art issues would assume, if not priority, a major rhetorical importance. Though the Black Panthers, the Chicago Seven and other radical causes have been supported; [...] the AWC, like its predecessor and sometime colleague, the Artists and Writers Protest, has concentrated its political energies on peace, as did the May 1970 Art Strike. On the first Moratorium Day (15 October 1969) the AWC managed to get the Modern, the Whitney and the Jewish museums and most of the galleries to close, and (with the crucial help of the participating artists) the Metropolitan to postpone the opening of its big American painting and sculpture show till a more auspicious date, though the museum itself stayed open and, with the Guggenheim, was picketed. [...]

For the most part, however, the artist's dilemma: Is this the kind of society I can make art in? What use is art in this or any society? Should it have no use, even morally? remains unsolved in or out of the AWC. [...]

It is frequently criticized for not representing enough of the art community to be listened to; we in turn frequently criticize the rest of the art community for nor speaking up, with or against us. [...] In June 1969, during an exchange with artists who had (we charged) been pressured to donate works to MoMA for a 'historical' show that just incidentally had to come from the museum's collections, we wrote: 'Our actions should not be mistaken for those of the community as a whole, but rather as a "conscience" in regard to the existing system. We represent the present membership (of the AWC) and, by default, the passive element in the art community. Anyone who does not speak for himself will be spoken for by us until he does take a position [...].'

The real value of the AWC is its voice rather than its force, its whispers rather than its shouts. It exists both as a threat and as a 'place' (in people's heads, and in real space as a clearing house for artists' complaints). More important than any of our 'concrete' achievements is the fact that whether or not we are popular for it, the Coalition has brought up issues that American artists (since the 1930s) have failed to confront together, issues concerning the dignity and value of art and artist in a world that often thinks neither has either. If the American artist looks with increased awareness at his shows, sales, conferences, contracts as an autonomous and independent member, even mover, of his own system, the AWC has made sense. [...]

Lucy R. Lippard, extracts from 'The Art Workers' Coalition: Not a History', *Studio International* (November 1970) 171–4.

Claire Bishop
Delegated Performance: Outsourcing Authenticity//2012

Let's begin with a generalization: one of the most conspicuous manifestations of the 'social turn' in contemporary art since the 1990s has been the hiring of non-professionals to do performances. This stands in sharp contrast to a tradition of performance from the late 1960s and early 1970s in which work is undertaken by the artists themselves; think of Vito Acconci, Marina Abramovic, Chris Burden and Gina Pane. If this tradition valorized live presence and immediacy via the artist's own body, in the last two decades this presence is no longer attached to the single performer but instead to the *collective* body of a social group.[1] Although this trend takes a number of forms, some of which I will describe below, all of this work maintains a comfortable relationship to the gallery, taking it either as the frame for a performance or as a space of exhibition for the photographic and video artefacts that result. I will refer to this tendency as 'delegated performance': the act of hiring non-professionals or specialists in other fields to undertake the job of being present and performing at a particular time and a particular place on behalf of the artist, and following his or her instructions. This strategy differs from a theatrical and cinematic tradition of employing people to act on the director's behalf in the following crucial respect: the artists I discuss below tend to hire people to perform *their own socio-economic category*, be this on the basis of gender, class, ethnicity, age, disability, or (more rarely) profession. [...]

My first type of delegated performance comprises actions outsourced to non-professionals who are asked to perform an aspect of their identities, often in the gallery or exhibition. This tendency, which we might call 'live installation', can be seen in the early work of Paweł Althamer (working with homeless men in *Observator*, 1992, and with female guards for the Zacheeta exhibition *Germinations*, 1994), or Elmgreen & Dragset's hiring, variously, gay men to lounge around in the gallery listening to headphones (*Try*, 1997) or unemployed men and women to be gallery guards (*Reg[u]arding the Guards*, 2005). [...]

Consider, for example, one of the earliest examples of this tendency, by Maurizio Cattelan. In 1991, the Italian artist assembled a soccer club of North African immigrants, who were deployed to play local matches in Italy (all of which they lost). Their shirts were emblazoned with the name of a fictional sponsor, RAUSS: the German word for 'get out', as in the phrase *Ausländer raus*, or 'foreigners out'. The title of the project, *Southern Suppliers FC*, alludes to immigrant labour ('suppliers' from the south), but also to the trend, then hotly debated in the Italian press, of hiring foreign footballers to play on Italian teams.

Cattelan's gesture draws a contrast between two types of foreign labour at different ends of the economic spectrum – star soccer players are rarely perceived in the same terms as working-class immigrants – but without any discernible Marxist rhetoric. Indeed, through this work, Cattelan fulfils the male dream of owning a football club, and apparently insults the players by dressing them in shirts emblazoned RAUSS. At the same time, he nevertheless produces a confusing image: the word RAUSS, when combined with the startling photograph of an all-black Italian football team, has an ambiguous, provocative potency, especially when it circulates in the media, since it seems to blurt out the unspoken EU fear of being deluged by immigrants from outside 'fortress Europe'. *Southern Suppliers FC* is a social sculpture as cynical performance, inserted into the real-time social system of a soccer league. [...].

A second strand of delegated performance, which began to be introduced in the later 1990s, concerns the use of professionals from other spheres of expertise: think of Allora and Calzadilla hiring opera singers (*Sediments, Sentiments, Figures of Speech*, 2007) or pianists (*Stop, Repair, Prepare*, 2008); of Tania Bruguera hiring mounted policemen to demonstrate crowd-control techniques (in *Tatlin's Whisper #5*, 2008); or of Tino Sehgal hiring university professors and students for his numerous speech-based situations (*This Objective of That Object*, 2004; *This Progress*, 2006). These performers tend to be specialists in fields other than those of art or performance, and since they tend to be recruited on the basis of their professional (elective) identity, rather than for being representatives of a particular class or race, there is far less controversy and ambivalence around this type of work. Critical attention tends to focus on the conceptual frame and on the specific activities or abilities of the performer or interpreter in question, whose skills are incorporated into the performance as a readymade. [...]

A third strand of delegated performance comprises situations constructed for video and film; key artists might include Gillian Wearing, Artur Zmijewski and Phil Collins. Recorded images are crucial here since these examples frequently capture situations that are too difficult or sensitive to be repeated. (Here it should be reiterated that my interest is not in artists working in a documentary tradition, but on works where the artist *devises* the entire situation being filmed, and where the participants are asked to perform themselves.) Depending on the mode of filming, these situations can trouble the border between live and mediated to the point where audiences are unsure of the degree to which an event has been staged or scripted. Because the artist assumes a strong editorial role, and because the work's success often relies on the watchability of the performers, this kind of work also tends to attract ethical criticism both from over-solicitous leftists and from the liberal and right-wing media. [...]

[T]he repeatability of delegated performance – both as a live event or as a video loop – is central to the economics of performance since 1990, enabling it to be bought and sold by institutions and individuals, performed and re-performed in many venues.[2] It is not coincidental that this tendency has developed hand in hand with managerial changes in the economy at large, providing an economic genealogy for this work that parallels the art historical one outlined above. 'Outsourcing' labour became a business buzzword in the early 1990s: the wholesale divesting of important but non-core activities to other companies, from customer-service call centres to financial analysis and research. With the growth of globalization, 'offshore outsourcing' became a term that refers – with not altogether positive connotations – to the use of hired labour and 'virtual companies' in developing countries, taking advantage of the huge differences in wages internationally. Business theorists present outsourcing as a tool for maximizing profits; in the US, this led to some controversy as outsourcing was perceived to threaten domestic employment figures (as well as security). For those sceptical of globalization, outsourcing is little more than a legal loophole that allows national and multinational companies to absolve themselves of legal responsibility for unregulated and exploitative labour conditions. It is strange and striking that most UK guides to outsourcing emphasize the importance of *trust*: companies give responsibility for some aspect of their production to another company, with all the risks and benefits that this shared responsibility entails. In the light of the present discussion, it is telling that all of these textbooks agree that the primary aim of outsourcing is to 'improve performance' (understood here as profit). But there are also important differences: if the aim of outsourcing in business is to *decrease* risk, artists frequently deploy it as a means to *increase* unpredictability – even if this means that a work might risk failing altogether.[3] […]

If I seem to be overstressing these economic changes, it's because they not only provide the contextual backdrop for contemporary art but also affect our reception of it. Financial transactions have become increasingly essential to the realization of delegated performance, as anyone who has organized an exhibition of this work can corroborate: contractual wage labour for performers is the largest outgoing expense in such shows, which operate with an inverse economy to that of installing more conventional art: as Tino Sehgal points out, the longer a steel sculpture by Richard Serra is on display, the cheaper the cost of its installation becomes, whereas Sehgal's own works cost more for the institution the longer they are exhibited. But despite the centrality of economics to delegated performance and the impact it has upon our understanding of duration, it is rare for artists to make an explicit point about financial transactions; usually such arrangements tend to be tacit. Unlike theatre, dance and film, where there are long-established codes for experiencing a performer's relationship to labour, contemporary art until recently has been comparatively artisanal, based on the romantic persona of the singular (and largely unpaid) artist-performer. It is only in the past twenty years that performance art has become 'industrialized', and this shift – from festival to museum space, mobilizing large numbers of performers, unionized modes of remuneration and ever larger audiences – means that contemporary art increasingly exists in a sphere of collaboration akin to that of theatre and dance, even while it retains art's valorization of individual authorship. [...]

It should be clear by now that I am trying to argue for a more complicated understanding of delegated performance than that offered by a Marxist framework of reification or a contemporary critical discourse rooted in positivist pragmatics and injunctions to social amelioration, all of which reduce these works to standard-issue questions of political correctness. The perverse pleasures underlying these artistic gestures offer an alternative form of knowledge about capitalism's commodification of the individual, especially when both participants and viewers appear to enjoy the transgression of subordination to a work of art. If one is not to fall into the trap of merely condemning these works as reiterations of capitalist exploitation, it becomes essential to view art not as part of a seamless continuum with contemporary labour but as offering a specific space of experience where those norms are suspended and put in service of pleasure in perverse ways (to return to Sade, a space not unlike that of BDSM sex). Rather than judging art as a model of social organization that can be evaluated according to pre-established moral criteria, it is more productive to view the conceptualization of these performances as properly *artistic* decisions. This is not to say that artists are uninterested in ethics, only to point out that ethics is the ground zero of any collaborative art. To judge a work on the basis of its preparatory phase is to neglect the singular approach of each artist, how this produces specific aesthetic consequences, and the larger questions that he or she might be struggling to articulate.[4]

And what might these larger questions be? Artists choose to use people as a medium for many reasons: to challenge traditional artistic criteria by reconfiguring everyday actions as performance; to give visibility to certain social constituencies and render them more complex, immediate and physically present; to introduce aesthetic effects of chance and risk; to problematize the binaries of live and mediated, spontaneous and staged, authentic and contrived; to examine the construction of collective identity and the extent to which people always exceed these categories. In the most compelling examples of this work, a series of paradoxical operations is put into play that impedes any simplistic accusation that the subjects of delegated performance are reified (decontextualized, and laden with other attributes). To judge these performances on a scale with supposed 'exploitation' at the bottom and full 'agency' at the top is to miss the point entirely. The difference, rather, is between 'art-fair art' and work that reifies *precisely in order to discuss reification*, or that exploits precisely *to thematize exploitation itself*. In this light, the risk of superficiality that occasionally accompanies the reductive branding or packaging of social identities in a work of art ('the unemployed', 'the blind', 'children', 'brass band players', etc.) should always be set against the dominant modes of media representation in opposition to which these works so frequently intend to do battle. This, for me, is the dividing line between the facile gestures of so much gala and art-fair art and those more troubling works that do not simply take advantage of contemporary labour conditions but trouble our relationship to them through the presentation of conventionally underexposed constituencies. It is true that at its worst, delegated performance produces quirkily staged reality designed *for* the media, rather than paradoxically mediated presence. But at its best, delegated performance produces disruptive events that testify to a shared reality between viewers and performers, and which defy not only agreed ways of thinking about pleasure, labour and ethics, but also the intellectual frameworks we have inherited to understand these ideas today.

1   Of course there are exceptions, such as Cildo Meireles's hiring five 'bodyguards' to watch over his flammable sculpture *Fiat Lux for 24 hours* (1979), or Sophie Calle hiring a detective to follow her (*Detective*, 1980). The difference between these and more recent examples is one of degree: the extent to which the identity of the hired labourer becomes a central and visible component of the work of art.

2   [footnote 28 in source] As Philip Auslander has argued, 'Despite the claim … that performance's evanescence allows it to escape commodification, it is performance's very evanescence that gives it value in terms of cultural prestige.' Auslander, *Liveness: Performance in a Mediatized Culture* (London and New York: Routledge, 1999) 58. He continues: 'Even within our hyper-mediatized culture, far more symbolic capital is attached to live events than to mediatized ones.'

3   [29] For the exhibition 'Double Agent' (ICA London, 2008), Mark Sladen and I attempted to commission a new work from Phil Collins. His proposal, *Ghost Rider*, involved hiring a ghostwriter to write a feature on ghostwriters, which would appear in *The Guardian* newspaper, signed by Phil Collins. The resulting article was considered unsuitable by Collins in both tone and content, since the ghostwriter had decided to try to mimic the artist's language and vocabulary, and the feature did not go to press.

4   [43] For example, a distinction can be made between those artists whose work addresses ethics as an explicit theme (e.g. Artur Zmijewski's *80064* [2004]) and those who use ethical discomfort as a technique to express and foreground questions of labour (such as Santiago Sierra) or control (Tania Bruguera).

Claire Bishop, extracts from 'Delegated Performance: Outsourcing Authenticity', *October*, no. 140 (Spring 2012) 91, 92–3, 95–6, 98, 104–5, 111–12.

Robert Smithson
Donald Judd//1965

Donald Judd has set up a 'company' that extends the technique of abstract art into unheard-of places. He may go to Long Island City and have the Bernstein Brothers, Tinsmiths, put 'Pittsburgh' seams into some (Bethcon) iron boxes, or he might go to Allied Plastics in Lower Manhattan and have cut-to-size some Rohm-Haas 'glowing' pink Plexiglas. Judd is always on the look-out for new finishes, like Lavax Wrinkle Finish, which a company pamphlet says 'combines beauty and great durability'. Judd likes that combination, and so he might 'self' spray one of his fabricated 'boxes' with it. Or maybe he will travel to Hackensack, New Jersey, to investigate a lead he got on a new kind of zinc-based paint called Galvanox, which is comparable to 'hot-dip' galvanizing. These procedures tend to baffle art-lovers. They either wonder where the 'art' went or where the 'work' went, or both. It is hard for them to comprehend that Judd is busy extending art into new mediums. This new approach to technique has nothing to do with sentimental notions about 'labour'. There is no subjective craftsmanship. Judd is not a specialist in a certain kind of labour, but a whole artist engaged in a multiplicity of techniques. […]

Robert Smithson, extract from 'Donald Judd', in *7 Sculptors* (Philadelphia: Institute of Contemporary Art, 1965); reprinted in *Robert Smithson: The Collected Writings*, ed. Jack Flam (Berkeley and Los Angeles: University of California Press, 1996) 4–6.

Marisa Jahn
Producing and Its Byproducts//2010

[…] Incorporated in 1966 by Ingrid Baxter and IAIN BAXTER& (formerly known as Iain Baxter), N.E. Thing Co. Ltd. (NETCO) operated in its early years as a business that offered services ranging from 'visual sensitivity' consultations to the integration of informatic technology. Through their rapport with the Canadian Board of Trade and their endorsement by Ronald Basford, Canada's then Minister of Corporate Affairs, NETCO worked to meet the needs of varied companies, responding in turn with the proliferation of 'departments' entitled 'Thing', 'Research', 'Movie', 'Project', 'ACT & ART', 'Service', 'COP', 'Printing', 'Photography', 'Communications' and 'Consulting'. To recruit they set up booths in trade fairs of diverse fields. The Baxters' experimental approach is emblematized in their use of the Telex, a new form of technology at the time that shocked the cultural sphere and ignited artistic possibilities. In an interview with Grant Arnold Ingrid Baxter describes the Telex machine as a means to transgress the traditional barriers of the art world: 'We could send images and penetrate into companies at night, and they would receive it in the morning'.[1] […]

A shared interest in transcending disciplinary divides drove the formation of Experiments in Art and Technology (E.A.T.), founded in New York City in 1966 by Billy Klüver, Fred Waldhauer, Robert Rauschenberg and Robert Whitman. Active until the 1980s, with Klüver at its forefront, E.A.T'.s mission was to fuse art, science and industry around different projects. For Klüver, experimentation was both a means and an end for an artist's collaboration with other disciplines:

> Today, the artist moves into working with materials where unfamiliarity with the material and its physical limitations become an important element of his work. The old assumption that the artist must know his material before he acts no longer has the same meaning. The contemporary artist is developing an attitude toward his new materials similar to that of the experimental scientist. Experimentation and process become an integral part of the artist's work.[2]

To meet the demands of the contemporary artist, E.A.T. actively recruited members from major research institutions (Bell, MIT, National Standards, etc.), and through a booth set up at the annual engineering trade fair – the IEEE (Institute of Electrical and Electronics Engineers). E.A.T., then, was made possible through the training and technical resources developed in corporate research laboratories. […]

The self-same need to discover models of working with non-art sectors was heralded as one of the chief outcomes of the Artist Placement Group (APG, now known as O+I or Organization and Imagination), founded by Barbara Steveni and John Latham in 1966, and active until 1991. The scope of APG's placements is impressive, claiming dozens of successful placements in corporations such as British Airways, ICI Fibres Ltd., the Milton Keynes Development Corporation, Brunei University, the National Coal Board, and the Intensive Care Unit of Clare Hall Hospital. Barbara Steveni, founder of APG/O+I, describes this gradual discovery of 'optimal' associations between art and industry in an interview with Josephine Berry Slater and Pauline van Mourik Broekman: 'It was only by doing the industrial placements that we [APG] began to find out how art activity, or how as artists, an optimum association might be developed which complied with making an artwork in these contexts — so that both sides were getting something out of it.' Steveni also mentions the challenges and discoveries of work-placements:

> So, after the industrial placements, which were seen as kind of terrible by the majority of the art world, for tangling with this 'dirt' so to speak – I was personally, and artists that we worked with, able to find out just what sort of exchange and engagement could be had in these situations. What we discovered was that we have to take great care to preserve the integrity of art's motivation vis-à-vis the commercial and political interests around.[3]

By 'preserv[ing] the integrity of art's motivation', Steveni refers to APG/O+I's insistence that an artist's critical position is at times uncoincident with the immediate goals of the organization, but that this difference should be valorized. As APG/O+I declare in their manifesto written in 1980, 'The status of the artist within organizations is independent, bound by the invitation, rather than by any instruction from authority within the organization, and to the long-term objectives of the whole of society'. [...]

[The] *modus operandi* of creating artwork from the margin of existing workplaces lends valence to the notion of the 'byproduct', or artwork produced from within and as a result of existing systems.

1   Interview with Grant Arnold, in *Byproduct: On the Excess of Embedded Art Practices* (Toronto: YYZBOOKS, 2010) 59–62.

2   Billy Klüver, 'The Artist and Industry', talk at The Museum of Modern Art, New York, 16 December 1968.

3   Pauline van Mourik Broekman and Josephine Berry Slater, Countdown to Zero, Count up to Now: An Interview with the Artist Placement Group', in *Byproduct*, op. cit., 42–8.

Marisa Jahn, extracts from 'Producing and Its Byproducts', in *Byproduct: On the Excess of Embedded Art Practices* (Toronto: YYZBOOKS, 2010) 34, 35, 35–6, 38.

Andrea Fraser
How to Provide an Artistic Service:
An Introduction//1994

In our initial proposal for 'Services', Helmut Draxler and I offered the term 'service' to describe what appeared to be a determining feature of what has come to be called 'project work'. We wrote:

> It appears to us that, related variously to institutional critique, productivist, activist and political documentary traditions as well as post-studio, site-specific and/or public art activities, the practices currently characterized as 'project work' do not necessarily share a thematic, ideological or procedural basis. What they do seem to share is the fact that they all involve expending an amount of labour which is either in excess of, or independent of, any specific material production and which cannot be transacted as or along with a product. This labour, which in economic terms would be called service provision (as opposed to goods production), may include:
> the work of the interpretation or analysis of sites and situations in and outside of cultural institutions;
> the work of presentation and installation;
> the work of public education in and outside of cultural institutions;
> advocacy and other community-based work, including organizing, education, documentary production and the creation of alternative structures.

'Providing a service', in this sense, is neither an intention (such as benefiting society), attributed to particular artists, nor a content (such as museum education or security), characterizing a group of works. Rather, we proposed 'service provision' to describe the economic condition of project work as well as the nature of the social relations under which it is carried out. On the most basic level we could even claim that the prevalence of practices such as the payment of fees to artists by cultural institutions indicates that the emergence of art as 'service provision' is simply an historical fact (a fee is by definition payment for services). We went on to write:

There seems to be a growing consensus among both artists and curators that the new set of relations [emerging around project work] ... needs clarification. While curators are increasingly interested in asking artists to produce work in response to specific existing or constructed situations, the labour necessary to respond to those demands is often not recognized or adequately compensated. Conversely, many curators committed to project development are frustrated by finding themselves in the role of producers for commercial galleries, or a 'service department' for artists ... [...]

While many of us had taken up, in our work, the positions and activities of curators, gallerists, educators, public relations and employee-management relations consultants, security consultants, architects and exhibition designers, researchers, archivists, etc., we certainly did not do so to have our practices reduced to the functions of these professions. What would – should – differentiate our practices from them is precisely our autonomy. This autonomy is represented, most importantly, in our relative freedom from the functionalization of our activity – that is, from its rationalization in the service of specific interests defined by the individuals or organizations with which we work. Included in this is freedom from the rationalization of the language and forms we use – a freedom which may or may not manifest itself in recognizably 'aesthetic' forms. Also included is the freedom of speech and conscience – guaranteed by accepted professional practice – which is supposed to safeguard our right to express critical opinions and engage in controversial activity.

The logic of the question is pretty clear. We are demanding fees as compensation for work within organizations. Fees are, by definition, payment for services. If we are, then, accepting payment in exchange for our services, does that mean we are serving those who pay us? If not, who are we serving and on what basis are we demanding payment (and should we be demanding payment)? Or, if so, how are we serving them (and what are we serving)? [...]

Am I really serving my own interests? According to the logic of artistic autonomy, we work only for ourselves; for our own satisfaction, for the satisfaction of our own criteria of judgement, subject only to the internal logic of our practice, the demands of our consciences or our drives. It has been my experience that the freedom gained in this form of autonomy is often no more than the basis for self-exploitation. Perhaps it is because the privilege of recognizing ourselves and being recognized in the products of our labour must be purchased (like the 'freedom' to labour as such, according to Marx), at the price of surplus labour, generating surplus value, or profit, to be appropriated by another. In our case, it is primarily symbolic profit that we generate. And it is conditioned precisely on the freedom from economic necessity we express in our self-exploitation.

Because we are working for our own satisfaction, our labour is supposed to be its own compensation. It often feels as if all our professional relations are organized as if the entire art apparatus – including cultural institutions and galleries – was established to provide us so generously with the opportunity of fulfilling our exhibitionistic desires in a public presentation. […]

If we are always already serving, artistic freedom can only consist in determining for ourselves – to the extent that we can – who and how we serve. This is, I think, the only course to a less contradictory principle of autonomy.

Andrea Fraser, extracts from 'How to Provide an Artistic Service: An Introduction' (1994), in *Museum Highlights: The Writings of Andrea Fraser*, ed. Alexander Alberro (Cambridge, Massachusetts: The MIT Press, 2005) 153–61.

Chto Delat
A Declaration on Politics, Knowledge and Art//2008

Our Principles: Self-Organization, Collectivism, Solidarity
The Chto Delat? platform unites artists, philosophers, social researchers, activists, and all those whose aim is the collaborative realization of critical and independent research, publication, artistic, educational and activist projects.

All of the platform's initiatives are based on principles of self-organization and collectivism. These principles are realized through the political coordination of working groups, the contemporary analogue of soviets. The projects undertaken by any of these groups represent the entire platform and are closely coordinated with one another. At the same time, the existence of the platform creates a common context for interpreting the projects of its individual participants.

We are likewise guided by the principle of solidarity. We organize and support mutual assistance networks with all grassroots groups who share the principles of internationalism, feminism and equality.

Demanding the (Im)possible
At this reactionary historical moment, when elementary demands for the possible are presented as a romantic impossibility, we remain *realists* and insist on certain simple, intelligible things. We have to move away from the frustrations occasioned by the historical failures to advance *leftist ideas* and discover anew their *emancipatory potential*.

We say that it is natural for each person to be free and live a life of dignity. All that we have to do is to find the strength within ourselves to fight for this. The first thing that motivates us is the rejection of all forms of oppression, the artificial alienation of people, and exploitation. That is why we stand for a distribution of the wealth produced by human labour and all natural resources that is just and directed towards the welfare of everyone.

We are internationalists: we demand the recognition of the equality of all people, no matter where they live or where they come from.

We are feminists: we are against all forms of patriarchy, homophobia and gender inequality.

Capitalism is Not a Totality

We believe that capital is not a totality, that the popular thesis that 'there is nothing outside capital' is false. The task of the intellectual and the artist is to engage in a thoroughgoing unmasking of the myth that there are no alternatives to the global capitalist system. We insist on the obvious: a world without the dominion of profit and exploitation not only can be created but always already exists in the micropolitics and microeconomies of human relationships and creative labour. We have to reveal this joyous space of life to the greatest number of people. The historical becoming of this economic, political, intellectual and creative emancipation is communism.

The Communist Decoding of Capitalist Reality

The person who is genuinely free, who lives in the fullness of their being, is a person who is alive to various sciences and disciplines, who critically examines themselves and the world. However, the narrow specialization of scientific knowledge in capitalist society places knowledge in the service of the dominant class. Individual research serves private interests, while research of society, research based on the universality of critical utterance, is not supported institutionally. We affirm that there is only one form of knowledge – knowledge that enables the discovery that the calling of human beings is to be free with other human beings. Critical knowledge should not be a commodity, and its maximally widespread distribution – enlightenment and education – is the cause of each intellectual and cultural worker. This synthesis of theory and practice, knowledge of the world and its transformation, we call the communist decoding of capitalist reality. We repeat along with Marx: 'We do not say to the world: Cease your struggles, they are foolish; we will give you the true slogan of struggle. We merely show the world what it is really fighting for, and consciousness is something that it has to acquire, even if it does not want to.' (Letter to Arnold Ruge, September 1843.)

Faithfulness to the Twentieth-Century Intellectual and Artistic Avant-Gardes
We recognize the importance of twentieth-century avant-garde thought for the
rethinking and renewal of leftist philosophical and political tradition. We believe
that for this renewal to happen we need a maximally open, non-dogmatic
approach that presupposes a critical reception of ideas, concepts and practices
that have formed outside the framework of doctrinal Marxism. Our urgent task
is to reconnect political action, engaged thought and artistic innovation.

Class Composition
One of the basic problems of theory remains the definition of contemporary
society's class structure. At present, when labour relations are in a process of
radical transformation, the very notion of classes is changing as well. We can no
longer rely wholly on the previous definitions of proletariat and bourgeoisie, or
on old forms of organizing the struggle for liberation. We believe that we have to
continue to re-examine class theory by considering the contemporary
development of the antagonism between labour and capital. We affirm that this
antagonism remains the central one. The transformation of society has not only
not made it disappear; on the contrary, this antagonism has only been exacerbated
and therefore needs to be interpreted anew. We are also faced here with the
question of rethinking the strategies and tasks of the critical intellectual in a
conjuncture where the configuration of productive forces is changing.

The Tasks of Contemporary Art
Contemporary art that is produced as a commodity form or a form of
entertainment is not art. It is the conveyor-belt manufacture of counterfeits and
narcotics for the enjoyment of a 'creative class' sated with novelty. One of our
most vital tasks today is unmasking the current system of ideological control
and manipulation of people. The pseudocreativity of this system is no more
than the commodification not only of the fruits of their labour, but also of all
forms of life. We are convinced that genuine art is art that de-automates
consciousness – first, that of the artist, then that of the viewer. And because art
is an activity open to everyone, neither power nor capital can have a monopoly
on the 'ownership' of art.

One answer to the perennial debate on art's autonomy is the possibility that
it can be produced independently of art institutions, whether state or private. In
the contemporary conjuncture, the self-negation essential to art's development
happens outside institutional practices. As a public form of the unfolding of each
person's creative potential, the place of art during moments of revolutionary
struggle has always been and always will be in the thick of events, on the squares
and in the communes. At such moments, art takes the form of street theatre,

posters, actions, graffiti, grassroots cinema, poetry and music. Renewing these forms at this new stage in history is the task of the genuine artist.

What is the Place of Revolutionary Art in a Time of Reaction?

Although mass movements for the transformation of society are temporarily absent, art's place is nevertheless still on the side of the oppressed. Its central task is the elaboration of new forms for the sensual and critical apprehension of the world from the perspective of collective liberation. Art should exist not for museums and dealers but in order to develop and articulate a new mode of 'emancipated sensuality'. It should become an instrument for seeing and knowing the world in the totality of its contradictions. The museums and institutions of art should function as depositories and laboratories for the aesthetic exploration of the world. We should, however, shield them from privatization, economization and subordination to the populist logic of the culture industry.

That is why we believe that right now it would be wrong to refuse to work in any way with cultural and academic institutions – despite the fact that the majority of these institutions throughout the world are engaged in the flagrant propaganda of commodity fetishism and servile knowledge. The political propaganda of all other forms of human vocation either provokes the system's harsh rejection or the system co-opts it into its spectacle.

At the same time, however, the system is not homogeneous – it is greedy, stupid and dependent. Today, this leaves us room to use these institutions to advance and promote our knowledge. We can bring this knowledge to a wide audience without succumbing to its distortion. That is why we need to develop clear criteria for deciding in which venues we can conduct our struggle, which projects should be boycotted and denounced, and with whom and on what conditions we can collaborate.

Our Basic Programme

In the current situation, we propose that self-governed collectives use the following basic programme as their guide:

Don't allow external factors to intervene as you develop your ideas and realize your projects. Don't give away exclusive rights to the distribution of your work. Don't directly or indirectly advertise the institutions of power and capital within your projects.

Economic relations have to be built in a political way. You need collectively to demand that your labour be compensated fairly and with dignity. By entering into a working relationship with the institutions of power, you demonstrate their capitalistic, exploitative nature.

Don't participate in projects whose results (symbolic capital, surplus value) can be instrumentalized for political ends that contradict the internal tasks of your collective's work.

As you realize your project you should try to make your work as 'non-transparent' as possible. At the same time, you should strive to produce situations whose meaning can be fully manifested only outside the limited frame of concrete relations of production. This means that you should construe the use value of the work in such a way that institutions of power will be hard pressed when they try to convert it into exchange value.

At the same time, we insist on an uncompromising critique of and struggle against all institutions of culture that base their work on corruption and the primitive servicing of the interests of commercial structures, the state and ideology. We must constantly 'slap' these dimwits and prostitutes 'on the wrist' and show them their shameful place in history. We will use all the means at our disposal to make this happen.

The Local Aspect of the Struggle

We demand, as a minimum, the abolition of tacit censorship and an end to all repression of political and cultural activity. It follows from this demand that we need state and public support for social research projects and critical art practices in Russia that are independent of private interests.

Avoiding the traditional choice between 'reformism' and 'radicalism', we insist on the search for a specific, local configuration of demands and transformational programmes. For a start we demand a few concrete things. Public funds should be transparently distributed for the support of research and art in public space, as well for grassroots initiatives. They should also be used to support work based on the harsh criticism of contemporary institutions of power, both in culture and in politics. On the other hand, this is possible only as part of a radical social transformation that would undermine the entire system of authoritarian capitalism. In order to foster conditions for this transformation, we need new forms of coordination with all other fronts of the struggle – with workers, trade unions, environmentalists, feminists and anti-authoritarian activists. We have to propagate models of activist self-education and the politicization of artistic and intellectual practices. These are the bases for a future broad consolidation of leftists and the hegemony of our ideas in society.

Chto Delat, 'A Declaration on Politics, Knowledge and Art', in *Chto Delat?* (November 2008).

Paolo Virno
Ten Theses on the Multitude and Post-Fordist Capitalism//2004

I have attempted to describe the nature of contemporary production, so-called post-Fordism, on the basis of categories drawn from political philosophy, ethics, epistemology and the philosophy of language. I have done so not as a professional exercise, but because I am truly convinced that, in order for it to be described clearly, the mode of contemporary production demands *this* variety of analyses, *this* breadth of views. One cannot understand post-Fordism without having recourse to a cluster of ethical-linguistic concepts. [...]

In order to name with a unifying term the forms of life and the linguistic games which characterize our era, I have used the notion of 'multitude'. This notion, the polar opposite of that of 'people', is defined by a complex of breaks, landslides and innovations which I have tried to point out. Let me cite some of them here, in no particular order: the life of the stranger (*bios xenikos*) being experienced as an ordinary condition; the prevalence of 'common places' in discourse over 'special' places; the publicness of the intellect, as much an apotropaic device as a pillar of social production; activity without end product (that is, virtuosity); the centrality of the principle of individuation; the relation with the possible in as much as it is possible (opportunism); the hypertrophic development of the non-referential aspects of language (idle talk). [...]

Thesis 9
The multitude throws the 'theory of proletarianization' out of the mix.
In Marxist theoretical discussion, the comparison between 'complex' (intellectual, that is) labour and 'simple' (unskilled) labour has provoked more than a few problems. What is the unit of measurement which permits this comparison? The prevalent answer is: the unit of measurement coincides with 'simple' labour, along with the pure waste of psychophysical energy; 'complex' labour is merely a multiple of 'simple' labour. The ratio between one and the other can be determined by considering the different cost of education (school, varied specializations, etc.) for the intellectual labour-power as opposed to the unskilled labour-power. Little of this old and controversial question interests me; here I would like, however, to capitalize on the terminology used in its regard. I hold that the intellectuality of the masses in its totality is 'complex' labour – but, note carefully – 'complex' labour which is *not reducible* to 'simple' labour. The complexity, as well as the irreducibility, comes from the fact that this labour-power mobilizes, in the fulfilling of its work duties, linguistic-cognitive

competencies which are generically human. These competencies, or faculties, cause the duties of the individual to be characterized *always* by a high rate of sociability and intelligence, even though they are not all specialized duties (we are not speaking of engineers or philologists here, but of ordinary workers). That which is not reducible to 'simple' labour is, if you will, the *co-operative quality* of the concrete operations carried out by the intellectuality of the masses.

To say that all post-Ford era labour is complex labour, irreducible to simple labour, means also to confirm that today the 'theory of proletarianization' is completely out of the mix. This theory had its peak of honour in signalling the potential comparability of intellectual labour to manual labour. Precisely for this reason, the theory ends up unsuited to accounting for the intellectuality of the masses, or, and this is the same thing, for accounting for living labour as *general intellect*. The theory of proletarianization fails when intellectual (or complex) labour cannot be equated with a network of specialized knowledge, but becomes one with the use of the generic linguistic-cognitive faculties of the human animal. This is the conceptual (and practical) movement which modifies all the terms of the question.

The lack of proletarianization certainly does not mean that qualified workers retain privileged niches. Instead it means that the sort of *homogeneity by subtraction* which the concept of 'proletariat' usually implies does not characterize all post-Fordist labour-power, as complex or intellectual as it may be. In other words, the lack of proletarianization means that post-Ford labour is *multitude*, not *people*.

Paolo Virno, extracts from *A Grammar of the Multitude: For an Analysis of Contemporary Forms of Life* (Los Angeles and New York: Semiotext[e], 2004) 97, 109–10.

Artur Żmijewski
In Conversation with Joanna Sokołowska//2010

Joanna Sokołowska As a part of the *Swiecie* open-air exhibition, you created a situation in which artists and industry workers worked collectively on a portrait of a modern workman; artists, vested with powers to work on collective imagery and language, were helping the workers in articulating their own subjectivity.

Artur Żmijewski It's the other way round – it is workers who help the artists to understand their incompetence in talking about workers. Artists use stereotypical imagery and are conservative in them, and therefore are just incompetent, but, on the other hand, they have no doubt that they can define defining who/what a modern workman is. This video is a 'dead language lesson' – the language of Social Realism. This language functioned as a kind of Esperanto – regardless of its violent character, it was understood by the majority of people. Surprisingly, it survived in artistic imagination. And now it was waken up on my demand. The sculptures in *Swiecie* were set on the streets of the town, and its citizens claimed it was for the first time for a long time they liked art so much.

Sokołowska Why have you evoked this language?

Żmijewski I reckon we still miss clear language in art, artistic Esperanto, a kind of pidgin English accessible for everybody. Critical texts often say that this artist cannot be easily defined or categorized, and that his/her art is constantly slipping away. For me, chasing eluding meanings takes away all our energy; it's all just a lot of hot air. And so, what would happen if artists became more palpable, and sometimes chose a transparent language with a well-known grammar? What would happen if they were able to speak it well? Most likely art wouldn't be over because of it.

Sokołowska You undertake interventions in various fields of knowledge, politics and economy; you also make use of opportunities offered by artistic autonomy. It means that no large-scale realizations of critical, emancipatory artistic experiments are expected, nor it is believed that they will contribute to real social changes.

Żmijewski Autonomy is not my fetish. I don't take an interest in either critical, emancipatory projects for nobody, or in such a description of my work. A finished film means the end of working with people; what we see as a film in a gallery was first a two-week long operation on a living, social organism – in a factory, based on everyday relations between workers, their employers and artists. For them, it was daily, hard work from 6 a.m. to 7 p.m. This factory employs about 200 people. Is the scale satisfactory? Does a project work among people, or just revivify the white cube's walls? [...]

Artur Żmijewski and Joanna Sokołowska, extracts from interview, 'Artur Zmijewski: Dead Language Lesson', in *Workers Leaving the Workplace* (Lódz: Muzeum Sztuki w Lodzi, 2010) 220–23.

Irit Rogoff
WE – Collectivities, Mutualities, Participations//2002

Collectivity is something that takes place as we arbitrarily gather to take part in different forms of cultural activity, such as looking at art. If we countenance that beyond all the roles that are allotted to us in culture, such as those of being viewers, listeners or audience members in one capacity or another, there are other emergent possibilities for the exchange of shared perspectives, or insights, or subjectivities, then we allow for some form of emergent collectivity. [...]

Despite the prevailing mythologies that continue to link the experience of art to individual reflection, we look at art and inhabit its spaces in various forms of collectivity. In the process, we produce new forms of mutuality, relations between viewers and spaces, rather than between viewers and objects. Beyond the shared categories of class, taste, political or sexual orientation, another form of 'WE' is produced in these processes of viewing, and this in turn shifts the very nature of meaning and its relation to the notion of displayed visual culture. [...]

By introducing the notion of WE as central to the experience of art I am insisting on several elements, such as the facts that:

Meaning is never produced in isolation or through isolating processes, but rather through intricate webs of connectedness.

Audiences produce meaning not simply through the subjectivities they project onto artworks whose circuits of meanings they complete, but through relations with one another and through the temporality of the event of an exhibition or display.

Artworks, and thematic exhibitions that continue to re-produce them into view, do not have immanent meanings but function as fields of possibilities for different audiences in different cultural circumstances and wildly divergent moods, to produce significance.

In a reflective shift from the analytical to the performative function of observation and participation we can agree that meaning is not excavated for, but 'takes place' in the present. [...]

I make these claims and observations in the wake of Jean-Luc Nancy's *Being Singular Plural* [...]. Nancy proceeds to take on the proper names of collectivity, 'we' and 'us', and their relation to meaning, and does so against the grain of the claims of identity and their ability to separate and segregate. He takes up the notion of meaning precisely because of this proliferation that has no other meaning than the indeterminate multiplication of centripetal meanings, meanings closed in on themselves and supersaturated with significance, no longer meaningful because they refer to their own closure, to their horizon of appropriation, and spread nothing but destruction, hatred and the denial of existence. To these ends he has to return to both 'we' and 'meaning' as the building blocks of another form of relatedness that is not founded on the articulation of identity.

> We do not 'have' meaning any more, because we ourselves are meaning – entirely, without reserve, infinitely, with no meaning other than 'us'. (*Being Singular Plural* [Stanford, 2000] 1) [...] There is no meaning if meaning is not shared, and not because there would be an ultimate or first signification that all beings have in common, but because meaning is itself the sharing of Being. (Ibid., 2) [...]

In Nancy's assertion that 'everything, then, passes *between us*', do we not also have the condition of the exhibition? And in this condition do we not have the possibility of shifting the gaze away from artworks that might critically alert us to certain untenable states of the world, away from exhibitions that make those states of hegemonic breach and unease the subject and focal point of saturated vision, and towards everything that passes between us in the process of those confrontations. [...] I am not arguing for the centrality of the art exhibition as a political space on the basis of what it exhibits, of the kind of work that the objects on display might do in the world, or the kinds of issues the thematic exhibition might alert us to. I am arguing instead for the art exhibition as what Nancy has termed 'the spectacle of society'.

> If being-with is the sharing of a simultaneous space-time, then it involves a presentation of this space-time as such. In order to say 'we' one must present the 'here and now' of this 'we'. [...] We can never simply be the 'the we' understood as a unique subject ... 'We' always expresses a plurality, expresses 'our' being divided and entangled [...].
> (Hannah Arendt, *The Human Condition* [Chicago, 1968] 199)

On this stage, as part of this spectacle, we can begin to perceive the possibilities for some form of action that is not the planned demonstrations of political activism, with their binaries of the blamed and the blaming. This stage functions as the 'space of appearance' that Hannah Arendt invoked in attempting to enlarge an understanding of how and where political action takes place. The peculiarity of this 'space of appearance', says Arendt,

> is that unlike the spaces which are the work of our hands, it does not survive the actuality of the movement which brought it into being, but disappears, not only with the dispersal of men ..., but with the disappearance or the arrest of the

activities themselves. Wherever people gather together; it is potentially there, but only potentially, not necessarily, and not forever. [...]

What I am proposing, then, is that the space of the exhibition is Arendt's 'Space of Appearance', in which a form of political action takes place that is not just ephemeral and based in speech as action but also founded on 'acting without a model', and on making 'its means as visible as possible'. If we can accept the space of the exhibition as the arena for such enactments, in which it is we, the audience, who produce the meanings through our 'being' and our acknowledgement of mutualities and imbrications, then what WE have is the possibility of another political space. Instead of an occasion for the translation of various sets or politics into the realm of aesthetics and language, instead of a series of exercises in moral navigations that take place in and through the art exhibition, we have the possibility of an actual political space *tout court*.

Irit Rogoff, extracts from 'WE – Collectivities, Mutualities, Participations', in *I Promise It's Political*, ed. Dorothea von Hantelmann and Marjorie Jongbloed (Cologne: Museum Ludwig, 2002) 127, 128, 129–31, 133 [footnotes not included].

WE CONSTANTLY
BECOME WHAT
OTHER PEOPLE
WANT US TO BE,
BUT STARTING
A HUMAN STRIKE
MEANS INVERTING
THAT MOVEMENT
AND REFUSING
TO ACT UPON
THE ACTIONS
OF OTHERS
THROUGH THE
USE OF POWER

Claire Fontaine, 'Human Strike Has Already Begun', 2009

ON STRIKE

Hito Steyerl
Politics of Art: Contemporary Art and the Transition to Post-Democracy//2011

A standard way of relating politics to art assumes that art represents political issues in one way or another. But there is a much more interesting perspective: the politics of the field of art as a place of work.[1] Simply look at what it does – not what it shows. [...]

[T]he production of art presents a mirror image of post-democratic forms of hypercapitalism that look set to become the dominant political post-Cold War paradigm. It seems unpredictable, unaccountable, brilliant, mercurial, moody, guided by inspiration and genius. Just as any oligarch aspiring to dictatorship might want to see himself. [...]

Thus traditional art production may be a role model for the nouveaux riches created by privatization, expropriation and speculation. But the actual production of art is simultaneously a workshop for many of the nouveaux poor, trying their luck as jpeg virtuosos and conceptual impostors, as gallerinas and overdrive content providers. Because art also means work, more precisely strike work.[2] It is produced as spectacle, on post-Fordist all-you-can-work conveyor belts. Strike or shock work is affective labour at insane speeds, enthusiastic, hyperactive and deeply compromised.

Originally, strike workers were excess labourers in the early Soviet Union. The term is derived from the expression *udarny trud* for 'superproductive, enthusiastic labour' (*udar* for 'shock, strike, blow'). Now, transferred to present-day cultural factories, strike work relates to the sensual dimension of shock. Rather than painting, welding and moulding, artistic strike work consists of ripping, chatting and posing. This accelerated form of artistic production creates punch and glitz, sensation and impact. Its historical origin as format for Stalinist model brigades brings an additional edge to the paradigm of hyperproductivity. Strike workers churn out feelings, perception and distinction in all possible sizes and variations. Intensity or evacuation, sublime or crap, readymade or readymade reality – strike work supplies consumers with all they never knew they wanted.

Strike work feeds on exhaustion and tempo, on deadlines and curatorial bullshit, on small talk and fine print. It also thrives on accelerated exploitation. I'd guess that – apart from domestic and care work – art is the industry with the most unpaid labour around. It sustains itself on the time and energy of unpaid interns and self-exploiting actors on pretty much every level and in almost every function. Free labour and rampant exploitation are the invisible dark matter that keeps the cultural sector going. [...]

Contemporary art's workforce consists largely of people who, despite working constantly, do not correspond to any traditional image of labour. They stubbornly resist settling into any entity recognizable enough to be identified as a class. While the easy way out would be to classify this constituency as multitude or crowd, it might be less romantic to ask whether they are not global lumpenfreelancers, deterritorialized and ideologically free-floating: a reserve army of imagination communicating via Google Translate.

Instead of shaping up as a new class, this fragile constituency may well consist – as Hannah Arendt once spitefully formulated – of the 'refuse of all classes'. These dispossessed adventurers described by Arendt, the urban pimps and hoodlums ready to be hired as colonial mercenaries and exploiters, are faintly (and quite distortedly) mirrored in the brigades of creative strike workers propelled into the global sphere of circulation known today as the art world. If we acknowledge that current strike workers might inhabit similarly shifting grounds – the opaque disaster zones of shock capitalism – a decidedly un-heroic, conflicted and ambivalent picture of artistic labour emerges.

We have to face up to the fact that there is no automatically available road to resistance and organization for artistic labour. That opportunism and competition are not a deviation of this form of labour but its inherent structure. That this workforce is not ever going to march in unison, except perhaps while dancing to a viral Lady Gaga imitation video. The international is over. Now let's get on with the global. [...]

The art field is a space of wild contradiction and phenomenal exploitation. It is a place of power mongering, speculation, financial engineering and massive and crooked manipulation. But it is also a site of commonality, movement, energy and desire. In its best iterations it is a terrific cosmopolitan arena populated by mobile shock workers, itinerant salesmen of self, tech whiz kids, budget tricksters, supersonic translators, PhD interns, and other digital vagrants and day labourers. It's hard-wired, thin-skinned, plastic-fantastic. A potential commonplace where competition is ruthless and solidarity remains the only foreign expression. Peopled with charming scumbags, bully-kings, almost-beauty-queens. It's HDMI, CMYK, LGBT. Pretentious, flirtatious, mesmerizing.

This mess is kept afloat by the sheer dynamism of loads and loads of hardworking women. A hive of affective labour under close scrutiny and controlled by capital, woven tightly into its multiple contradictions. All of this makes it relevant to contemporary reality. Art affects this reality precisely because it is entangled into all of its aspects. It's messy, embedded, troubled, irresistible. We could try to understand its space as a political one instead of trying to represent a politics that is always happening elsewhere. Art is not outside politics, but politics resides within its production, its distribution and its reception. If we take this on, we might surpass the plane of a politics of representation and embark on a politics that is there, in front of our eyes, ready to embrace.

1   I am expanding on a notion developed by Hongjohn Lin in his curatorial statement for the Taipei Biennial 2010. Hongjohn Lin, 'Curatorial Statement', in *10TB Taipei Biennial Guidebook* (Taipei: Taipei Fine Arts Museum, 2010) 10–11.

2   I am drawing on a field of meaning developed by Ekaterina Degot, Cosmin Costinas and David Riff for their 1st Ural Industrial Biennial, 2010.

Hito Steyerl, extracts from 'Politics of Art: Contemporary Art and the Transition to Post-Democracy', in *Are You Working Too Much? Post-Fordism, Precarity and the Labour of Art*, ed. Julieta Aranda, Brian Kuan Wood, Anton Vidokle (Berlin: Sternberg Press, 2011) 30, 31–3, 33–4.

Gustav Metzger
Years without Art//1974

Artists engaged in political struggle act in two key areas: the use of their art for direct social change; and actions to change the structures of the art world. It needs to be understood that this activity is necessarily of a reformist, rather than revolutionary, character. Indeed this political activity often serves to consolidate the existing order, in the West and in the East.

The use of art for social change is bedevilled by the close integration of art and society. The state supports art, it needs art as a cosmetic cloak to its horrifying reality, and uses art to confuse, divert and entertain large numbers of people. Even when deployed against the interests of the state, art cannot cut loose the umbilical cord of the state. Art in the service of revolution is unsatisfactory and mistrusted because of the numerous links of art with the state and capitalism. Despite these problems, artists will go on using art to change society.

Throughout the century, artists have attacked the prevailing methods of production, distribution and consumption of art. These attacks on the organization of the art world have gained momentum in recent years. This struggle, aimed at the destruction of existing commercial and public marketing and patronage systems, can be brought to a successful conclusion in the course of the present decade.

The refusal to labour is the chief weapon of workers fighting the system; artists can use the same weapon. To bring down the art system it is necessary to call for years without art, a period of three years – 1977 to 1980 – when artists will not produce work, sell work, permit work to go on exhibition, and refuse collaboration with any part of the publicity machinery of the art world. This total withdrawal of labour is the most extreme collective challenge that artists can make to the state.

The years without art will see the collapse of many private galleries. Museums and cultural institutions handling contemporary art will be severely hit, suffer loss of funds, and will have to reduce their staff. National and local government institutions will be in serious trouble. Art magazines will fold. The international ramifications of the dealer/museum/publicity complex make for vulnerability; it is a system that is keyed to a continuous juggling of artists, finance, works and information – damage one part and the effect is felt worldwide.

Three years is the minimum period required to cripple the system, whilst a longer period of time would create difficulties for artists. The very small number of artists who live from the practice of art are sufficiently wealthy to live on their capital for three years. The vast majority of people who produce art have to subsidise their work by other means; they will, in fact, be saving money and time. Most people who practise art never sell their work at a profit, do not get the chance to exhibit their work under proper conditions, and are unmentioned by the publicity organs. Some artist may find it difficult to restrain themselves from producing art. These artists will be invited to enter camps, where making of artworks is forbidden, and where any work produced is destroyed at regular intervals. In place of the practice of art, people can spend time on the numerous historical, aesthetic and social issues facing art. It will be necessary to construct more equitable forms for marketing, exhibiting and publicizing art in the future. As the twentieth century has progressed, capitalism has smothered art – the deep surgery of the years without art will give it a new chance.

Gustav Metzger, 'Years without Art', in *Art into Society – Society into Art: Seven German Artists* (London: Institute of Contemporary Arts, 1974) 79.

Walter Benjamin
Critique of Violence//1921

[...] Organized labour is, apart from the state, probably today the only legal subject entitled to exercise violence. Against this view there is certainly the objection that an omission of actions, a non-action, which a strike really is, cannot be described as violence. Such a consideration doubtless made it easier for a state power to conceive the right to strike, once this was no longer avoidable. But its truth is not unconditional, and therefore not unrestricted. It is true that the omission of an action, or service, where it amounts simply to a 'severing of relations', can be an entirely nonviolent, pure means. And as in the view of the state, or the law, the right to strike conceded to labour is certainly not a right to exercise violence but, rather, to escape from a violence indirectly exercised by the employer, strikes conforming to this may undoubtedly occur from time to time and involve only a 'withdrawal' or 'estrangement' from the employer. The moment of violence, however, is necessarily introduced, in the form of extortion, into such an omission, if it takes place in the context of a conscious readiness to resume the suspended action under certain circumstances that either have nothing whatever to do with this action or only superficially modify it. Understood in this way, the right to strike constitutes in the view of labour, which is opposed to that of the state, the right to use force in attaining certain ends. The antithesis between the two conceptions emerges in all its bitterness in face of a revolutionary general strike. In this, labour will always appeal to its right to strike, and the state will call this appeal an abuse, since the right to strike was not 'so intended', and take emergency measures. For the state retains the right to declare that a simultaneous use of strike in all industries is illegal, since the specific reasons for strike admitted by legislation cannot be prevalent in every workshop. In this difference of interpretation is expressed the objective contradiction in the legal situation, whereby the state acknowledges a violence whose ends, as natural ends, it sometimes regards with indifference, but in a crisis (the revolutionary general strike) confronts inimically. For, however paradoxical this may appear at first sight, even conduct involving the exercise of a right can nevertheless, under certain circumstances, be described as violent. More specifically, such conduct, when active, may be called violent if it exercises a right in order to overthrow the legal system that has conferred it; when passive, it is nevertheless to be so described if it constitutes extortion in the sense explained above. It therefore reveals an objective contradiction in the legal situation, but not a logical contradiction in the law, if under certain circumstances the law meets the strikers, as perpetrators of violence, with violence. For in a strike the state fears above all else that function of violence which it is the object of this study to identify as the only secure foundation of its critique. For if violence were, as first appears, merely the means to secure directly whatever happens to be sought, it could fulfil its end as predatory violence. It would be entirely unsuitable as a basis for, or a modification to, relatively stable conditions. The strike shows, however, that it can be so, that it is able to found and modify legal conditions, however offended the sense of justice may find itself thereby. It will be objected that such a function of violence is fortuitous and isolated. This can be rebutted by a consideration of military violence. [...]

As regards class struggles, in them strike must under certain conditions be seen as a pure means. Two essentially different kinds of strike, the possibilities of which have already been considered, must now be more fully characterized. Georges Sorel has the credit – from political, rather than purely theoretical, considerations – of having first distinguished them. He contrasts them as the political and the proletarian general strike. They are also antithetical in their relation to violence. [...] 'The political general strike demonstrates how the state will lose none of its strength, how power is transferred from the privileged to the privileged, how the mass of producers will change their masters.'1 In contrast to this political general strike [...], the proletarian general strike sets itself the sole task of destroying state power. [...] 'This general strike clearly announces its indifference toward material gain through conquest by declaring its intention to abolish the state; the state was really ... the basis of the existence of the ruling group, who in all their enterprises benefit from the burdens borne by the public.' While the first form of interruption of work is violent since it causes only an external modification of labour conditions, the second, as a pure means, is nonviolent. For it takes place not in readiness to resume work following external concessions and this or that modification to working conditions, but in the determination to resume only a wholly transformed work, no longer enforced by the state, an upheaval that this kind of strike not so much causes as consummates. For this reason, the first of these undertakings is lawmaking but the second anarchistic. [...]

1   Georges Sorel, *Reflexions sur la violence*, 5th ed. (Paris, 1919) 250.

Walter Benjamin, extracts from 'Zur Kritik der Gewalt' (1921), in *Walter Benjamin: Gesammelte Schriften*, vol. 2, no. 1, ed. Rolf Tiedemann and Hermann Schweppenhäuser (Frankfurt am Main: Suhrkamp Verlag, 1999) 179–204; trans. Edmund Jephcott, 'Critique of Violence', in *Reflections* (New York: Schocken Books, 1969) 281–3, 291–2.

Rasheed Araeen
How Does/Could/Would the Withdrawal of Art Affect the World?//2002

1) Withdrawal of art will not affect the world, as what is being produced as art has nothing to do with the world.

2) Withdrawal of art can strike a blow to the economic structure of the art market, but this will not happen, as this withdrawal will never take place within the prevailing system.

Rasheed Araeen, 'How Does/Could/Would the Withdrawal of Art Affect the World?', in *Strike*, ed. Gavin Wade (Wolverhampton: Wolverhampton Art Gallery/London Alberta Press, 2002) 61.

Sarah Lehrer-Graiwer
Lee Lozano: *Dropout Piece*//2014

Lee Lozano's legendary and legendarily elusive *Dropout Piece*, begun around 1970, may or may not be precisely equivalent to her dropping out of the New York art world. It is among Lozano's most challenging works and notorious, lasting achievements. Yet in many ways there is no piece to speak of, not in any conventional sense of an artwork we can exhibit and study, nor of a performance that took place as an event for an audience. If those who should be best acquainted with Lozano's body of work – the artist's estate, her former dealers Jaap van Liere and Barry Rosen – question outright whether or not *Dropout Piece* exists at all, we must position our study in uncomfortably close relation to not knowing, continually asking ourselves what status the work occupies and how is it a piece. In talking about *Dropout Piece*, we are talking around an absence – the artist's absence and the void of information it created. Lozano teased Duchamp's question 'Can one make works which are not works of "art"?' This ontological experiment is built into the work: through dropping out Lozano posed major problems of recognition. As much as this investigation will elucidate, we ought to preserve the fundamental quality of doubt in her thinking that produced *Dropout Piece* and was to be its desired effect.

We can begin by saying that *Dropout Piece*, first and foremost, is a title – a concise fragment of language indicating, with the word 'piece', the application of art's frame around a certain zone of defiant, difficult and joyously (ce)rebellious thinking represented by the ambiguous but decisive compound 'dropout'. Being a title, the piece functions as a verbal object to be considered in the literary context of the artist's writings. *Dropout Piece* is the name Lozano gave to her wrenching transformation from insider to outsider, her declaration of willed marginality. She named her position to the world, or rather to the art world, as a designation of otherness and refusal, rejection and critical defection.

As a title, *Dropout Piece* takes material form only in a few notes the artist wrote to herself in a private notebook on 5 April 1970 – not in an art object, drawing, document or discretely prepared entity of any kind. Nor is it contained as an event, being imprecisely located in time and having no connection to a viewing audience except in the abstract. Lozano never prepared *Dropout Piece* for exhibition, as she had earlier art actions such as *Investment Piece* and *Grass Piece* (both 1969); but then again, the dropping out of the art world which the piece entails precluded that very possibility of exhibition. Formlessness followed function (or dysfunction) in order to enact content: Dropout's immateriality as art had to be consistent with the negation it enacted in life. As an uncommodified action, it couldn't be sold (and hasn't been yet), and that's a key part of its point. [...]

Lozano's dropping out of the New York art world, which coincides with but may not be entirely equal to *Dropout Piece*, cannot be pinned down definitively in the historical record. The artist did not give *Dropout Piece* a starting date; it can be attributed to either 1970 or 1972, or both. It might depend on whether a work's life begins at conception or on realization, not that those are the only options. 1970 is the earliest extant mention of the piece by name found written in her hand, although she likely articulated the desire to drop out in some other impermanent, unrecorded way earlier. Conflicting reports have her losing her Grand Street studio loft either at the very start of 1972 or as late as 1974, and 1971 was the last year she took an active interest in exhibiting her work. [...]

Dropout identified with the counterculture's fascination and utopian/ dystopian fantasy, at least since Timothy Leary's call in 1967 for the youth to 'turn on, tune in, drop out' in their psychedelic summer of love, and then again later with more anger and defiance as punk surged in the 1970s. It was a time of paradigm shifts and endgame strategies all around. From our historical vantage point, Lozano's piece is significantly representative of a collective turning, when protest culture and critique translated into radical acts or inwardness and refusal for artists.

There's a case to be made for 1969 as the year Lozano began formalizing withdrawal in her 'Life-Art' practice by rehearsing withdrawal in another, proto-dropout piece called *General Strike Piece* (8 February 1969): GRADUALLY BUT

DETERMINEDELY AVOID BEING PRESENT AT OFFICIAL OR PUBLIC 'UPTOWN' FUNCTIONS OR GATHERINGS RELATED TO THE 'ART WORLD' IN ORDER TO PURSUE INVESTIGATION OF TOTAL PERSONAL & PUBLIC REVOLUTION.

There's still another case to be made for 1982, when Lozano, the Lone Star, relocated to Texas, marking her final, physical departure from the New York scene. [...]

Dropout Piece is the culmination of Lozano's 'Life-Art' project, what she had been working towards: a metamorphosis. Its power is contextual, coming from where her practice was before and where it went after. The very grammar of dropping out is relational, prepositional and reactive. Alone and out of context, dropping out hardly signifies at all. It is all about connections and relationships and their severing. *Dropout Piece* was crucially both a rupture, a break, a schism and a contiguous extension of the trajectory the artist was on. This contradiction, at once climactic and incremental, produced an extraordinary, complex tension that throws light on the fundamental and dialectical opposition of 'Life-Art'. [...] Life matters as a function of art. Lozano's self-experimentation not only took real risks and suffered heavy consequences, but her very concept of art became explicitly predicated on danger and disruption. [...]

It is tricky to speak of the time following *Dropout Piece*. To begin with, I can't even say when *after* the piece was – when, exactly, its posterity commenced. As established, this work evades dating and duration. Beyond problems of pinning it down temporally (let alone chronologically), there is scant record of the artist's whereabouts and activities in her post-*Dropout* period. Then again, that inscrutability, that opacity, was at least partly the point of Lozano's self-exile. *Dropout Piece* works to delineate the edges of art's economy and history: its limits, blind spots, forgetfulness and aporia. [...]

Sarah Lehrer-Graiwer, extracts from *Lee Lozano: Dropout Piece* (London: Afterall Books, 2014) 13–14, 15–16, 76 [footnotes not included].

Kata Krasznahorkai
Tamás St. Auby's Strikes//2016

Since 1972 Tamás St. Auby has been concerned theoretically and practically with various manifestations of the art (and as he understands it from Duchamp, non-art art) strike. By refusing work, but through an active practice of striking, St. Auby tries to combat the economic sin of excessive consumption. In his argument, work is the punishment for overproduction. For St. Auby, strikes become artistic material that enables independence from state, Church and capital. However, strikes as a means of liberating oneself from state structures as an artist is not suggested by St. Auby from a political or economic perspective, but rather from a 'cultural', 'basic mythical attitude'.[1] St. Auby understands the concept of a complex strike system as an 'aesthetic, ethical act', opposed to the 'myth of Church and state'.[2] Strikes are to be offset by the *Subsistence Level Standard Project 1984 W – Make a Chair!* and become a survival strategy on a parallel path to non-working.

To date the *Subsistence Level Standard Project 1984 W – Make a Chair!* conceives this survival in five phases. In the first phase of the Subsistence Level Project a mutant is brought to life that submits to neither state nor Church structures, and so mutates into a free being. In the second phase a whole mutant class is brought to life, and in the third the 24th canton of Switzerland is defined as their geographical habitat. St. Auby describes the fourth phase as a 'history of salvation',[3] and in St. Auby's artistic concept excessive consumption is compared to Biblical sin.

The new social class of mutants is characterized by strikes: 'And in light of the fact that according to the Marxist myth humans in pre-history became human through work, the new class, the mutant class, becomes what it is through strikes'.[4] In 1979, in the context of an intercalation of technology and strikes, St. Auby designed a *Subsistence Level Strike Machine*, the *BioSt.rike Robot*, which was only actually manufactured in 1996. It is an experimental design, a modified bio-feedback machine, that functions as the model of a mind-reading automaton. With this bio-feedback instrument various states of consciousness can be registered and influenced, such as wakefulness or deep sleep. St. Auby's strike robot, which translates free will into physical/mechanical work, acts to a certain extent as a surrogate worker, and yet embodies the refusal to work of the striker, whose will it carries out. This can be understood as a subversive, critical allusion to the Taylorist model of labour and its equation of human and machine. By contrast in St. Auby's piece, the robot becomes the motor of spiritual development and represents the power (and labour) of thought.

Going on strike as an artistic instrument was particularly resonant in Eastern European communist countries as, in accordance with post-1946 Soviet labour laws, no right to strike existed. Any strike was considered a crime against the state, an act of sabotage.[5] Moreover in Hungary the horrors of the 1956 General Strike as a political instrument opposing Soviet rule were still deeply ingrained. In 1957 after the bloody end of the revolution, participation in strikes in Hungary carried the death penalty. Refusal to participate in socialist work structures, while at the same time taking part in artistic activity that cannot be fitted into this system, was a factor in generating and provoking the implementation and perpetuation of the State's repressive structures and strategies, if not actually legitimizing the perpetuation of the extensive surveillance system that provided employment to thousands. One of the arguments for St. Auby's surveillance was that he refused the socialist world of work. Ultimately his actions and strike actions led to St. Auby being expelled from Hungary in 1975 and emigrating to Switzerland, following accusations of having smuggled samizdat literature out of the country.

The unique aspect of St. Auby's concept of strikes is that the strike itself becomes the material for an artistic refusal to produce. In this way the strike becomes a parable of art by contrast to the withdrawal scenarios and retreat campaigns of many artists who are associated with the notion of strike. In this case strikes are not a scenario of withdrawal from art, but rather a scenario of access to art.

The strike is not inactivity and does not mean the discontinuation of engagement with artistic production processes or artistic material, but is itself the material and the instrument from which and through which (artistic) activity emerges. Instead of the discontinuation of production, the strike becomes the material for a production machine with objects, robots and drawings. Moreover, by contrast with other artists who called for strikes such as Gustav Metzger, St. Auby's strike is not time-limited and stands for an ongoing existential state of uncompromising independence and freedom on the part of the artist – both in socialist and in capitalist society.

1   Tamás St. Auby, 'Létminimum Standard Projekt 1984 W (IV. Fázis): Katabasis Soteriologike, St.Auby Tamás, a TNPU V. – *ad interim* – diszpécserének tárlatvezetése a MĐcsarnokban 1996 május 9-én. Átirat videófelvétel alapján.' [Subsistence Level Standard Project 1984 W (4th phase: Katabasis Soteriologike, led by Tamás St. Auby, 5th *ad interim* dispatcher at the International Parallel Union of Telecommunication in Budapest Palace of Art on 9 May 1996, typescript from video recording] (http://www.sztaki.hu/providers/nightwatch/szocpol/stauby/tarlatvez/) accessed on 3 September 2016.

2   Cf. International Parallel Union of Telecommunication, BiRo, 'The Butterfly Effect', exhibition text

in the exhibition, Budapest Palace of Art, 20 January–25 February 1996. (http://www.c3.hu/scca/ butterfly/IPUT/projecthu.html) accessed on 17 July 2016.

3   Tamás St. Auby, 'Subsistence Level Standard Project 1984 W (4th phase)' (http://www.sztaki.hu/ providers/nightwatch/szocpol/stauby/tarlatvez/) accessed on 3 September 2016.

4   Tamás St. Auby in 'Beszélgetés az IPUT-ról és a 24. Kanotonról' [A conversation about IPUT and the 24th canton]. Interview by Júlia Láng with the dispatcher of the International Parallel Union of Telecommunication, Tony Putr, Geneva, 1 August 1981. A corrected version appeared in *Artpool Levelek 5* (Summer 1983) 18–23. (http://www.artpool.hu/Al/al05/IPUT.html) accessed on 18 October 2016.

5   Georg Jahn, ed., *Die Wirtschaftssysteme der Staaten Osteuropas und der Volksrepublik China. Untersuchungen der Entstehung, Entfaltung und Wandlung sozialistischer Wirtschaftssysteme*, vol. 2 (Berlin: Duncker & Humblot, 1962) 235.

Kata Krasznahorkai, 'Tamás St. Auby's Strikes'. Commissioned for this volume, 2016. Translated by Philippa Hurd, 2017.

Precarias a la Deriva
A Very Careful Strike: Four Hypotheses//2005

[O]nly if the maids, the whores, the phone sex operators, grant-holding students or researchers, telephone operators, social workers, nurses, friends, mothers, daughters, *compañeras*, lovers … only if the caregivers, which all women are and everyone should be (*que somos todas y que habríamos de ser todos*) rediscover the fundamental role of the labour (remunerated or not) of care and of the social wealth it produces and we withdraw from the invisibilization, hyperexploitation, infravalorization or social stigma of which care is the object, only then will we be prepared to extract from care its transformative force.

Once brought into the light, the revolutionary potential of care could become the logic that governs our lives, replacing not only the securitary logic but also that other logic which underlies it: that of the imperatives of profit. Now the interests of capital determine production (what, how and when one produces), spaces (the houses we inhabit, the design of our cities and towns, the very global geography and its borders) and times (labour and leisure, haste, the intensification of time). But why not begin to imagine and construct an organization of the social that prioritizes persons, that attends to our sustainability – from access to healthcare to the right to affect – which orients towards our enrichment as human beings – from the access to knowledge, education and information to the freedom to move around the world – that listens to our desires? This is the biopolitical challenge.

And we need tools to bring it about. One of these is the caring strike. It seems a paradox, because the strike is always interruption and visibilization, and care is the continuous and invisible line whose interruption would be devastating. But all that is lacking is a change of perspective, to see that that there is no paradox: the caring strike would be nothing other than the interruption of the order that is ineluctably produced in the moment in which we place the truth of care in the centre and politicize it.

Thus the strike appears to us in the first place as interpellation: 'what is your caring strike?' Interpellation launched to all: to those of us that act as maids, as housewives, as whores, as nurses, as telephone operators ... launched also to those of us that think the cities, in order to facilitate encounters, to those of us that invent bridges, so affects can come through, to those of us that imagine worlds, in order that the profit economy could be replaced by the ecology of care ... and, of course, to the men – are we going to end with the mystique that obliges women to care for others even at the cost of themselves and obliges men to be incapable of caring even for themselves? Or are we never going to cease to be sad men and women and begin to degenerate the imposed attributions of gender?

In second place, the strike appears to us as an everyday and multiple practice: there will be those who propose transforming public space, converting spaces of consumption into places of encounter and play, preparing a 'reclaim the streets'; those who suggest organizing a work stoppage in the hospital when the work conditions don't allow the nurses to take care of themselves as they deserve; those who decide to turn off their alarm clocks, call in sick and give themselves a day off as a present; and those who prefer to join others in order to say 'that's enough' to the clients who refuse to wear condoms ... There will be those who oppose the deportation of miners from the 'refuge' centres where they work, those who dare – like the 11 March Victims' Association (la asociación de afectados 11M) – to bring care to political debate, proposing measures and refusing utilizations of the situation by political parties; those who throw the apron out of the window and ask, Why so much cleaning? And those who join forces in order to demand that they be cared for as quadriplegics and not as 'poor things' to be pitied, as people without economic resources and not as stupid people, as immigrants without papers and not as potential delinquents, as autonomous persons and not as institutionalized dependents. There will be those who ...

Because care is not a domestic question but rather a public matter and generator of conflict.

Precarias a la Deriva, extracts from 'A Very Careful Strike: Four Hypotheses' (Madrid, 2005), trans. Franco Ingrassia and Nate Holdren, in *The Commoner: A Web Journal for Other Values*, no. 11 (Spring 2006) 42–3.

Adrian Melis
In Conversation with Friederike Sigler//2016

Friederike Sigler For *Dreams Production Plan for State-run Companies in Cuba* (2010–12) you asked workers to write down the dreams they have while falling asleep during their work time. To sleep during work seems a paradox, especially in the context of modern production logics. Can the sleeping workers be considered as strikers?

Adrian Melis Sleeping at work seems like a paradox in the western world; in Cuba, however, it is completely normal. In the work of *Dreams Production Plan* as well as in all my works I select and deal with existing issues within established socio-economic structures. In Cuba the state has complete control over the economic structures and means of production. It projects the illusion of productivity, even if these structures it has set are useless and do not function. I call these structures 'ghost production structures'. Cuba is an island where the paradoxical occurs naturally. It is prohibited to fight for your labour rights – even just placing a complaint is usually not an option – and no one has the courage publicly to make a demand for change. Simply put, we pretend to be productive within an unproductive system, and for this reason sleeping during working hours changes nothing; we wake up caught in the same cycle. The system is not affected in any way, because productivity is dispensable for it to continue working as it is. Imagine that your duty is to be in a battlefield, provided with the right ammunition, well prepared, eager, everything is set but there is no war happening and no war is coming. The workers' 'dormant' state is a consequence of the State, since there are no means to protest for one's labour rights as there are in other countries, so sleeping is the only thing you can do.

In addition to showing the dreams of Cubans, one of my main objectives for this project was to achieve a production line that would allow me to demonstrate in tangible form that the dreams of socialism are a marketable product, a merchandise that can be mass produced and exported. *Dreams Production Plan* is a critique of the establishment. It presents an alternate system that allows for productivity to happen using the existing structures, without changing or interfering with the day-to-day work rituals. The workers know by now how to use the system to their own benefit. In fact, it is not the workers who are striking, it is the government that is striking and struggling to stop western ideologies from infiltrating Cuba. The government is in constant 'strike' and the workers are the pawns of this power play. In a capitalist system no margin exists to question the definition of productivity, since it has already been firmly established through an ideology of growth, advancement, evolution, expansion, etc. Productivity in Cuba is still a fluid term.

Sigler A similar version of 'non-work' is presented in *The Value of Absence* (2010–12), a collection of various excuses for staying away from work.

Melis The difference between *Dreams Production Plan* and *The Value of Absence* is that in the former, I created a product without intervening or changing the employees' regular day at work. In *The Value of Absence* the excuses of the workers become the engine that drives the work beyond this façade of our reality and into a platform wherein the workers don't only stop working but are paid to do it. The payment was equal to the amount they would be paid had they gone to work. If we consider the consequences that this activity could bring, *The Value of Absence* could be considered as an attack against the establishment, in Cuba as well as in the rest of the world. The excuses allowed 114 people to miss out on work, to be precise altogether 327 working days, with approximately 90 euros which at the time was close to 127,70 Cuban pesos. Imagine if I had a budget of 3,000 euros at my disposal. I could have paralysed Havana. In a capitalist context I would have been put in jail but in Cuba, I could have paralysed the capital without anyone noticing, because the system is already paralysed.

The Value of Absence highlights a secondary dimension of the Cuban reality that changes the rules of the game that other westernized countries are playing, and that is the significant lack of motivation. The worker decides to miss work because he/she just doesn't want to go, and that is a form of protest, a silent underhanded protest. Whether he/she goes to work will not affect the existing structures or change her/his life. Reality in Cuba is different, it cannot be analysed through the eyes of capitalism; such a comparison would just be too simple an approach to take. The capitalist system drives people to work, and if you systematically miss work you will be fired and considered as lacking work ethic. However, in Cuba, if you are being too productive and complain about the inefficiency of the system you are extracted from it and considered to be an obstruction to the system. The government knows people don't show up for work but it ignores this phenomenon, because it acknowledges that this is how the system they have created functions: here and there people will wander. Ironically we have some freedoms in Cuba that do not exist anywhere else.

Sigler The subject of *The Making of Forty Rectangular Pieces for a Floor Construction* (2008) are workers, who – 'due to a shortage of materials to produce' – are basically waiting for the end of their worktime as there's nothing to work on.

Melis In *The Making of Forty Rectangular Pieces* something peculiar occurs. When I went to the factory to produce the work, I had to go through the administrator. He took me directly to the workers who were sitting, drinking rum, playing dominos and not doing much else. He ordered them: 'Hey, listen up. Since I can't put you to work, he (the artist) will put you to work.' At that moment they exhaled a sigh of relief. I guess they were happy to do something useful, something that would motivate them and that was not related to their routine. That day they worked incessantly for eight hours to achieve the best outcome, a perfect soundtrack simulating a faint memory of a reality now nonexistent. They were the musicians in an orchestra of which I was the conductor. The work acquired another conceptual dimension, a parallel dimension, in which they could be productive within the confines of art instead of reality. When the workers saw the final cut they exclaimed: 'Look! Everything works! We're working! You've done it! You're a genius.'

That's when I realized that the concept of work is more closely related to art than reality itself. To be unproductive is not a mode of protest, it is a way of creating a parallel reality, where it is possible that art is a motor for productivity within a paralysed context. My work does not pretend to change anything but I believe that it is a way to question not only those who believe that work dignifies man, but also a point of reference for the Cuban establishment to observe through the eyes of the Cubans how the system they have created operates, or doesn't.

Adrian Melis, interview with Friederike Sigler for this volume, 2016.

Anthony W. Lee
Trace//2009

In 2007 Simon Starling began to conceive of an installation for the Massachusetts Museum of Contemporary Art (MASS MoCA), a large museum once home to a factory in the northern Berkshires. He based his ideas on an old photograph of Chinese factory workers taken by the photographer Henry D. Ward, now little known. The photograph belonged to an earlier moment in the region's history, a mostly forgotten time whose stories remain tucked in archives and whose images can be found, here and there, in pictures like Ward's. [...]

In the spring of 1870, Calvin T. Sampson, a shoe manufacturer and owner of one of the most successful businesses in North Adams, Massachusetts, dispatched his chief assistant, George Chase, to San Francisco.[1] Chase's charge was to find and deliver a group of workers who could man the berths in the bottoming room of Sampson's large factory. Their job would be to 'bottom', to affix the lasts and soles of the shoes to the uppers. It was a physical job, the kind that demanded constant twisting and bending at the hips and crooking and flexing of the arms. [...] The previous bottomers had demanded better wages – in fact, merely living wages – and, when Sampson refused, went on strike. Rather than fall to the pressures of organized labour, Sampson sent Chase to find strikebreakers. The shoe manufacturer's goal was not to force organized labour but simply to replace it altogether.

Sampson's decision to import non-union labour was controversial enough [...] but the decision had an added layer of scandal: the choice to import a new kind of worker, Chinese immigrants. [...] More boys than men, the Chinese workers represented the first large contingent of the working class to venture east of the Mississippi River. [...]

The 'Chinese experiment', as it soon came to be called, was debated seemingly everywhere. [...] The events became big drama, and occasionally turned violent. [...] By the decade's end, the opponents of the Chinese experiment had gained increasing sway and consensus, overcoming the arguments proposed by men like Sampson and his class of embattled manufacturers. 'Yellow', they decreed, had no place in the variegated spectrum between black and white. Finally, in 1882, the working classes needing jobs and politicians needing votes combined to pass an Exclusion Act in Congress, which simply forbade working-class Chinese entry into the country. [...]

For *The Nanjing Particles*, the large installation at MASS MoCA, Starling extracted silver particles from a copy photograph of Ward's stereo view of the

North Adams Chinese. He placed the particles in an electron microscope to discover their peculiar shapes, and then used those shapes, magnified 25,000 times, as the basis for two monumental sculptures, scaled up to a million times the size of the original trace particles. Finding the cost of labour to fashion the sculptures too exorbitant in the US, Starling had them manufactured at the Shanghai State Art Foundry in Nanjing. At the foundry, the sculptures' shapes were first formed with clay and plaster moulds, over which Chinese workers fitted a stainless steel skin. Then the workers' hands polished the steel surfaces to a mirror-like finish. The completed sculptures were shipped to North Adams for display, where they are now installed next to an enormous enlargement of Ward's photograph showing the two locations, on the stereo view, from which the silver particles had been extracted. [...]

Photographs picture things, but in Starling's understanding they also contain things, literally. More to the point, though, in exploring the materials of photography, the artist discovers connections between representation and labour, art and industry, history and display. [...] Where Sampson sought cheap Chinese labour to bypass more costly labour, so too has Starling. Where Sampson used photographs to celebrate (or flaunt) that labour, so in a sense has Starling. The parallels court risk. No doubt Sampson's decision to hire the Chinese had an element of risk, but it also included courage, lunacy, desperation and pride. His was an unenviable example. But where Sampson, in reaping the benefits of that labour, was happy to keep the Chinese men's specific identities unknown (and to use that anonymity to his advantage when dealing with the irate), the same cannot be said of Starling and his relation to the Chinese. They are carefully named in the installation, and their labour is celebrated in [the accompanying] book: Cai Haiming, Huang Xiaohui, Jin Binghui, Li Gaodao, Li Renwei, Li Weibing, Lin Bingli, Lin Gaosong, Lin Guohua, Lin Qiang, Ma Xiaopan, Wang Jinxing, Wang Xiting, Wang Zhengwei, Xu Benben, Yuan Wenwei, and Yuan Youjun.

1   See Anthony W. Lee, *A Shoemaker's Story: Being Cheifly about French Canadian Immigrants, Enterprising Photographers, Rascal Yankees and Chinese Cobblers in a Nineteenth-Century Factory Town* (Princeton: Princeton University Press, 2008).

Anthony W. Lee, extracts from 'Trace', in *Simon Starling: The Nanjing Particles*, ed. Susan Cross (North Adams, Massachusetts: MASS MoCA, 2009) 17–20, 21, 23.

Paolo Magagnoli
Moulène, Rancière and *24 Objets de Grève*//2012

In his 1996 book *Gargantua: Manufactured Mass Culture* art historian Julian Stallabrass celebrated the critical value of rubbish. Rubbish, he argued, may reveal the deceptive nature of capitalism and advertising. In Stallabrass's account, the physical decay of the product is sufficient to dispel the commodity fetishism which is typical, according to Marx, of capitalism. Yet, what if the object is an expression of the worker's momentary appropriation of the means of production? Should it undergo a similar process of disintegration in order to be redeemed? This conundrum is exemplified by the objects photographed by French artist Jean-Luc Moulène for his archive *24 Objets de Grève Présentés par Jean-Luc Moulène* (24 Strike-Objects Presented by Jean-Luc Moulène, 1999). The objects were produced by French factory workers during strike occupations in the period between 1968 and 1999. They range from scarves, dresses and maps to watches, cigarette packs, newspapers and train tickets. Each of them represents a different dispute. Some were circulated to the general public in order to raise awareness about the workers' grievances (the map of the Paris metro); some were used to demonstrate the workers' technical skills (the Novacore suite); others had a merely symbolic function (the doll symbolizing the dispute 'Bella'). Despite their differences, they all stand for the workers' appropriation of the means of production.

The strike-objects distinguish themselves from standard commercial goods in that they were manufactured in small quantities and were supposed to express craft, know-how and pleasure of work. They were clearly marked as 'different' from reified commodities through visible details. So, for example, the cigarette packet 'La Pantinoise', made in 1982 by the workers of the Pantin tobacco factory in Janco, differs from Gauloises packets through the inscription 'Not For Sale. Made by the workers in dispute'; the Manufrance frying pan has the slogans 'Relax' and 'Employment, solidarity, liberty, justice' engraved on its back. Moreover, several of the objects are red, the colour of revolution. Whereas it is true that some of the goods looked like counterfeits of standard commodities, their ambiguous appearance never reached a point of total uncertainty. The form of the products made ostensibly clear that they were made by workers on strike.

Instead of highlighting the difference between strike-objects and ordinary commodities, Moulène's photographs depict them as ambiguous things. In *24 Objets de Grève*, the objects have a kind of mute, opaque presence that is quietly unsettling. The artist shot the products in front of grey backgrounds, using a high contrast and highly saturated colour film. He printed the images on large-sized Plexiglas, which gives photographs a glaring, almost reflective surface, reminiscent of advertisement billboards; it is only through understated captions – printed in the exhibition catalogue – that the viewer can learn about the singular history of the products. [...]

[T]he conceptual affinities between the artist's photographs and the strike-objects – both being the outcome of strategies of détournement – suggests a resemblance between the artist and the worker. This is the reading made by Jacques Rancière in a conversation with Fulvia Carnevale and John Kelsey published in *Artforum* in 2007. Here Rancière argued that Moulène's series epitomizes an attempt 'to give form to a continuity between artistic creativity and the forms of creativity manifested in objects and behaviours that testify to everyone's capacities and to our inherent powers of resistance'. For Rancière, Moulène's photographs exemplify the model of a truly emancipatory art, whereby the conventional division of competences – such as those between artist and spectator, producer and consumer of images – are overturned. [...]

For Rancière, the emancipatory value of a work of art does not reside in the explicit content of the message it conveys, but rather in the ways that the common divisions of labour and competences are unsettled. In other words, the problem of an emancipatory, political art has to do with the question: who has the right to produce art? Politics is conceptualized by Rancière as a dissenting event enacted by those 'who have no place' and 'no time', by which he means those who, on the one hand, are defined as deprived of *logos*, and yet, on the other hand, are taken to share in the universal capacity of aesthetic judgement. 'Politics occurs', he writes, 'when those who "have no" time take the time necessary to front up as inhabitants of a common space and demonstrate that their mouths really do emit speech capable of making pronouncements on the common which cannot be reduced to voices signalling pain.'1 In relation to Rancière's aesthetics, *24 Objets de Grève* emerges as an example of an emancipatory and political art. The project describes the strikers as subjects capable of occupying a different place from that usually prescribed to them by the capitalist order and, therefore, it affirms the universal claim of equality that constitutes the radical message at the heart of his aesthetics. In *24 Objets de Grève* the strikers appear as ingenious producers and their creations as conceptually sophisticated works of art. Elaborating on this Rancèrian reading, one can argue that Moulène's aestheticization of the strike-objects does not abstract them from their social history but, on the contrary, makes a statement that calls for the equality of all subjects.

One may wonder whether this reading is too optimistic. The photographs in *24 Objets de Grève* may, in fact, convey less the subjectivity of the anonymous strikers than that of the artist. Representing the strike-objects according to his trademark style, Moulène, perhaps inadvertently, transforms them into an allegory of his own practice. [...] Rather than acting as testimony to the workers' capacity for resistance, as Rancière suggests, the project may be viewed as an undue appropriation of the strikers' work which serves to conceal class hierarchies. The series resonates with the practice of some other contemporary artists who deploy anonymous assistants as labour to produce works of art, while retaining their authorship and ownership. Ultimately, it is impossible to decide which one of these conflicting readings is more appropriate. Perhaps, part of *24 Objets de Grève*'s considerable achievement is that it can operate within and reveal these different, contradictory interpretations and, perhaps, Moulène's work should be seen as an art of subversive mimesis. [...]

1   Jacques Rancière, *Aesthetics and Its Discontents* (Cambridge: Polity Press, 2009) 24.

Paolo Magagnoli, extracts from 'Moulène, Rancière and 24 Objets de Grève: Productive Ambivalence or Reifying Opacity?', *Philosophy of Photography*, vol. 3, no. 1 (2012) 156, 163–4.

Antonio Negri
Notes on the Abstract Strike//2015

[...] What is an abstract strike today? That is to say, what is a strike that is measured against both the new nature of living labour and the neoliberal constitution of production and reproduction? What is a social struggle that has the capacity to 'do harm' by showing itself to be newly in possession of a material, biopolitical and effective power? First of all, we must ask if and how living labour can today rebel and interrupt the flow of valorization. In contrast to the tradition of the workers' struggle, which ruptured productive relations through walkouts, sabotage, etc., one must observe that the situation is different today, when labour has taken over life, when someone works all day outside of any set hours, when the productive capacities of every worker are taken into command networks. How is it possible under these circumstances to rediscover that independence of action demanded by the call to strike within both the spatial and the temporal properties of cooperation and its continuous flow? How is it possible, for example, to occupy and close down the productive hub of the metropolis and/or interrupt the flow of social networks that never stop to take a break?

Here the answer can only lead us back to that singular composition that today is represented by the intimate algorithmic connection between production and command – where workers build meaningful and productive relations whose meaning is extracted by capital. In this case the strike can succeed when it not only breaks the valorization process, but when it also recovers its independence: the substance of living labour as a productive act. In a strike, machinic living labour breaks the algorithm for creating new networks of signification. It can do it because without production on the part of living labour, without subjectification, there is no algorithm. It must do it because, within capitalism, there are neither wages nor social progress, neither welfare nor the possible enjoyment of life without resistance. The strike reveals the future, breaking with the wretchedness of and subjection to command. The strike reclaims the workers' tradition, carried over to the entire terrain of life – the social strike. This is the figure of the strike against the capitalist techniques of the extraction of value from an entire society.

But there is a second, equally or perhaps even more important point of entry. It is found where the processes of society's reproduction intersect with financial capital, with the process of monetization. Consumption is always a good thing when one knows how to consume in relation to the reproductive needs of the species – not the natural, generically human species so much as that of the productive, 'post-human' worker. Now, this is the ground of welfare as the organization of the dominion over services and consumption, and it should be crossed as the battleground where the abstract strike becomes a materialist strike. The abstract strike, at the level of production, thus imposes the restoration of the independence of living labour at the level of reproduction. It demands the construction and the imposition of a new sequence of needs-desires-consumption.

At the moment, we find an abundance of research dedicated to building spaces of labour independence within the productive networks most invested in the capitalist mode of value extraction. This rebirth of mutualism and the growth of online cooperation are only the first steps in the struggle. With regard to breaking the sequence of desire-consumption (and its forced monetization), there are widespread efforts to create currencies like Bitcoin and to build autonomous communication networks and/or independent consumption networks, and these efforts are partial but significant. They cannot become decisive, however, without offensively seizing that crucial point where capitalist production transforms productive subjectification into the autocratic production of subjects.

It is clear that the strike against the extraction of value and the strike that operates at the level of the capitalist abstraction of social exploitation are not the same thing. In the first case, the struggle is directed at the appropriation of profit;

in the second, at the overturning of models of the reproduction of society, of its capitalist rule, and of the contextual minting of functional currency. Today it is clear that these two levels of struggle are not identical, but they are nonetheless closely connected. The first one is horizontal; the second is vertical. The first is a struggle for the emancipation of labour; the second for liberation from labour. From the point of view of the struggles, it would be impossible to distinguish them. Nor, however, can they be conflated – because the one struggles and the other builds. They must do it separately; they must do it together.

Therein lies the task. […]

Antonio Negri, extract from 'Notes on the Abstract Strike' (2015); trans. Phillip Stephen Twilley, in *Supercommunity: e-flux journal 56th Venice Biennale* (2015). (supercommunity.e-flux.com)

Claire Fontaine
Human Strike Has Already Begun//2009

'Grève humaine' is the French expression for 'human strike', designating the most generic movement of revolt against any oppressive condition. It's a more radical and less specific strike than a general strike or a wildcat strike.

Human strike attacks the economic, affective, sexual and emotional positions within which subjects are imprisoned. It provides an answer to the question 'how do we become something other than what we are?' It isn't a social movement, although within the uprising and agitations it can find a fertile ground upon which to develop and grow, sometimes even against these.

For example, it has been said that the feminist movement in Italy during the 1970s demolished the leftist political organizations, but what hasn't been said is what leftist political organizations were doing to the women who were part of them. Human strike can be a revolt within a revolt, an unarticulated refusal, an excess of work or the total refusal of any labour, depending on the situation. There is no orthodoxy for it. If strikes are made in order to improve specific aspects of the workers' conditions, they are always a means to an end. But human strike is a pure means, a way to create an immediate present here where there is nothing but waiting, projecting, expecting, hoping. […]

'We need to change ourselves': everyone agrees on this point, but who to become and what to produce are the first questions that arise as soon as this discussion takes place in a collective context. The reflex of refusing any present that doesn't come with the guarantee of a reassuring future is the very mechanism of the slavery we are caught in and that we must break. To produce the present is not to produce the future.

'How do I do it and where do I start?' Surely everyone knows this better for oneself than anybody else ever could: no more leaders, no more teachers, no more students, here comes the time of inventing new mediations between people, and we are already in the midst of the work of the human strike. There are no preliminaries, no intermediary steps, no organizers in charge of the logistical aspects. The work of the human strike strikes against itself. It transforms at the same time what we see and the organs we see with. It transforms both ourselves and the people who made this transformation possible. It kills the bourgeois in all of us, liberating unknown forces. […]

There are no lessons of human strike, it is nothing but a disquieting possibility that we must remain intimate with. We are remunerated neither for the work of love nor for being able to find the right words to bridge the social fractures that separate all of us. We do not get paid for making everyday life more enjoyable or simply possible for ourselves and for other people. The unremunerated labour of the affects continuously crushes the insulting pyramid of capitalistic values but this conflict is effaced day after day. […]

No mourning of the impossible revolutions can get in the way of the human strikers because human strike is not a mission, nor a project or a programme. It is the gesture that makes legible the silent political element in everything: women's lives, the dissatisfaction of rich people, the anger of privileged teenagers, the refusal to submit to the mediocrity of necessity, ordinary racism, and so on.

When we inhabit language we place ourselves on the permeable membrane between life and desires, where it clearly appears that life and desires are made of the same fabric. Desiring together makes things come true even when they are not technically true. Witches were burned for having truly been flying in the night and for having actually kissed Satan's ass. When we come out of prison we are delinquents, even if we were innocents when they first arrested us by mistake.

We constantly become what other people want us to be, but starting a human strike means inverting that movement and refusing to act upon the actions of others through the use of power; it means opposing a philosophy of management with the material presence of potentiality. Reality can be more than what any realistic representation of the facts offers. The very concept of reality progressively starts to fade when we lose touch with the possible and the impossible that human strike points to.

Claire Fontaine, extracts from 'Human Strike Has Already Begun' (New York, 2009), in *Human Strike Has Already Begun & Other Writings, ed. Claire Fontaine* (Lüneburg: Mute Books/PLM Books, 2009) 27–33.

IF THE FACTORY IS EVERYWHERE, THEN THERE IS NO LONGER A GATE BY WHICH TO LEAVE IT — THERE IS NO WAY TO ESCAPE RELENTLESS PRODUCTIVITY

Hito Steyerl, 'Is a Museum a Factory?', 2009

FACTORY

Harun Farocki
Workers Leaving the Factory//2001

The film *Workers Leaving the Lumière Factory in Lyon* (1895) by the brothers Louis and Auguste Lumière is 45 seconds long and shows the roughly one hundred workers at the factory for photographic goods in Lyon-Montplaisir leaving the factory through two gates and exiting the frame to both sides. Over the past twelve months, I set myself the task of tracking down the theme of this film, workers leaving the workplace, in as many variants as possible. Examples were found in documentaries, industrial and propaganda films, newsreels and features. [...]

Berlin, 1934: Siemens factory workers and employees leave the premises in marching order to attend a Nazi rally. There is a column of war invalids, and many are wearing white overalls as if to bring the idea of militarized science into the shot.

German Democratic Republic, 1963 (without precuse localization): A *Betriebskampfgruppe* – a works combat unit or militia made up of workers under the leadership of the party – turn out for manoeuvres. Very serious men and women in uniform get onto military light vehicles and drive to the woods where they will encounter men who themselves wear caps and pose as saboteurs. As the convoy drives out through the gate, the factory has the appearance of a barracks.

Federal Republic of Germany, 1975: A small loudspeaker van is parked in front of the Volkswagen plant in Emden and plays music with lyrics by Vladimir Mayakovsky and vocals by Ernst Busch. A man from the labour union calls on the workers leaving the early shift to attend a meeting protesting against the plan to transfer production to the US. The labour union uses optimistic, revolutionary music as backing for the image of industrial workers in the Federal Republic of 1975; music echoing from the actual scene [...].

The first camera in the history of cinema was pointed at a factory, but a century later it can be said that film is hardly drawn to the factory and even repelled by it. Films about work or workers have not become one of the main genres, and the space in front of the factory has remained on the sidelines. Most narrative films take place in that part of life where work has been left behind. [...] Cameras and projectors are essentially mechanical inventions, and in 1895 the heyday of mechanical inventions had passed. The technical processes which were emerging at the time – chemistry and electricity – were almost inaccessible to visual understanding. The reality based on these methods was hardly ever characterized by visible movement. The cine camera, however, has remained fixated on movement. [...]

In the Lumière film of 1895 it is possible to discover that the workers were assembled behind the gates and surged out at the camera operator's command. Before the film direction stepped in to condense the subject, it was the industrial order which synchronized the lives of the many individuals. They were released from this regulation at a particular point in time, contained in the process by the factory gates as in a frame. The Lumières' camera did not have a viewfinder, so they could not be certain of the view depicted; the gates provide a perception of framing which leaves no room for doubt.

The work structure synchronizes the workers, the factory gates group them, and this process of compression produces the image of a workforce. As may be realized or brought to mind by the portrayal, the people passing through the gates evidently have something fundamental in common. Images are closely related to concepts, thus this film has become a rhetorical figure. [...]

The appearance of community does not last long. Immediately after the workers hurry past the gate, they disperse to become individual persons, and it is this aspect of their existence which is taken up by most narrative films. If after leaving the factory the workers don't remain together for a rally, their image as workers disintegrates. [...]

Because the image of community cannot be maintained once the workplace is left behind, the rhetorical figure of leaving the factory is often found at the beginning or the end of a film, like a slogan, where it is possible to leave it detached, like a prologue or epilogue. It is astonishing that even this first film already had something not easily surpassable. It makes a statement which defies immediate extension. [...]

I have gathered, compared and studied these and many other images which use the motif of the first film in the history of cinema, 'workers leaving the factory', and have assembled them into a film, *Arbeiter Verlassen die Fabrik* (Workers Leaving the Factory, video, 37 min., 1995). The film montage had a totalizing effect on me. With the montage before me, I found myself gaining the impression that for over a century cinematography had been dealing with just one single theme. Like a child repeating for more than a hundred years the first words it has learned speak in order to immortalize the joy of first speech. Or as though cinema had been working in the same spirit as painters of the Far East, always painting the same landscape until it becomes perfect and comes to include the painter within it. When it was no longer possible to believe in such perfection, film was invented.

In the Lumière film about leaving the factory, the building or area is a container, full at the beginning and emptied at the end. This satisfies the desire of the eye, which itself can be based on other desires. In the first film, the aim was to represent motion and thus to illustrate the possibility of representing movement. [...]

Immediately after the command had been given to leave the factory back in 1895, the workers streamed out. Even if they sometimes got in each other's way – one young woman is seen to tug at another's skirt before they part in opposite directions, knowing that the other will not dare to retaliate under the stern eye of the camera – the overall movement remains swift and nobody is left behind. That this is the case is perhaps because the primary aim was to represent motion, maybe signposts were already being set. Only later, once it had been learned how filmic images grasp for ideas and are themselves seized by them, are we able to see in hindsight that the resolution of the workers' motion represents something, that the visible movement of people is standing in for the absent and invisible movement of goods, money and ideas circulating in industry.

The basis for the chief stylistics of cinema was given in the first film sequence. Signs and symbols are not brought into the world, but taken from reality. It is as though the world itself wanted to tell us something.

Harun Farocki, extracts from 'Workers Leaving the Factory', in *Harun Farocki: Imprint – Writings*, ed. Susanne Gaensheimer, Nicolaus Schafhausen, trans. Laurent Faasch-Ibrahim (Berlin: Verlag Vorwerk 8/New York: Lukas & Sternberg, 2001) 230–32, 234–5, 244–6.

Gerald Raunig
The University-Factory as a Site of Reterritorialization//2013

Once the factory was the exemplary site of condensation – not only condensing the time and space of production, but also condensing resistance. It was in the place of the exploitation they shared that workers also found the conditions for collectively discussing, assembling and constituting assemblages of resistance. Today, in the setting of the factory of knowledge, in the universities as well as in the diffuse places of dispersed knowledge production, a mode of radically dispersed production is crystallizing, and occupation, strike, spatial and social condensation, to the extent they are not declared completely impossible at all, turn into mysterious and puzzling matters.

Factories of knowledge: fashionable metaphor for the self-proletarization of intellectuals, misinterpretation of ephemeral Marx marginalia, terminological makeshift solution for the situation of precarious knowledge work? There is no doubt that the General Intellect has been increasingly seized by capitalist valorization in recent decades. Knowledge economy, knowledge age, knowledge-based economy, knowledge management, cognitive capitalism – these terms for the current social situation speak volumes. Knowledge becomes a commodity, which is manufactured, fabricated and traded like material commodities. Immaterial flows of know-how and finances, cooperation and coordination, collective forms of the intellect seem to combine in some regions of the world into a tendency to transform modes of production. This tendency could be called cognification, and this is not necessarily coupled with an improvement of working conditions or a substantialization of cognitive labour. […]

The factory is – Marx already alluded to this in his analysis of the large factory in the nineteenth century – the container of partial machines, their assemblage, not simply a mere accumulation of partial machines, a machine park; it grows into a machinery that is more than the sum of its parts. The concept of machinery indicates exactly this tendency to ascribe a surplus to the machinic assemblage of the factory, a life of its own. This life of its own can be interpreted in the paradigm of the sorcerer's apprentice, in which the factory worker is reduced to a part of a self-moving and self-governing partial machine. If only this paradigm comes into view, the technical apparatuses must be attacked, there must be a luddite battle against the enslavement of human beings under the yoke of the partial machine and the factory machinery.

In machinic thinking, on the other hand, the factory implies a concatenation of human bodies, their intellectuality and sociality, and the technical apparatuses. The 'machinery's' independent existence is then less a matter of the technical apparatuses and the factory as a whole becoming independent, and conversely the worker-engineer does not rule over apparatuses gloriously as *homo faber*. The power of movement that seems to move itself consists specifically and exclusively in the relation of the mechanical and intellectual parts of what is now a *social* machine. Instead of the mechanical and human components of the factory being strictly separated, their effect for the production process is to be investigated specifically in the interweaving and interrelating of the components. It is the physical concatenation of bodies and things, the attachment of the body-machines to the technical machines that allows the flows of production and of desire.

This change of perspective also has consequences for the old question of who serves whom, machines serving people, or people serving machines. In *Capital* Marx drew a clear line of separation between manufacture and craft, in which the worker takes the tool *into service*, and the factory, in which the worker *serves* the machine. In these two modes of service, opposing relations of subordination contrast with each other: either a dead mechanism as an arrangement of technical apparatuses retains the upper hand, or a living mechanism consisting in the communication and the machinic-social intellect of the workers. If the relation between serving and taking into service has ever existed in this pure dissociation, the division between dead and living partial machines is dissolving. The distinction cannot be maintained consistently for the factory of the nineteenth century, and even less so now in the twenty-first.

Whereas the factory in the classic view meant the hierarchical setting of relations between technical apparatuses and humans and humans with other humans, a machinic approach understands the composition of the factory as a multidimensional exchange among bodies, apparatuses and their environments. In this sense, the factory still remains a site of disciplining, exploiting and subjugating living labour, even though not under mechanical components, but rather under the relation of capital. At the same time, however, the factory is also a quasi horizontal site of machinic subservience, linking aspects of government and self-government together. Concepts such as serving, service, subservience take on the full spectrum of their vivid colourations in their different possible connections between human and machine. [...]

Gerald Raunig, extracts from *Factories of Knowledge: Industries of Creativity* (Los Angeles: Semiotext[e], 2013) 17–18, 21–3.

Jasmina Metwaly and Philip Rizk
In Conversation with Heinz-Norbert Jocks//2015

According to [curator] Florian Ebner [the film Out on the Street *(2015) about the privatization of a Cairo factory] by the Egypt-based artist duo Jasmina Metwaly and Philip Rizk, in the German pavilion [at the 2015 Venice Biennale] presented an artistic attitude that arose outside the established, Western art market.*

Norbert Jocks Why do you work together?

Philip Rizk Because we both think we can complement each other's work. Over the last ten, fifteen years Jasmina has worked in the art world, while I was busy making films and being an activist. We conceived the film together, we did the filming, directing and even some of the film editing ourselves. That characterizes the essence of the film, as well as working with workers from poor housing estates who have never acted professionally before. The work itself is about collective efforts. The actors not only play their roles, they also improvise them.

There is no screenplay that's written in stone. From start to finish the work on the rooftop with the workers focused powerfully on the everyday experience of work itself.

Jasmina Metwaly [...] The idea for it came when we were both making short videos about industrial disputes in Cairo and elsewhere. We drove to the various workplaces and filmed factory occupations and protests, in order to create a short video about it afterwards. At the time we were part of a larger collective called Mosireen (meaning 'determined'), which had emerged from the 18-day revolution. A group of friends had access to a huge archive of film material of these 18 days, shot by people with mobile phones, FlipCams, but also by filmmakers with more professional cameras. After the 18 days the idea emerged of taking this further. So the collective was formed and we joined a month later. We were already working on the short videos that dealt with topics in the ongoing political situation in Egypt. Our focus was on the industrial disputes, and we were visiting factories and privatized plants in Suez and Cairo to find out what the workers were actually demanding and what they hoped to change in their own work situations. Almost nothing of this was being made public. No one really knew what was going on in the factories, in particular in those that are located far away from the cities, near the Red Sea, in the region of Suez, those that are very cut off. Here, at the end of the world, we discovered thousands of people protesting. They had erected tents on the factory site and occupied factories. [...]

Rizk Over time it became clear how ephemeral such videos are, as soon as they are uploaded online and then again when they are screened. [We] wanted to make something that is of a different length that is not necessarily expressed in this urgent, activist language or form. Our question was, how do you talk about a struggle without talking about it? For us it was no longer about taking part in a demonstration.

Jocks But rather?

Metwaly About making something that neither addresses a problem specifically nor illustrates a particular political event. Thinking about the different narrative forms for fictionalizing truth, we then looked at the Theatre of the Oppressed as well as the theories of Grotowski and Stanislavski. Much of what they had done turned out to be unsuitable for what we had in mind. But we learned how to create something with non-professionals.

Rizk As we already mentioned, our work consisted of documenting on-going struggles. Doing this we reached a turning point when we recognized the limitations inherent to this kind of images, because they were too much reduced to the level of news. For example, if you film workers during a particular struggle, the message is limited to the immediate demands at a particular workplace and at a particular time. For us it was high time to go beyond this kind of immediate urgency in a struggle, towards a more open realm of the imaginary. [...] In the early stages of the project the situation in Egypt changed considerably, as people began taking back control of the streets. Occupying public space, they resisted the state and its security apparatus. Initially it was important for us to find some form of public performance, and so we planned to prepare workshops that we wanted to hold on the street in the districts our actors come from. When the security and political situation in Egypt changed and became even more catastrophic than before 2011, we had to drop the idea. Ultimately the project took place in a tent in a private space on the eleventh floor of a building in the centre [...].

Jocks What does it mean to you to screen this project in the German pavilion?

Rizk From the very beginning for us this work meant something global. While shooting we didn't make much of the fact that the film was being made in Egypt. The problems we addressed such as police violence, the politics of exploitation and social exclusion of the underclasses are widespread. Rich countries play a specific role in this regarding the events in Egypt, in so far as the policies adopted here [in Egypt] were invented and theoretically justified in places such as London or New York. The trade relations between Egypt and Europe, for example, are to a great extent part of this kind of organization between societies here and those in the North. This is why we would like to allow the public to take part in this story – a public that doesn't experience this kind of narrative immediately but certainly plays a role in it.

Metwaly Our work was based on the discovery of what it means to be on the other side of power relations. There's the man who plays the role of a foreman, as well as various interactions between boss and workers within the fictionalized reality. In real life it would never come to such a confrontation. In this way we can imagine how it would be if you said something or tried to speak with the person who acts out or claims this authority. What would happen if you spoke the truth and faced up to it in person?

Jasmina Metwaly, Philip Rizk, Heinz-Norbert Jocks, extracts from 'Jasmina Metwaly & Philip Rizk: Auf dem Dach von Kairo' (Interview), *Kunstforum International*, no. 233 (2015) 268–273. Revised for this volume. Translated by Philippa Hurd, 2017.

Kodwo Eshun
It's Her Factory//2012

The appearance of the Patti Smith Group at 2:33 [in Dan Graham's video *Rock My Religion*] shifts the oppressiveness of labour into the near present of the 1970s. The poor-quality recording shows the group performing at an outdoor concert. Smith holds her thin arms in front of her, walking forward in time to the beat. She sings 'Piss Factory', the B-side of 'Hey Joe', her debut single, recorded in June 1974. *Rock My Religion* returns to this scene three times. What seems of interest to Graham on this first occasion are the opening sentences of the song, in which Smith judges herself and her co-workers at the toy factory where she worked as a teenager with pitiless clarity. *Rock My Religion* draws attention to these words by transcribing them in a capitalized yellow font that scrolls upwards on the screen. Reading is complicated by images of Smith performing behind the text and the simultaneous but not synchronous bootleg recording of the song.

Smith's pungent account of work on the assembly line at the Dennis Mitchel Toy Factory in Pitman, South Jersey, in the summer of 1964 becomes a modern case study of low-paid female work. When Smith sings, 'You do your piece work and you do it slow', she is ventriloquizing the words of the factory foreman that warned her teenage self to fall into line. He is telling her to slow down her rate of productivity; the young Patti Smith must learn to adjust her pace to match that of other female workers.

Factory work forces its workers to adopt its repetitive rhythms. The rhythms of the assembly line enforce themselves upon the psyche as much as the body: bored by repeating the same gestures hour after hour, female workers fall into daydreaming. As Herbert Marcuse wrote, 'The machine process in the technological universe breaks down the innermost privacy of freedom and joins sexuality and labour in one unconscious rhythmic automatism'.[1] Marcuse envisioned a world inhabited by subjects psychically enslaved by their desires, their unconscious wishes programmed on an industrial scale. These unconscious desires could not be changed by moral appeal or critical dialogue. To reprogramme the unconscious, one would have to invent methods capable of entering into the 'one unconscious rhythmic automatism' and hacking its mechanisms. In its surging beat and insistent words, 'Piss Factory' articulates Smith's liberation from those rhythms. In the context of *Rock My Religion*, this argument takes shape by means of a preoccupation with the relationship between the rhythms of work and the beat of rock. For Graham, hardcore punk provided one method of remembering the injuries inflicted on the spirit by industrial rhythms and transducing them at the same time. [...]

1   [footnote 35 in source] Herbert Marcuse, *One Dimensional Man: The Ideology of Industrial Society* (1964) (London: Sphere Books, 1968) 37.

Kodwo Eshun, extract from *Dan Graham: Rock My Religion* (London: Afterall Books, 2012) 18–19.

John A. Walker
On Kay Fido Hunt, Margaret Harrison and Mary Kelly: *Women and Work//2002*

[...] Female labour was the theme of a show entitled *Women and Work: A Document of the Division of Labour in Industry* held at the South London Art Gallery in May 1975. It was the result of a lengthy investigation conducted by Kay Fido Hunt, Margaret Harrison and Mary Kelly, three artists who had decided to collaborate. Issues debated within the Women's Movement concerned them all and, since they were members of the recently formed Artists' Union, they were conscious of the need for artists to unionize like industrial workers. Between 1973–75, funding of £1,500 was made available by the Greater London Arts Association and the Thames Television Artists' Fund to record the experience of women factory workers in the Southwark works of the Metal Box Company. (Traditionally, the tin box trade had been predominantly women's work since the time of the First World War.) None of the artists had any training in the research methods sociologists might have employed and so they learnt by doing.

Hunt was born in South London in 1931 into a working-class family. She studied sculpture at Camberwell College of Art and taught at Guildford at the time of the 1968 student occupation; she was one of 40 staff sacked at that time for supporting the students' cause. Hunt had a strong personal motivation for the project: it was a way of honouring living workers' experience and the lives of her own mother and aunts who had all laboured in South London factories.

Harrison (born in 1940) came from Wakefield, Yorkshire, and had studied at Carlisle College of Art, 1957–61, and the Royal Academy Schools in London, 1961–64. She has recalled that her motivation for undertaking research in Companies House and in archives of the Trade Unions' headquarters was political activism. Mary Kelly (born 1941), an American, came to London to undertake postgraduate study at St Martin's, 1968–70, and was to remain in Britain for two decades.

The three artists visited the factory, gained the cooperation of a Public Relations officer, filmed and took photographs and interviewed employees. The exhibition that followed was overwhelmingly factual in character: there were images and sounds of the noisy assembly lines, portraits of the women workers, photographs of their hands engaged in fiddly, repetitive tasks plus timetables of their daily routines before, during and after work. Two colour films were projected side by side so that male and female labour could be compared. Another section displayed folders of documents and sound recordings supplying information about the company and industrial injuries suffered. A further display recorded the numbers of men and women (and their grades) who performed the various tasks in the factory.

In terms of its style of presentation, the exhibition reflected the influence of minimal and conceptual art – the use of grids for the arrangement of photographs, for example. Harrison has also argued that Conrad Atkinson's exhibition/work *Strike at Brannans* (Institute of Contemporary Arts, London, 1972) had established a precedent for documentary-type displays as art.

What the three artists discovered was that men were more mobile within the factory, had the more interesting jobs and enjoyed higher wages, and that many women experienced problems when expected to work a shift system because of their additional responsibility of caring for children. At the time, British employers were applying the Equal Pay Act, passed in 1970. Jane Kelly has summed up what happened in the case of Metal Box:

> … the management were restructuring the work force to keep profits intact. The female work force was not simply downgraded; a much more complicated reshuffling process was introduced, including token female representation in the top grades, automatic machinery and therefore redundancies in the second, and eventually the phasing out of all part-time work (traditionally a married woman's province) and the introduction of a double-day shift with the concomitant anti-social hours … the exhibition documented a labour force on its way out, showing the way in which industry copes with problematic, liberal legislation by either restructuring or ignoring its stipulations.'[1] [...]

Metal Box's employees were invited to the opening of the exhibition and were pleased and flattered to find their portraits on the walls of the local art gallery – a place most of them did not normally visit. The critical information in the show, on the other hand, displeased the all-male management and the artists were banned from visiting the factory again.

A sympathetic review appeared in *Spare Rib*. Rosalind Delmar found the presentation low-key but lucid and concluded that the exhibition was 'a stimulating and thought-provoking experiment'.[2] It was indeed a worthy attempt by three artist-intellectuals to address a real life issue and to connect with working women outside the world of art. Predictably, the socialist realists of the LSA [League of Socialist Artists] were hostile to a documentary-type exhibition and they distributed a critical pamphlet to coincide with it.[3] They objected to the 'generous hand-outs' given to three members of the Artists' Union and doubted that 'mere reporting' counted as 'real art'. They found the display marked by 'barrenness and monotonous paucity of material' and sarcastically dismissed its 'facile reformist message'. [...]

However, the critical work [of *Women and Work* and similar other artists' projects] did prompt some viewers to wonder: 'Having called public attention to the problem of exploitation, what can or should be done? Can art also propose a solution?' Hunt has claimed that *Women and Work* had one positive effect, that is, it persuaded some female employees of Metal Box to join a union. However, it seems that many of them subsequently lost their jobs because part-time employment was phased out.[4]

1   [foonote 7 in source] Jane Kelly,'Mary Kelly', *Studio International*, vol. 193, no. 987 (1977) 186–8.

2   [8] Rosalind Delmar, 'Woman and Work ...', *Spare Rib*, no. 40 (1975) 32–3.

3   [9] LSA, Do you really know what this exhibition is all about? (London: LSA, 1975) 7 pages, reprinted in *Class War in the Arts!* (London: LSA, 1976) 52-page pamphlet.

4   [10] Interview conducted with Kay Fido Hunt in South London in June 2000.

John A. Walker, extracts from *Left Shift: Radical Art in 1970s Britain* (London and New York: I.B.Tauris, 2002) 144–7.

Giovanna Zapperi
Against Domesticity: Artists and Feminists in the Kitchen//2015

We identify unpaid domestic work as being the service that allows capitalism, both private and of the state, to substist. [...] Equal pay is our right, but our freedom is something else. Is equal pay enough after we've also chalked up hours of housework?
– *Manifesto* of Rivolta Femminile, 1970

The first manifesto of the Rivolta Femminile group, one of the first feminist groups in Italy, clearly revealed the link between housework and female oppression in the radicalness that characterized the writing of Carla Lanzi, its main author, along with Carla Accardi and Elvira Banotti. For Rivolta Femminile, freedom was inseparable from an awareness of all the roles that turned a woman into a subsidiary being and someone who worked for others, whose activity was valorized only in so far as it was related to the unpaid areas of motherhood, housework and caretaking. The private area to which female existences are so often relegated thus became a conflictual area to be reinvented collectively [...].

The chance to rethink the domestic space – the site of woman's oppression – was in most cases associated with a performative practice that allowed for the elaboration of critical points of view with respect to the way in which women were defined via the stereotyped roles linked to motherhood and caretaking. The private spaces and the houses in which the artists lived thus became places of experimentation and self-invention, opening up to cross-fertitlization and sharing. [...]

An example of the feminist deconstruction of the kitchen space is the 1972 group project *Womanhouse*, in which a series of young artists – students enrolled in the Feminist Art Program directed by Judy Chicago and Miriam Shapiro at California Institute of the Arts – created seventeen ambiences inside an abandoned building whose purpose was to reflect on the stereotypes linked to domestic activities, at the same time abolishing the distinction between public and private space, domestic environment and expository space. Inside the building was the *Nurturant Kitchen* realized by Susan Frazier, Vickie Hodgetts and Robin Weltsch collectively, who had painted the kitchen walls and the objects and appliances inside them pink: refrigerator, oven, jars of preserves, sink, toaster and other items, too. Hanging from the ceiling and on the walls were a series of sculptures in the shape of a fried egg. These appeared to be soft and spongy, which made them terribly realistic, especially in the way they alluded to the female breast. Hence, if on the one hand, the 'breasts/fried eggs' ironically pointed to the social function of the female gender represented in terms of care and nourishment, on the other, the kitchen space as a whole was englobed in a totalizing and equally oppressive femininity, marked by the colour pink that covered each single element. [...]

As was recently observed by [Paul B.] Preciado, the environments of Womanhouse teach us to look at domestic space as though it were a technology of production and domination in which the institutions that regulate women's lives (marriage, care and sexuality) emerge as just as many regimes of containment and discipline of the body.[1] [...]

In reconfiguring the space of the kitchen, starting from the body and women's experiences, several artists produced works that explored, not without irony, the objective and alienating dimension linked to domestic work and to the role assigned to women in the private sphere. A series of performative works made in the 1970s reveal the woman's body grappling with a highly technological domestic environment, in which the kitchen is represented and experienced as the site that contains female subjectivity. In the video *Semiotics of the Kitchen* (1975), Martha Rosler identifies the space of the kitchen with the stereotype of the White middle-class suburban American housewife, literally imprisoned inside her domestic existence. The video stages a sort of demonstration of the use of a series of utensils in which the kitchen is literally represented as though it were a battlefield: the parodic repetition of daily gestures conceals the alienation of housework. Martha Rosler thus embodies a dehumanized character who lists all the various utensils in alphabetical order – apron, ladle, grater, and so on – like a robot incapable of expressing itself completely, limited to mechanically repeating a series of standardized gestures. In her demonstration-parody, however, Rosler exaggerates the juxtaposition between the housewife's body and the modern utensils that fill American kitchens. Her gestures reflect the instrumental function of a woman in the domestic sphere, to the point of transforming the woman herself into a utensil in the last scenes of the video, when she, not having the corresponding instruments, mimes the letters V, W, X, Y, Z directly. In the crescendo of paroxysm that characterizes the finale of the video, the letters are literally 'written' by the female body and end up identifying the object of the demonstration with the woman herself.[2]

1   [footnote 2 in source] [Paul] B. Preciado, 'Revenir à la Womanhouse', *Le Magazine du Jeu de Paume* (October 3, 2013).

2   [4] See Silvia Eiblmayr, 'Martha Rosler's Characters', in *Martha Rosler: Positions in the Life World*, ed. Catherine de Zegher (Cambridge, Massachusetts: The MIT Press 1998) 153.

Giovanna Zapperi, extracts from 'Against Domesticity: Artists and Feminists in the Kitchen', in *Kitchens & Invaders*, ed. Germano Celant and Silvana Annicchiarico (Milan: Triennale Design Museum, 2015) 169–75.

Dietmar Rübel
Factories as Places of Knowledge: Richard Serra and the Production Process//2010

We actually know very little about what happens in a factory. It is clear what goes into factories and what comes out of them. But the production process, the actual work process, is hardly ever shown [...]: it is a blank space in the collective pictorial memory. [...] Movie narratives that take place in factories are extremely rare, and if a film ever locates its characters in a steel mill – Michael Cimino's *The Deer Hunter* of 1978, for example – the setting is merely used as a backdrop.[1] Where can we find concepts of the complex, cooperative production processes that go on within factories from? Who can supply the images?

We owe most of our knowledge to slapstick, as this body-related sub-genre plays a central role in the popular presentation of images of industry. To put it bluntly, everything we know about the factory in our mass media society we know because of slapstick. Modern slapstick makes the factory a place of knowledge. In this context, the entertainment film, in particular the comedy, reveals itself to be a paradox, as Bertolt Brecht [...] wrote about the cinema: 'Those who buy tickets transform themselves in front of the screen into idlers and exploiters. Since the object of exploitation is put inside them, they are, so to speak, victims of "imploitation".'[2] Slapstick's main approach is [...] the density of time, space and body. In the chronotopic density of film, industrial rationalization finds its aesthetic correlation. Charlie Chaplin's 1936 film *Modern Times* provided the images for the view of generations that the factory worker – as Marx wrote – was merely an appendage of the machine.[3] In his early experimental films, Richard Serra addressed these heteronomous processes [...] together with the black pedagogy of slapstick. In these films the artist submits to the mechanized rhythm of factories – and acts as a dystopian worker–artist.[4] For example, in Richard Serra's 1968 black-and-white film, *Hand Catching Lead*, we see the artist's right forearm alone in front of a light-coloured brick wall. The palm and fingers of the powerful hand are blackened. For three-and-a-half minutes, at a consistent pace, angular pieces of lead fall from above. Occasionally, one of the scraps of metal catches the light [...]. Again and again the hand grasps at the malleable lead, but only rarely succeeds in catching an object. If it does, the hand immediately lets it drop, only for it to open again a fraction of a second later to grasp with lightning speed at another piece of lead.

This [...] pulsating action correlates with the projection of a cinematographic machine. The pace and the impulses of the falling objects seem to reflect the mechanical succession of images on a celluloid strip. The sluggishness of the eye that cannot follow the increased momentum of time in the cinematography is juxtaposed with the tension of the working hand. The artist's grasping hand recalls Frederick W. Taylor's notorious chronometry that aimed to increase work capacity – for which scientific time-and-motion studies for optimizing production processes were undertaken[5] – intensified by the absolute inevitability of the mechanized flow of images. As Chaplin, in the famous machines scene in *Modern Times*, slides through the gear wheels like a strip of celluloid, Serra's motion picture drives the number of units onwards, like an assembly line. *Hand Catching Lead* reduces work to a simple gesture, that nevertheless bears all the attributes of physical work – material, dirt, effort – whose purpose, however, is unrecognizable in the clip, like modern manufacture where the individual often no longer sees the final product he has just been working on. In the exaggerated alienation of work – reduced to the opening and closing of the hand – Serra's grasping at lead becomes an absurd action that even bears the characteristics of slapstick for a moment in its collapse of repetition into the repetitive action. For example, as a consequence of a minimal hesitation in the flow of lead, the index finger makes a playful gesture demanding more pace, so that its stupid piecework can be maintained. To my knowledge this playful gesture is the only touch of humour that Serra has allowed himself over his entire artistic career.

In its exaggerated reduction and uniformity Serra's film recalls *Modern Times*. In the opening episode […], Charlie, the tramp with his cane and bowler hat, struggles desperately against the monotony of his work, typically enough in a factory called 'Electric Steel'. The camera shows how the workers on the assembly line are scarcely able to follow the rhythm of the machines. Each one must carry out the same manipulation with breakneck uniformity, relentlessly and with incessant repetition: assembly-line work in a 'system of machines to which motion is communicated […] from an automatic centre'.[6] Even during the short breaks Charlie's body carries on moving. His arms still twitch in piecework, and search desperately for suitable objects to adjust.

Obviously the basic principle of the machine age is rationalization – the human being becomes a mere cog in the machine. Through this visual metaphor, which Chaplin explores in *Modern Times* and Serra addresses in *Hand Catching Lead*, a critical view of the rationalization of production, management and entertainment has had a long-lasting impact.[7] The assembly line above all stands for this dark side, but no less for the fascination with technological modernity, around which the stages of work are dismantled and arranged in such a way that all manipulations are coordinated and can be or must be carried out without losing time – as Charlie's heteronomous body demonstrates. This extremely efficient process forces the people on the assembly line to adapt themselves substantially to the monotonous, phased rhythms of the machines;

the worker becomes an appendage. Even Charlie's simple scratching or swatting a fly is [...] impossible, as it brings the entire production process to a standstill. Its high symbolic value notwithstanding, the assembly line nevertheless came to the fore in industrial manufacture only around the mid twentieth century. The large steel mills of classical modernity were the first places where the division of labour and standardization became decisive factors. This extreme, highly productive concentration produced heteronomous processes, which the worker could avoid only selectively. Or indeed not at all, as we can see in the case of Chaplin: the monotony and the conveyor belt's high-speed compulsion rob the tramp of his mental stability, or as Sigfried Giedion writes in *Mechanization Takes Command* about the film's assembly-line sequence: 'The mechanized individualist goes mad and proceeds to turn the factory into the madhouse that it really always had been'.[8]

In Serra's short film the absurd mechanics of work are emphasized by the peculiarity of the hand still grasping at every piece of lead without really wanting to stop the falling fragments. Rather, in his absurd educational film a mysterious test – just as compulsive as Chaplin's piecework twitching – takes place as a valorized production process. Although the activity seems to obey a strict division of labour, there is a growing impression that the hand's work is aiming at dedifferentiation. Thus much more chaos than order is created, ultimately devaluing the work itself. Outside of the image it is impossible that the energy used in the exhausting grasping can lead to any meaningful use. Thus the material result of *Hand Catching Lead* can only be an accidental accumulation of alienated work.

1   Exceptions are, for example, Jean-Luc Godard's *Passion* (1982) or Aki Kaurismäki in *Tulitikkutehtaan tyttö* (The Match Factory Girl, 1990), and today alongside children's TV programmes primarily the evening programmes of news channels, which broadcast documentaries about food production as a form of advertising.

2   Bertolt Brecht, 'The Threepenny Lawsuit' in *Bertolt Brecht on Film & Radio*, trans. and ed. Marc Silberman (London: Bloomsbury, 2000) 170.

3   Karl Marx, *Capital: A Critique of Political Economy, vol. 1, book I: The Process of Production of Capital*, trans. Ben Fowkes (Harmondsworth: Penguin, 1976) 614.

4   On these films in general see Rosalind E. Krauss, *Passages in Modern Sculpture* (Cambridge, Massachusetts: The MIT Press, 1977) 279 ff; and subsequently Benjamin H.D. Buchloh, 'Prozessuale Skulptur und Film im Werk Richard Serras' in *Richard Serra: Arbeiten 66-77* (Tübingen: Kunsthalle Tübingen, 1978) 175–88; as well as O. Pascheit and D. Rübel, *Richard Serra in der Hamburger Kunsthalle* (Hamburg: Christians Verlag, 2003).

5   See P. Hinrichs and I. Kolboom, 'Taylor, Ford, Fayol: Wissenschaftliche Arbeitsorganisation in Frankreich zwischen Belle Epoque und Weltwirtschaftskrise' in *absolut modern sein. Zwischen*

Fahrrad und Fließband. Culture technique in Frankreich 1889-1937 (Berlin: Neue Gesellschaft für Bildende Kunst, 1986) 75¬–94.

6   Marx, *Capital*, vol. 1, book I, op. cit., 503.

7   On Chaplin see the anthologies by D. Kimmich (ed.), *Charlie Chaplin. Eine Ikone der Moderne* (Frankfurt: Suhrkamp, 2003) and the uncredited source of W. Wiegand (ed.), *Über Chaplin* (Zurich: Diogenes, 1978). On *Modern Times* see J. Mellen's monograph, *Modern Times* (London: BFI, 2006).

8   Sigfried Giedion, *Mechanization Takes Command: A Contribution to Anonymous History* (New York: Oxford University Press, 1948) 126. Here Giedion is actually quoting an anonymous review from the *Herald Tribune* of 1936.

Dietmar Rübel, extracts from 'Fabriken als Erkenntnisorte: Richard Serra und der Gang in die Produktion', in *Topos Atelier: Werkstatt und Wissensform*, ed. Michael Diers and Monika Wagner (Berlin: Akademie Verlag, 2010) 111–35. Translated by Philippa Hurd, 2017.

Peter Weiss
The Aesthetics of Resistance//2005

[...] What my father wanted to examine and what he needed to systematize his impressions for were the beginning that appeared again and again, in which the relations to the workers deepened, in which the dimensions shifted, and the labourers were released from their significance, sometimes even dominating in a social constellation. Emphasizing a farmhand, a soldier over the lord, the knight, that was tantamount to heresy, which initially required secrecy, conspiracy. However, said my father, the depicted worker was never seen by himself, he was always seen only by the artist, by members of a different sphere of life. We, he said, expressed ourselves solely in our labour, we very seldom got to view what was captured of us in art. We dealt with our tools, our art was cultivating the soil, grafting the fruits, building the houses, these things called for songs, fables, fairy tales, handed down orally, we never made a fuss about the things we signed with our names. The secret art in temples and cathedrals, in manuscripts and statues said something about our presence, it was certainly allied with us, and it also helped us to gradually appreciate our achievements, but we mean something else when we talk about our culture, it is precisely this activeness that is the basis of everything surrounding us in the country and the cities. Our culture comes toward me, he said, whenever I see someone piling the chopped wood, sharpening the scythe, mending the net, joining the beams into the roof frame, polishing the pistons of the machine. He did not wish to idealize this, he added, but he saw no other possibility of arousing something of what links to the overall talent and knowledge of an era. Oddly enough, he said, it was only the artistic representation of a seamstress, a lacemaker, a mower and thresher, a servant girl picking grapes, or a blacksmith that gave value to labour. It was only in an artwork that labour had cultural meaning, it was only there that labour had become art, while the workers themselves remained without rank. I recalled this conversation so clearly because it was associated with a painting, Menzel's picture, eight feet wide, of an iron-rolling mill. Using a colour reproduction, my father had explained to me that because of the growth of a conscious working class the recognized official art had provided a place for workers, a place for them to make their presence felt, and that the establishment had, at the same time, skilfully reneged on its generosity. Menzel's picture, the original of which we saw later on, at the National Gallery, was ubiquitously hailed as the apotheosis of labour. The atmosphere of heavy industry had been convincingly rendered with great technical expertise. The steam, the booming of hammers, the screeching of cranes and drag chains, the rotating of the flywheels on the machines, the heat of the fires, the white glow of the iron, the bracing of muscles, all these things could be felt in the painting. The group of blacksmith trudged toward the centre of the picture, shoving the glaring metal block, taken from the raised cart, under the roll, at the right, protected by a dented disk of sheet metal, a few men were resting, spooning food from bowls, lifting bottles to their mouths, and at the left edge of the painting, bare-chested workers of the previous shift were washing their necks and hair. Every action, every twisting and bending over the tools, and also the weary, burned-out sitting in the corner were components of the gigantic hall, squeezed into the bars, the daylight shimmering through the haze at several points seemed unreachable. All that was stated by the rendering of this nonstop, sweaty intermeshing was that people were working here, hard and unprotesting. The force in the heaving and swinging, regulated and controlled, the moment of utmost concentration for holding the tongs, the alertness shown by the bearded foreman at the lever as the rolled part came through, the scrubbing of the soot-caked bodies, the exhaustion on a brief pause, all these things pointed to a single theme, to labour, to the principle of labour, and it was a specific principle, which could be defined only after detailed observation. This was not a matter of work as my father spoke about it, nor was it work as a system of self-realization, it was work done at the lowest possible price and with the highest profit for the work buyer. Since only the workers were visible, committing their entire existence to the activities, the viewer had the impression that they controlled the work. Dynamically sculpted by the glow of the fire, they filled out the space. At first sight, said my father when we were at the art museum, they are presented in the overwhelming dominance over the productive forces. And yet all they are doing is thoroughly confirming the rules of the division of labour. They appear to be acting on their own, but they exist only in their bond with the tools and the machines, which are the property of others. Now these others were nowhere to be seen, yet the workers were in their service. Even the ones crouching in the filthy corner, on their own for a while, almost in possession of their own lives, were merely waiting for the signal that would summon them back. They developed their strength purely in the handiwork, and even there the motions of their arms were not threatening, it was plain that they would use their arms exclusively to produce goods. The praise of labour was a praise of subordination. The men who, surrounded by spraying sparks, rallied about the white-hot mass of iron, who washed themselves at the trough, and the ones who, exhaustedly staring into space, sat at their meal, and in front of whom the young woman with the careworn face and the anxious upward glance packed the empty cups into the basket, they were all powerless. The depth of the factory was indeterminable, the rows of vertical and horizontal iron girders moved as a grid into infinity. The building, losing itself in smoke, was a world from which there was no escape. [...]

Peter Weiss, extract from *The Aesthetics of Resistance, Volume 1: A Novel*, trans. Joachim Neugroschel (Durham, North Carolina: Duke University Press, 2005) 309–12.

Jihoon Kim
Factory Complex: The Post-*Vérité* Turn of Korean Experimental Documentary//2015

Korean independent documentary during the last few years has been the richest and most vibrant territory of formal and aesthetic experimentations in Korean national cinema as many filmmakers and artists have attempted to renew and transcend its traditional ethos of *cinéma vérité*. A majority of Korean independent non-fiction films since the 1980s were predicated upon the priority of the director's engagement with the scenes of the various local conflicts, such as political struggles for democratization, ideological tensions, state violence, labour movements, and the resistance of villagers against demolition. By contrast, emerging directors and artists have developed an array of other formal devices than those in the participatory mode of documentary, including self-reflexive and essayistic approaches, reenactment, archival uses of found footage and poetic observation. These devices have resulted in various films, videos, and installations that fall under the rubrics of 'experimental documentary' or 'avant-doc'.

The new filmmakers and artists' growing attempts at the intersection of documentary and avant-garde cinema, and of documentary and contemporary art, however, do not mark a total departure from their predecessors. The works in the 2010s might break from the authentic assumption of the traditional Korean independent documentary, but their directors and artists ultimately aim at extending its traditional subjects, political responsibility and ethical problems into their formal experimentations. It is in this sense that the works are seen to mark the 'post-vérité' turn of Korean independent documentary. *Factory Complex* (2014), a feature-length film that recently gave the Silver Lion to its director Im Heung-Soon at the 56th Venice Biennale, emblematizes this tendency of the recent Korean independent documentary while also situating itself within the global trend of avant-doc.

As manifested in its end credit, the film is dedicated to Im's mother, 'who worked in the sewing factory and all the women who fought to defend their labour rights'. Based upon this, Im portrays a series of female workers' labour struggles in various workplaces since the 1970s, including textile and wig factories as part of Korea's labour-intensive industry, which played a major role in its rapid modernization. The voices of the former workers bear vivid testimony as to how the workplaces' poor and unequal working conditions, including overdue wages, overnight shifts, industrial diseases and unjustified layoffs, lead to their strikes and protests, as well as to the violence of the companies' repressions. Instead of chronicling this tumultuous history in a linear manner, the film constructs a non-chronological narrative, intersecting past with present, drawing the viewer's attention to the persistence of these conditions in contemporary local and translocal labours. For instance, Im associates industrial disease in the wig factory of the 1970s with the former semiconductor workers in Samsung Electronics, who suffered hair loss, leukemia and cancers. This non-linear intersection of the past and the present is also applied to the repetition of the labour protests in the 2000s, through Im's interviews with the former workers in Kiryung Electronics who went on hunger strike against overdue wage in 2005, and with Kim Jin-suk, a former welder of Hanjin Heavy Industries who protested on an aerial crane from 2010 to 2011 against the company's large-scale layoffs. Im's transhistorical view on the labour issues further demonstrates how they still persist in a time when the labour-intensive industries might be regarded as outdated in highly developed Korea, and its central force was moved to developing countries. The poor working conditions and the physical and mental exploitation of workers in the past, though taking different forms, are linked to various labourers in the contemporary transportation and service industries, encompassing market cashiers, cabin crew and public call centre tellers. They are also repeated in the transnational flow of labour, as Im's camera moves to Cambodia and frames interviews with several local workers in an OEM clothing factory who suffer extremely low wages. [...]

[Im employs and mixes] various formal devices of avant-doc in *Factory Complex*. Besides capturing the interviews with the workers, Im's camera poetically observes the past and present landscapes of the workplaces, as in the sequence where the former Guro Complex, as the centre of labour-intensive industries in Seoul, overlaps with the skyscrapers in its present, with its name changed to Gasan Digital Complex. This observational perspective competes ·with Im's subjective use of his camera, as it embodies the viewpoint of the female workers who show their past poor and overpopulated quarters that remain abandoned now. While drawing on photographic documents, newspaper photos and video footage, Im also uses several forms of reenactment, including a theatrical play and a girl in blindfold, to take an imaginary approach to the pains and traumas of the manual workers who engaged in the protests, and to establish the distance between the past and the present as his principle of constructing an alternative history.

While the variety of these formal innovations presents Im's concern with form and meditation as a characteristic of experimental documentary, it is significant to note that they demonstrate Im's idea of inheriting the realities of history and politics from the traditional Korean independent documentary. More than raising the validity and urgency of the labour issues in the contemporary Korean independent documentary, all the non-*vérité* devices ultimately serve to reinforce the power of the interview that the participatory mode of documentary, as well as the traditional Korean independent documentary, has long developed as a distinct form of social encounter. In *Factory Complex*, the viewer feels the power of the camera that vividly captures not simply the faces and voices of the workers but also their affective smiles, sighs and tears, which trigger his sympathy and awareness. By maintaining the centrality of these testimonies and articulating them through his critical subjectiveness, Im succeeds in reconciling his formal experiments with the vérité tradition of Korean independent documentary as a driving force of the 'post-*vérité*' turn.

Jihoon Kim, extracts from 'Factory Complex: The Post-Vérité Turn of Korean Experimental Documentary', in *Millenium Film Journal*, no. 62 (Fall 2015) 11–12.

Paweł Mościcki
Distortion, or the Gay Science According to Paweł Althamer//2011

[...] Paweł Althamer's hallmark is the attempt to make of the commonplace, deficient or marginal a space for reflection, creative activity and community. This type of space can also be evoked by direct confrontation with the mundane and the miserable. [...]

At the Deutsche Guggenheim, Althamer creates a bold heterotopia that recalls the concept of transpolarization. This term denotes the process of reversing the earth's magnetic poles, but in the context of [the 2011 installation] *Almech* it refers to the distortion of the relationship between the centre and its peripheries, the mythical West and East. Althamer transplants factory equipment from his father's small, Polish plastics-manufacturing company to the very heart of global capitalism. Two economics meet: that of the fluid exchange of knowledge and capital on a global scale and that of a peripheral economy, weighed down by family ties, which, from the point of view of late capitalism, seems an economy of the lowest rank. The basic symbols of this transpolarization – other than the displacement of factory equipment in the exhibition space – is the changed signage. For the duration of the exhibition, the logo of the Almech company hangs on Unter den Linden in Berlin, while that of Deutsche Guggenheim is on Slowicza Street in Wesola, on the outskirts of Warsaw.

This singular mccting of incompatible orders forces both institutions into new roles, enjoining them to borrow from each other's functions. The exhibition space becomes a temporary factory filled with entirely material objects and no longer simply a place of virtual financial exchange or transmission of knowledge. Meanwhile, in Wesola, production will be on a mass scale but with no regard for the principle of product standardization. The collision with the art world changes the appearance of the manufacturing process itself, as it approaches artistic production. With *Almech*, Althamer does not seek to 'catapult us all into creative new social constellations', but rather to hold us for a while in a moment of impasse, of distorted order, and to help us make the most of the opportunities that are presented to us in this moment.[1] [...]

The figures produced as part of the exhibition refer above all to the rich tradition and diverse connotations of the mask. The portraits evoke death masks, and tall figures placed on pedestals, larger than life, clearly indicate the phantasmal excess with which every such apparition is endowed. As Georges Bataille wrote, 'when the face is closed and covered by a mask, it no longer participates in stability or the ground. The mask communicates incertitude and the menace of unexpected changes, unforeseeable and as insupportable as death.'[2] The mask replaces the natural face with a fake shell that simultaneously tears us away from the natural world and inaugurates the mortification-based order of image and likeness.[3] Thus it appears on the threshold of the everyday world as an 'obscure incarnation of chaos'; it is 'chaos made flesh'.[4] However, the crux of Althamer's project seems to be whether this deathly context of the mask and its involvement in the most dead and forgotten elements of the psyche could find its place in the context of affirmative mythologizing. [...]

In the Deutsche Guggenheim exhibition space, Almech employees make casts of human faces together with the artist with no regard for the hierarchy of the institution. Management as well as security staff, cleaning staff and visitors are able to lend their faces to the project. Thus emerges a very particular, egalitarian community, all with eyes closed as if in deep sleep or agony. This is a real community of spirits that appears at the institution at the hour of transpolarization. It combines two opposing dimensions of time: the ephemeral present of the exhibition, the framework of which ruthlessly recruits new members, and the long-term duration of the fossils immortalized in the act of masking. *Almech* could perhaps be compared to Jacques Derrida's *Spectres of Marx*, in which the French philosopher seriously questions the future of radical political engagement by likening the figure of the spectre of communism that haunts Europe in Marx's letters to Hamlet's father's spirit, which requests that his son continue his difficult legacy, in Shakespeare's play. Althamer contrasts his own analogy to that of the father's spirit – Marx's spectre: between his father's logo and the unnamed community of spirits.[5]

1   [footnote 11 in source] Claire Bishop, 'Something for Everyone: Claire Bishop on the Art of Paweł
     Althamer', *Artforum* (February 2011) 181.

2   [19] Georges Bataille, 'Le masque', in *Oeuvres completes, vol. 2, Écrits posthumes, 1922–40* (Paris:
     Gallimard, 1970) 405.

3   [20] On the relationships among likeness, the death mask and the philosophical concept of the
     image in the context of Blanchot and Heidegger, see Georges Didi-Huberman, 'De ressemblance
     à ressemblance', in *Maurice Blanchot: Récits critiques*, ed. Christophe Bident and Pierre Vilar
     (Tours: Farrago/Paris: Léo Scheer, 2003) 143–67.

4   [21] Bataille, op. cit., 403.

5   [25] See Jacques Derrida, *Spectres de Marx* (Paris: Galilée, 1993) 41–6.

Paweł Mościcki, extracts from 'Distortion, or the Gay Science According to Paweł Althamer', in *Paweł Althamer: Almech* (Berlin: Deutsche Guggenheim, 2011) 77, 78, 83, 84.

Marwa Arsanios
Olga's Notes: This Whole New World//2015

'The Most Beautiful Industry in Our Country' is the title of an article that talks about a dance school. 'If you pass next to an industrial building, don't think this is a new metal or car factory! No! It is a big hangar but nothing of what you expect. It is a place where bodies get trained to dance in a certain manner and join the national troupe.'

Learning in a factory is a mass learning and producing a mass that has learned. Bodies in masses that have learned to dance ballet to become, or not become, ballerinas. The article describes the newly built ballet school as 'the biggest industry that has been built in the country', and continues, 'This is not a steel industry, this is a place that will surprise you. It is an industry of the body, it is a ballet school.' It promotes the school and the activities happening inside it in the way it would promote a building development project. Building bodies that could dance in a certain manner. The opera house and the ballet school become part of the modernization process of the nation. But why ballet? Ballet as a tradition coming from industrialized countries. But also ballet as a tradition that would disrupt the local folkloric and traditional dances. Ballet as a colonizer, ballet as a decolonizer from traditional dance.

The national dance school aimed at producing national dancers that would enter the national troupe and dance on official occasions. These bodies of dancers would become representatives of the country with its specific borders. Beyond borders, travelling to give spectacles and performances, the dancers' bodies freshly coming out of national industry will have to dance the dance that represents their country and their people. A specific gesture or a dance movement can be representative of a country and the people living within specific borders mapped by human hands and fingers – colonial hands. What do colonial hands look like?

In the same way, the spectators start identifying with the dance group who they think best represents their country. The ballet school was implemented in 1958 with the help of experts from the Bolshoi Ballet. In 1966, Leonid Lavrovsky flew to Cairo to stage *The Fountain of Bakhchisarai*, the first big production. Nasser attended the opening on 3 December 1966, and awarded Orders of Merit to the lead dancers. One year later, Lavrovsky died. A year after that, the Six Day War was fought. The bodies had to learn and adapt to this dance. The industrial body had to learn ballet. The body of the ballerina can fly. It learned to fly. After certain conditioning, it can do the jumpin-the-air-and-fly.

If the modern project has given birth to democracy and totalitarianism at the same time, then perhaps the dancer's body was trapped in between those two projects. But don't worry, we are not here to save it. Perhaps the dancer will decide to break away when she rebels against the choreographer. But in any case we are not here to save her.

Carita and Natasha were my neighbours. Older than me, they were trained as ballerinas but joined the national folkloric dance troupe in the 1980s. The Twins. They were known as the twins. Born to Greek parents, they moved to Beirut with their mother after she remarried. Their stepfather owned the building where I lived as a child. This is what Carita writes next to a photo she posts on Facebook: 'The war was in full swing but for the time of a lull we would take a break on the balcony of my room, seen by the photographer Houda.'

The pose of the ballerina on her balcony when the fighting paused.

The ballerina with her *pointe* in a funny fashion comes out and poses. She doesn't dance, she poses. She poses the moment the fighting stops. She simulates the act of being a dancer for a moment on the balcony. She seduces. She is a dancer even if she is not dancing for the moment, or she had to stop dancing for a while. As soon as the fighting stops she steps out on her balcony and becomes a dancer again. The body of the dancer on the balcony means that the fighting has stopped. At least for a while. The time to take a picture. Twenty years later she can write the comment and post it on Facebook. 'That moment twenty years ago the fighting stopped for a bit and I went out on my balcony and posed.' […]

Marwa Arsanios, extracts from 'Olga's Notes: This Whole New World', *ArtMargins*, vol. 4, no. 1 (February 2015) 61–78.

Hito Steyerl
Is a Museum a Factory?//2009

The film *La hora de los hornos* (The Hour of the Furnaces, 1968), a Third Cinema manifesto against neocolonialism, has a brilliant installation specification.[1] A banner was to be hung at every screening with text reading: 'Every spectator is either a coward or a traitor.'[2] It was intended to break down the distinctions between filmmaker and audience, author and producer, and thus create a sphere of political action. And where was this film shown? In factories, of course.

Now, political films are no longer shown in factories.[3] They are shown in the museum, or the gallery – the art space. That is, in any sort of white cube.

How did this happen? First of all, the traditional Fordist factory is, for the most part, gone.[4] It's been emptied out, machines packed up and shipped off to China. Former workers have been retrained for further retraining, or become software programmers and started working from home. Secondly, the cinema has been transformed almost as dramatically as the factory. It's been multiplexed, digitized and sequelized, as well as rapidly commercialized, as neoliberalism became hegemonic in its reach and influence. [...] Now, political and experimental films alike are shown in black boxes set within white cubes – in fortresses, bunkers, docks and former churches. [...]

On the other hand [...], the displacement from factory to museum never took place. In reality, political films are very often screened in the exact same place as they always were: in former factories, which are today, more often than not, museums. A gallery, an art space, a white cube with abysmal sound isolation. Which will certainly show political films. But which also has become a hotbed of contemporary production. Of images, jargon, lifestyles and values. [...] A flagship store of Cultural Industries, staffed by eager interns who work for free.

A factory, so to speak, but a different one. It is still a space for production, still a space of exploitation and even of political screenings. It is a space of physical meeting and sometimes even common discussion. At the same time, it has changed almost beyond recognition. So what sort of factory is this?

The typical set-up of the museum-as-factory looks like this. Before: an industrial workplace. Now: people spending their leisure time in front of TV monitors. Before: people working in these factories. Now: people working at home in front of computer monitors. [...]

In the museum-as-factory, something continues to be produced. [...]

In this economy, even spectators are transformed into workers. As Jonathan Beller argues, cinema and its derivatives (television, the Internet, and so on) are factories, in which spectators work. Now, 'to look is to labour'.[5] Cinema, which integrated the logic of Taylorist production and the conveyor belt, now spreads the factory wherever it travels. But this type of production is much more intensive than the industrial one. The senses are drafted into production, the media capitalize upon the aesthetic faculties and imaginary practices of viewers.[6] In that sense, any space that integrates cinema and its successors has now become a factory, and this obviously includes the museum. While in the history of political filmmaking the factory became a cinema, cinema now turns museum spaces back into factories. [...]

While the classical space of cinema resembles the space of the industrial factory, the museum corresponds to the dispersed space of the social factory. Both cinema and Fordist factory are organized as locations of confinement, arrest and temporal control. Imagine: Workers leaving the factory. Spectators leaving the cinema – a similar mass, disciplined and controlled in time, assembled and released at regular intervals. As the traditional factory arrests its workers, the cinema arrests the spectator. Both are disciplinary spaces and spaces of confinement.

But now imagine: Workers leaving the factory. Spectators trickling out of the museum (or even queuing to get in). An entirely different constellation of time and space. This second crowd is not a mass, but a multitude.[7] The museum doesn't organize a coherent crowd of people. People are dispersed in time and space – a silent crowd, immersed and atomized, struggling between passivity and overstimulation.

This spatial transformation is reflected by the format of many newer cinematic works. [...] While the traditional cinema set-up works from a single central perspective, multi-screen projections create a multifocal space. While cinema is a mass medium, multi-screen installations address a multitude spread out in space, connected only by distraction, separation and difference. [...]

Without notice, the question of political cinema has been inverted. What began as a discussion of political cinema in the museum has turned into a question of cinematic politics in a factory. Traditionally, political cinema was meant to educate – it was an instrumental effort at 'representation' in order to achieve its effects in 'reality'. It was measured in terms of efficiency, of revolutionary revelation, of gains in consciousness, or as potential triggers of action.

Today, cinematic politics are post-representational. They do not educate the crowd, but produce it. They articulate the crowd in space and time. They submerge it in partial invisibility and then orchestrate their dispersion, movement and reconfiguration. They organize the crowd without preaching to it. They replace the gaze of the bourgeois sovereign spectator of the white cube with the incomplete, obscured, fractured and overwhelmed vision of the spectator-as-labourer. [...]

Cinema inside the museum thus calls for a multiple gaze, which is no longer collective, but common, which is incomplete, but in process, which is distracted and singular, but can be edited into various sequences and combinations. This gaze is no longer the gaze of the individual sovereign master, nor, more precisely, of the self-deluded sovereign (even if 'just for one day', as David Bowie sang). It isn't even a product of common labour, but focuses its point of rupture on the paradigm of productivity. The museum-as-factory and its cinematic politics interpellate this missing, multiple subject. But by displaying its absence and its lack, they simultaneously activate a desire for this subject.

But does this now mean that all cinematic works have become political? Or rather, is there still any difference between different forms of cinematic politics? The answer is simple. Any conventional cinematic work will try to reproduce the existing set-up: a projection of a public, which is not public after all, and in which participation and exploitation become indistinguishable. But a political cinematic articulation might try to come up with something completely different.

What else is desperately missing from the museum-as-factory? An exit. If the factory is everywhere, then there is no longer a gate by which to leave it – there is no way to escape relentless productivity. Political cinema could then become the screen through which people could leave the museum-as-social-factory. But on which screen could this exit take place? On the one that is currently missing, of course.

1   Grupo Cine Liberación (Fernando E. Solanas, Octavio Getino), Argentina, 1968.

2   A quote from Frantz Fanon's *The Wretched of the Earth*. The film was of course banned and had to be shown clandestinely.

3   Or videos or video/film installations. Properly to make the distinctions (which exist and are important) would require another text.

4   [footnote 5 in source] At least in Western countries.

5   [9] Jonathan L. Beller, 'Kino-I, Kino-World', in *The Visual Culture Reader*, ed. Nicholas Mirzoeff (London and New York: Routledge, 2002) 61.

6   [10] Ibid., 67.

7   [16] For a more sober description of the generally quite idealized condition of multitude, see Paolo Virno, *A Grammar of the Multitude* (New York and Los Angeles: Semiotext[e], 2004).

Hito Steyerl, extracts from 'Is a Museum a Factory?', *e-flux journal*, vol. 7 (June–August 2009).

they criticized
me because I had
people sitting for
four hours a day,
but they didn't
realize that a
little further up
the hallway the
guard spends
eight hours a day
on his feet

Santiago Sierra, In conversation with Teresa Margolles

Santiago Sierra
In Conversation with Teresa Margolles//2004

Teresa Margolles What is the work like that you've done here in Madrid?

Santiago Sierra Lately I've done some pieces that have surprised me. I hid a hundred unemployed people in one street: in vacant apartments, empty commercial spaces, warehouses. Nobody saw any of this, because neither the people nor the places have any visibility. When you hide something instead of teaching or revealing it, you provoke a response in the imagination of the spectator. For instance, the museum watchman I paid to live for 365 hours behind a wall at PS1 in New York told me that no one had ever been so interested in him and that he had never met so many people. I realized that hiding something is a very effective working technique. The forgotten people want to communicate – something that you also express in your work. [...]

Well, I have been called an exploiter. At Kunstwerke in Berlin they criticized me because I had people *sitting* for four hours a day, but they didn't realize that a little further up the hallway the guard spends eight hours a day on his feet. You want to stick your finger in the wound and say that the work is definitely torture, that it is indeed a punishment of biblical proportions. And when you put your name on the work it seems that you're held responsible for the capitalist system itself. Many of the people who make those criticisms have never worked in their lives; if they think it's a horror to sit hidden in a cardboard box for four hours, they don't know what work is. Also, if I compensated these people more, they'd be talking about how 'good' I am. But if I find someone who does something that's hard for 50 euros and it usually costs 200, I use the person who does it for 50. And of course extreme labour relations shed much more light on how the labour system actually works. A yuppie is also a servant of capital and he also has a price, but he's sweetened by a certain glamour and is thus not useful in terms of what interests me.

If I thought about how to give real visibility to these people, I wouldn't have chosen the art world as a platform to do it, but rather a determined political activism – but I don't trust that either. Let's say that I do things because I think they should be included in the art world, but I don't have grandiose dreams that I'll actually achieve anyone's redemption, because that's absurd. When you sell a photograph for $11,000 you can't possibly redeem anyone except yourself.

Margolles Your work has also been called amoral.

Sierra It's possible to have dignity in society, but it costs money. A person without money has no dignity. Whenever you pay for your dignity, you put your body and your time in the hands of a third party. By saying these few things in my work, I think that, as an artist, I've achieved enough. In any case, I don't see a connection between politics and morality or between art and morality. A banker who buys one of my pieces is like a newspaper that accepts letters to the editor. Self-criticism makes you feel morally superior, and I give high society and high culture the mechanisms to unload their morality and their guilt.

Margolles Do you think the only viable anarchism is neoliberalism?

Sierra I think that happiness is not possible and unhappiness is. The rich man is in a state of tremendous slavery to money. His level of suffering is very much reduced, but it's slavery like any other form of it.

Margolles But has your work been censored?

Sierra In the US I have experienced a form of censorship that is now much more common: not someone saying 'Take that down', but people making it difficult for the piece to come out. I suppose I was censored at PS1. I wanted to line up all the PS1 workers according to the position they occupied and photograph their backs. Of course they knew that if I did that, there would be a perfect gradation from white to black, because the people who work at the door are black, but when you go upstairs, the watchmen are more Latino, and at the top, it's the paradise of the white man. So they stonewalled, telling me I was trying to create a problem that didn't exist. But I'm going to keep the idea and try to do it again.

Margolles What is the worst evil of society? You talk about racism, drugs, prostitution …

Sierra The worst evil of society is its broken promises. That's why I choose these themes. Equality and sexual liberation are a catalogue of promises of a liberation that has been taken away from us. What damages society is its structure: everyone works for the production of capital. The problem is not what you shoot into your veins, but what society you do it in.

Santiago Sierra and Teresa Margolles, extracts from interview, 'Santiago Sierra', *Bomb*, no. 86 (Winter 2004) 62–9.

Franco 'Bifo' Berardi
The Precarious Soul//2009

[...] Precariousness is not a particular element of the social relation, but the dark core of capitalist production in the sphere of the global network, where a flow of fragmented recombinant info-labour continuously circulates. Precariousness is the transformative element of the whole cycle of production. Nobody is shielded from it. The wages of workers on permanent contracts are lowered and broken down; everyone's life is threatened by an increasing instability.

Ever since Fordist discipline was dissolved, individuals find themselves in a condition of apparent freedom. Nobody forces them to endure subjection and dependency. Coercion is instead embedded in the technicalities of social relations, and control is exerted through the voluntary yet inevitable submission to a chain of automatisms. [...]

The neoliberal values presented in the 1980s and 1990s as vectors of independence and self-entrepreneurship revealed themselves to be manifestations of a new form of slavery, producing social insecurity, and most of all, a psychological catastrophe. The soul, once wandering and unpredictable, must now follow functional paths in order to become compatible with the system of operative exchanges structuring the productive ensemble. The soul hardens, and loses its tenderness and malleability. Industrial factories used the body, forcing it to leave the soul outside of the assembly line, so that the worker looked like a soulless body. The immaterial factory asks instead to place our very souls at its disposal: intelligence, sensibility, creativity and language. The useless body lies flabbily at the borders of the game field: to take care of it and entertain it, we put it through the commercial circuits of fitness and sex.

When we move into the sphere of info-labour, Capital no longer recruits people, it buys packets of time, separated from their interchangeable and contingent bearers. De-personalized time is now the real agent of the process of valorization, and de-personalized time has no rights. [...]

The multitude does not manifest itself as autonomy at all, but rather as dependence from the automatisms that biopower builds and activates in everyday life, in our sensibility and psyche: we become a swarm. According to Eugene Thacker, a swarm is an organization of multiple, individuated units with some relation to one another.[1] That is, a swarm is a particular kind of collectivity or group phenomenon that may be dependent upon a condition of connectivity. A swarm is a collectivity that is defined by relationality. This pertains as much to the level of the individual unit as it does to the overall organization of the swarm.

At some level 'living networks' and 'swarms' overlap. A swarm is a whole that is more than the sum of its parts, but it is also a heterogeneous whole. In the swarm, the parts are not subservient to the whole – both exist simultaneously and because of each other.

The swarm has no political soul, only an automatic and relational soul. […]

1   [footnote 6 in source] Eugene Thacker, 'Networks, Swarms, Multitudes', *CTheory* (May 2004).

Franco 'Bifo' Berardi, extracts from *The Soul at Work: From Alienation to Autonomy*, trans. Francesca Cadel and Giuseppina Mecchia (Los Angeles: Semiotext[e] 2009) 191–2, 194.

Haben und Brauchen
To Have and to Need Manifesto//2012

[…] The fact that artists are now being merchandized as figureheads of a new work culture – the creative industry – leads some to believe that artists possess the same money-making opportunities as other 'creative professionals'. That, however, is seldom the case. Artists deliver an image for an entire industry, but it is simply not the case that they are paid well (or paid at all) for their activities. As evidenced by current studies, the old, undignified tradition has largely remained unchanged: the majority of culture makers continue to lead lives at or under the poverty line. […]

Haben und Brauchen [To Have and to Need] wish to launch a widespread, general and collective discussion on how work should be understood and rightfully recognized and honoured throughout society as a whole.

Because everyone is talking about work. But even if we work ceaselessly, only some work is paid. Some is not. When all is said and done, payment is an expression of societal recognition. Today this form of recognition is primarily given, however, to work that can be measured by its productivity, that is, by the products it manufactures. Yet the commodity form is not necessarily the result art strives for. Even though it is often thus portrayed, only a marginal part of artistic work can be understood in terms of productivity. A large part of the time that artistic work consists of is determined by other activities: reflection, research, reading, communicating, linking one's own knowledge to that of others, trying things out, preparing, practising and coaching, and also having to throw things out, fail, gain distance so as to see more clearly again, to have experiences, deal with those experiences, reflect on them, let them ferment, and return to them in meandering processes, or not.

None of these activities are necessarily goal-oriented – they quite possibly do not even manifest as art – nor can they be judged according to standpoints that privilege efficiency. Nevertheless, all these activities are a prerequisite for artistic work, and they should be recognized as work.

Cultural work can be compared with scientific working processes: it is almost always self-motivated and self-contracted, and it costs time and money. Just as scientists need access to libraries, culture-makers require the possibility to examine the cultural life of the city which they contribute to and, therefore, need free entrance to museums, theatres and libraries. The continuity of artistic working processes conditions the quality of their output. Art is not societal decor. And likewise, artists are not virginal, spiritual beings who await their saviour in a place far removed from the theatre of capitalistic virility. Instead, critical and self-determined, they comprehend developmental processes in society as processes of formation. Cultural work produces cultural, social and interpersonal knowledge. It is within the incisive contradictions of art that society, in its emotions and in its thoughts, arrives at a concept of itself. Art creates spaces where societal actions can be experienced as worth. Hence it poses a challenge and a contradiction to the neoliberal agenda, as it strives to privatize the Commons and peddle collective rights (fundamental rights and land law rights) to the highest bidder.

Neoliberal populists' relationship to art is schizophrenic: on the one hand, artists are celebrated as 'creative', and on the other, art's role in the creation of the Commons (and its dependency therein) is denied while public support for culture makers, and the conditions that make work possible, are denied or withdrawn. This logic of denial and withdrawal must be opposed! Cultural activities must receive adequate recognition as work. Here 'recognition' means the right to demand fair payment and participation in societal decision making processes. [...]

Haben und Brauchen, extracts from 'To Have and to Need Manifesto' (January 2012).

Haben und Brauchen [To Have and To Need] is an informal platform for discussion and action founded in 2011. It advocates the recognition and preservation of a self-organized artistic practice that has grown out of the specific historical conditions in Berlin. The manifesto has been composed collectively by more than forty people. This act of collective writing was an experiment and an attempt to convey the diverse perspectives on the situation of the contemporary Berlin art scene and to put those perspectives forward for a broader public for discussion. The full manifesto can be read on: www. habenundbrauchen.de

Martha Rosler
For an Art against the Mythology of Everyday Life//1979

1. Where do ideas come from? All the myths of everyday life stitched together form a seamless envelope of ideology, the false account of the workings of the world. The interests served by ideology are not human interests properly defined; rather, ideology serves society by shoring up its particular form of social organization. Ideology in class society serves the interests of the class that dominates. In our society, that ideology is held up as the only possible set of attitudes and beliefs, and we are all more or less impelled to adopt them, and to identify ourselves as members of the 'middle class', a mystified category based on vague and shifting criteria, including income levels, social status and identification, that substitutes for an image of the dominant class and its real foundations of social power.

Historically, the advance of industrial capitalism has eradicated craft skills among working people and *economically productive* activity within the family, and thus lessened our chances to gain a sense of accomplishnent and worth in our work. More and more we are directed to seek satisfaction instead in 'private life', which has been redefined in terms of purchase and consumption, and which is supposed to represent, as the antithesis to the workaday world, all the things missing from work. As the opportunities for personal control diminish for all but a relative few, self-confidence, trust and pleasure conceived in straightforward terms are poisoned. In their place, advertising, the handmaiden of industry, promises personal power and fulfilment through consumption, and we are increasingly beguiled by an accordion-like set of mediations, in the form of commodities, between ourselves and the natural and social world.

Our mode of economic organization, in which people seem less important than the things they produce, prompts us to stand reality on its head by granting the aura of life to things and draining it from people: *we personify objects and objectify persons.* This fetishism of commodities, as Marx termed it, is not a universal mental habit; it has its origins in a productive system in which we are split off from our own productive capacities, our ability to make or to do things, which is transformed into a commodity itself, the abstract leveller 'labour power', which is saleable to the boss for wages. We experience this condition as alienation from ourselves as well as from others. We best comprehend ourselves as social entities in looking at pictures of ourselves, assuming the voyeur's role with respect to our own images; we best know ourselves from within in looking through the viewfinder at other people and things.

Those who aspire to move upward socially are led to develop superfluous skills – gourmet cooking, small-boat navigation – whose real cultural significance is extravagant, well-rationalized consumerism and the cultivation of the self. These skills, in seeking legitimation, mimic skills once necessary to life; skills which, moreover, were tied to a form of social organization that we think of as less alienated and more familial than our own. Things – in this case, skills – that once were useful and productive are now re-seen through the haze of commodification, and we are sold back what we imagine as our ancestral heritage. People's legitimate desire for meaningful, creative work and for self-determination is thus forced into a conformingly reactionary mode of expression.

At the same time, women, trapped in an economically unproductive and often unsatisfying activity or relegated to low-paying, low-status jobs on top of home and family maintenance, see entrance into the job and skill marketplace as an emancipation from economic dependency and as a chance to gain a social identity now mostly denied us. Yet many of us can see that moving from slavery to indentured status, so to speak – to 'wage slavery' or more privileged types of paying work – is only a partial advance. And arrayed against us now are not just an escalating right-wing reaction against our demands for equality with men and deceitful attacks on our bodily self-determination but also the marketing of new commodifications of our lives, resting on the language of liberation. While we achieve greater acceptance in the job market, we seem to slip back toward object status, accepting without complaint the new ways in which we remain defined by *how we look* and by the style in which we *perform* our lives. Meanwhile, merchandisers strive to extend an obligatory narcissism to men. New expressions of sexuality play upon pretend transferences of power from men to women and the symbolic acting out of rebellion and punishment. Again the desire for self-determination is drowned in a shower of substitutions and repressions.

2. How does one address these banally profound issues of everyday life, thereby revealing the public and political in the personal? It seems reasonable to me to use forms that suggest and refer to mass-cultural forms without simply mimicking them. Television, for example, is, in its most familiar form, one of the primary conduits of ideology, through its programmes and commercials alike. One of the basic forms of mass culture, including television and movies, is the narrative. Narrative can be a homey, manageable form of address, but its very virtue, the suggestion of subjectivity and lived experience, is also its danger. The rootedness in an I, the most seductive encoding of *convincingness*, suggests an absolute inability to transcend the individual consciousness. And consciousness is the domain of ideology, so that the logic of at least the first-person narrative is that there is no appeal from ideology, no *metacritical* level. Given the pervasive

relativism of our society, according to which only the personal is truly knowable and in which all opinions are equally valid outside the realm of science, the first-person narrative suggests the unretrievability of objective human and social truth. At most, one or another version of the dominant ideology is reinforced.

Yet this inability to speak truth is the failure not so much of narrative as of the naturalism that is taken as narrative's central feature. Break the bonds of that naturalism and the problem vanishes. One can provide a critical dimension and invoke matters of truth by referring explicitly to the ideological confusions that naturalism can only falsify through omission. A character who speaks in contradictions or who fails to manage the socially necessary sequence of behaviours can eloquently index the unresolvable social contradictions – starvation in the midst of plenty, gourmetism as a form of imperialism, rampant inflation and impoverishment alongside bounding corporate profits – that underlie ideological confusion, and make them stand out clearly.

3. In dealing with issues of personal life in my own work, in particular how people's thoughts and interests can be related to their social positions, I use a variety of different forms, most of which are borrowed from common culture, forms such as written postcards, letters, conversations, banquets, garage sales and television programmes of various forms, including human-interest interviews and cooking demonstrations. Using these forms provides an element of familiarity and also signals my interest in real-world concerns, as well as giving me the chance to take on those cultural forms, to interrogate them, so to speak, about their meaning within society. In video, for example, I see the opportunity to do work that falls into a natural dialectic with TV itself. A woman in a bare-bones kitchen demonstrating some hand tools and replacing their domesticated 'meaning' with a lexicon of rage and frustration is an antipodean Julia Child. A woman in a red-and-blue Chinese coat, demonstrating a wok in a dining room and trying to speak with the absurd voice of the corporation, is a failed Mrs Pat Boone or a low-budget appliance ad. An anachronistically young couple, sitting cramped and earnest in their well-appointed living room, attempting to present a coherent account of starvation, are any respectably middle-class couple visited by misfortune and subjected to an interview.

4. In choosing representational strategies, I have avoided the naturalism that I mentioned earlier as being that which locks narrative into an almost inevitably uncritical relation to culture. Rather, I aim for the distancing effect that breaks the emotional identification with character and situation that naturalism implies, substituting for it, when it is effective, an emotional recognition coupled with a critical, intellectual understanding of the *systematic meaning* of the work, its

meaning in relation to common issues. In video I tend to seek this effect with a wrenched pacing and bent space; an immovable shot or, conversely, the obvious movement or the unexpected edit, pointing to the mediating agencies of photography and speech; long shots rather than close-ups, to deny psychological intensity; contradictory utterances; humour and burlesque; and, in acting, flattened affect, histrionics, theatricality or staginess. In written texts I also use humour and satire, and I may move a character through impossible development or have her display contradictory thoughts and behaviour or, conversely, an unlikely transcendent clarity. In photography I pass up single-image revelations and often join photos with text.

5. There is another critical issue to consider: the choosing or seeking of an audience. I feel that the art world does not suffice, and I try to make my work accessible to as many people outside the art audience as I can effectively reach. Cultural products can never bring about substantive changes in society, yet they are indispensable to any movement that is working to bring about such changes. The clarification of vision is a first step toward reasonably and humanely changing the world.

Martha Rosler, 'For an Art against the Mythology of Everyday Life' (1979), in Martha Rosler, *Decoys and Disruptions: Selected Writings, 1975–2001* (Cambridge, Massachusetts: The MIT Press, 2004) 3–8.

Silvia Federici
On Affective Labour//2011

Coined in the mid 1990s by Marxist Autonomists reflecting on the new forms of work that the restructuring of the world economy has produced, 'affective labour' has become a common notion in radical circles, proving to be a protean concept. Through is brief lifespan, its latitude has expanded, making attempts to provide a precise definition a difficult task. 'Affective Labour' (AL) is presently used to describe new work-activities in the service sector, or conceptualize the nature of work in the 'post-Fordist' era; for some it is a synonym of reproductive work or a springboard for rethinking the fundamentals of feminist discourse. [...]

An analysis of AL must begin with the work of Antonio Negri and Michael Hardt because it is here that the concept of AL was first developed, and their treatment of it has set a frame that has shaped later discussions. AL, however, in

Negri and Hardt's writing is not a self-subsistent concept. Rather, it is an aspect of the theory of Immaterial Labour [IL] that is the core of their work. [...]

In the same way as the cognitive part of IL is concretized in the activities spawned by the computerization of work and the Internet, so AL is often said to describe activities in the service sector, especially referring to the commercialization of reproduction. In this respect, a clear influence on the theory of AL has been the work of the feminist sociologist Arlie Hochschild on the 'commodification of emotions' and 'emotional labour'. [...]

[In *The Managed Heart* (1983)] Hochschild had argued that with the decline of industrial production (reduced by 1983 to 6 per cent of all employment) and the rise of the service sector, 'nowadays most jobs call for a capacity to deal with people rather than with things, [and call] for more interpersonal skills rather than mechanical skills'. She had then put under the spotlight the 'emotional labour' that flight attendants in the airline industry must perform to dispel the passengers' anxiety, project a sense of confidence and ease, repress anger or irritation in front of abuse and make those they serve feel valorized. [...]

There are, however, significant differences between Hochschild's theory and Negri and Hardt's. Hochschild's analysis leaves no doubt that *women are the central subjects of emotional labour*, and though this is waged work performed on a public basis, she maintains that in essence it is work that women have always done. As she points out, lacking other resources and depending on men for money, women have always made an asset of their feelings, giving them to men in return for the material resources they lacked. The rise of the service sector has [in her words] made emotional work more systematized, standardized and mass produced, but its existence still capitalizes on the fact that from childhood, women have been trained to have an instrumental relation to their emotions.

Hochschild further establishes a direct connection between the commercialization of emotions and women's refusal of unpaid domestic work. Indeed, her analysis of emotional labour is part of a broader investigation into the effects of the 'feminist revolution' on women's social position and family relations. One of the main concerns is the crisis of care that women's waged employment has sparked off in the absence of changes in the (waged) workplace or increased institutional support for reproductive work or increased men's readiness to share the housework. [...]

On all these counts, Negri and Hardt's theory of AL is a departure from Hochschild's. Although examples for AL are drawn from service sector-jobs usually performed by women and though is often labelled 'women's work', AL does not describe a gendered form of work. On the contrary, as we have seen, it is said to be a component of most forms of IL, all forms of work presumably becoming more communicative, interactive and productive of social relations. It is in this sense that Negri and Hardt speak of the 'feminization of work'. Their reference here is not primarily to the massive entrance of women into (waged) labour-force, but to the becoming 'feminine' of the work done by men, which explains why there are nothing more than passing references to gender-specific forms of work, like procreation and child care, in any of their texts. Negri and Hardt are not interested in 'female labour' as such, whether paid or unpaid, inside or outside the home, though we may describe it as the largest pool of 'affective work' on the planet. Similarly, they seem unaware of the massive struggles, visible and invisible, that women have made against the blackmail of 'affectivity', culminating in the struggle of welfare mothers and the women's liberation movement. [...]

They also miss the fact that rather than merging with production, reproductive work, as reconfigured in the post-Fordist era, has largely been unloaded on the shoulders of immigrant women.

Indeed, AL [...] cannot speak to the key questions in women's lives today: the crisis that women are facing trying to reconcile paid labour with reproduction, the fact that social reproduction still relies on women's unwaged work, that as much reproductive work has returned to the home as has gone out of it, due to cuts in healthcare, hospital care, retail work, due also to the (worldwide) expansion of home-work but above all the continuing function of the home as a magnet for unpaid/low paid labour.

In view of the above, we can then draw some preliminary conclusions. The generalization of affective labor, i.e., its dispersal over every form of work, takes us back to a pre-feminist situation, where not only the specificity but the very existence of women's reproductive work and the struggle women are making on this terrain become invisible again. [...]

Silvia Federici, extracts from 'On Affective Labour', in *Cognitive Capitalism, Education and Digital Labour*, ed. Michael A. Peters and Ergin Bulut (New York: Peter Lang, 2011) 57, 58, 65, 66–7, 68 [references not included].

Siona Wilson
Nightcleaners: The Ambiguities of Activism and the Limits of Production//2015

[I]n 1970, the Pimlico branch of the London Women's Liberation Workshop – a local chapter of the London-wide network of feminist activists, consciousness-raising and study groups – was approached by May Hobbes, an activist for a group of night cleaning workers and a night cleaner herself, who was looking for help with the slow task of grassroots organization needed to unionize previously unrepresented immigrant and working-class women. Very early on in this activist alliance, in November of that year, the Berwick Street Film Collective was asked to make a film about the campaign. *Nightcleaners* (1972–75) began as a straightforward agitprop film, but after four years in postproduction editing, this was not what reached the screen. After the spectacular immediacy of the Miss World actions [of 1970], the night cleaners campaign went on to become one of the most significant activist campaigns in the early years of the British women's movement. [...] The night cleaners' struggle met the demands of an emerging women's movement that was grounded in New Left thinking wherein a gendered politics of class intersects with the complexities of postcolonial Britain. It sought to define a feminist politics that went beyond the confines of middle-class women's experience to include working-class and immigrant women. [...] When *Nightcleaners* was first screened in 1975 – after nearly four years in postproduction editing – it became controversial among some feminist audiences. On the one hand, many feminist activists harshly rejected it because it failed to deliver a straightforward campaign message: the intersections of race, class and gender remained intractably dissonant. On the other hand, when it was screened at the Edinburgh International Film Festival in August 1975, Claire Johnston and Paul Willemen claimed it was the apotheosis of a new feminist avant-garde. They argued that *Nightcleaners* was exceptional because it diverged so markedly from other documentary examples and fulfilled a Brechtian aesthetic.[1]

Much of the footage of *Nightcleaners* is not unfamiliar to expository documentary. The Berwick Street Film Collective spent eighteen months filming the women cleaners at work, in meetings with the feminist activists and the male union representative, in interviews with various figures involved, including the cleaning company boss, and at large-scale labour demonstrations. But it is the way the parts are connected together that caused much of the outcry. The film's documentary passages are continually interrupted by sections of black leader tape, an editing effect that makes the screen go dark. Instead of serving as a conventional spatio-temporal ellipsis – used either between different shots or directly prior to an intertitle, and permitting the smooth shift from one visual segment to the next – in *Nightcleaners* the black leader tape is present onscreen for much longer, and it appears between almost every segment of the film, marking the editorial cuts. [...] Rather than raising awareness about the campaign, this interruptive device alienated certain members of the feminist audience by precluding straightforward communicability. Further confusion occurred for the disgruntled activists because the filmmakers repeatedly isolated individual shots that had been processed and refilmed to emphasize the visual properties of 16mm film. These images included close-up head shots and isolated gestures, ambiguous visual details that further interrupt the expectations of documentary as a realist genre and connect *Nightcleaners* to the kinds of visual experimentation associated with avant-garde filmmaking. [...]

The complexity of the film's affective address *and* reception points to questions of (political) desire and psychical effects that reveal the deep significance of this collective project. [...]

With the inclusion of footage showing domestic labour, *Nightcleaners* makes clear that almost all the cleaners have children, and despite working all night, during the days they are still fully responsible for child care, cooking and cleaning. It is because of the responsibility they feel towards their children (also depicted in the film) that they take on the paid work, even though it is extremely physically demanding. Over and over again, the women interviewed describe how they are only able to catch a very few hours of sleep and frequently none at all; their daytime hours are almost as busy as at night. It becomes immediately apparent that the political issue here is not only the working wage but also the sexual division of labour. *Nightcleaners* explores how sexual difference determines the mutually dependent relationship between paid employment and non-paid domestic work and how the women's capacity as political agents is seriously constrained by this situation. Undoubtedly, many of the feminist activists felt particularly passionate about this issue, but the film is not able to offer any solutions; it can only indicate the limitations to conventional labour union activism in dealing with the women's wage-labour issues, and point towards the necessity for a radically different approach to political change. [...]

1   Claire Johnston and Paul Willemen, 'Brecht in Britain: The Independent Political Film (on *The Nightcleaners*)', *Screen*, vol. 16, no. 4 (June 1975) 62–80.

Siona Wilson, extracts from *Art Labour, Sex Politics: Feminist Effects in 1970s British Art and Performance* (Minneapolis: University of Minnesota Press, 2015) 3–4, 5–6, 47.

Gulf Labor Coalition
Artists' Boycott of Guggenheim Abu Dhabi//2011

We, the undersigned, are writing to demand that the Guggenheim Foundation obtain contractual guarantees that will protect the rights of workers employed in the construction and maintenance of its new branch museum in Abu Dhabi.

Human rights violations are currently occurring on Saadiyat Island, the location of the new museum. In two extensive reports on the UAE, Human Rights Watch has documented a cycle of abuse that leaves migrant workers deeply indebted, poorly paid and unable to defend their rights, or even quit their jobs. The UAE authorities responsible for developing the island have failed to tackle the root causes of abuse: unlawful recruiting fees, broken promises of wages, and a sponsorship system that gives employers virtually unlimited power over workers.

These violations, which threaten to sully the Guggenheim's reputation, present a serious, moral challenge to those who may be asked to work with the museum. No one should be asked to exhibit or perform in a building that has been constructed and maintained on the backs of exploited employees.

Human Rights Watch has expressed its concerns to the Foundation on several occasions, but so far, adequate steps have not been taken to ensure that workers' rights will be respected at the Abu Dhabi site. While the Guggenheim is franchising its name and is not a direct party to the subcontractors who employ the migrant labour, it can and should assert responsibility for the well-being of these workers.

We urge the Foundation and its partners in Abu Dhabi, TDIC (The Abu Dhabi Tourism and Development Investment Company), to conform rigorously to the various commitments made in the TDIC's Employment Practices Policy (EPP), dated June 2010, the TDIC/Guggenheim Statement of Shared Values, published 22 September 2010, and the recent EPP update, amended 11 March 2011. Moreover, we urge the Foundation and TDIC to address the current absence of independent monitoring of employers' compliance with international human rights and labour laws, and the lack of an effective enforcement mechanism. A monitor must be empowered to make random visits to work sites and maintain a relationship independent of employer influence. It must also determine if its findings conform to international laws and standards, and it must issue public reports on these findings.

In the absence of these conditions, violations will persist and continue to be under-reported. Similarly, without explicit mechanisms for enforcing the terms of the contract or clearly enumerated remedies in the event of breaches, all efforts to protect workers will be in vain. TDIC has announced that it will appoint a 'reputable independent monitor' in May. We demand that the appointment be made as soon as possible and that the conditions outlined above be observed as part of the monitor's mandate.

Our cooperation with the Guggenheim in Abu Dhabi (and, for many of us, at other Guggenheim locations) will not be forthcoming if the Foundation fails to take steps to safeguard the rights of the workers who will be employed in the museum's operations on Saadiyat Island. Human Rights Watch will determine if and when adequate monitoring measures have been established and effectively implemented. [...]

We are a coalition of international artists working to ensure that migrant worker rights are protected during the construction and maintenance of the Guggenheim's new branch museum on Saadiyat Island in Abu Dhabi, UAE. Artists should not be asked to exhibit their work in buildings built on the backs of exploited workers. Those working with bricks and mortar deserve the same kind of respect as those working with cameras and brushes.

Gulf Labor Coalition, extracts from 'Artists' Boycott of Guggenheim Abu Dhabi' (March 2011). (www.gulflabor.wordpress.com)

Achille Mbembe
Necropolitics//2003

This essay assumes that the ultimate expression of sovereignty resides, to a large degree, in the power and the capacity to dictate who may live and who must die. Hence, to kill or to allow to live constitute the limits of sovereignty, its fundamental attributes. To exercise sovereignty is to exercise control over mortality and to define life as the deployment and manifestation of power. One could summarize in the above terms what Michel Foucault meant by biopower: that domain of life over which power has taken control.[1] But under what practical conditions is the right to kill, to allow to live, or to expose to death exercised? [...]

Any historical account of the rise of modern terror needs to address slavery, which could be considered one of the first instances of biopolitical experimentation. In many respects, the very structure of the plantation system and its aftermath manifests the emblematic and paradoxical figure of the state of exception.[2] This figure is paradoxical here for two reasons. First, in the context of the plantation, the humanity of the slave appears as the perfect figure of a shadow. Indeed, the slave condition results from a triple loss: loss of a 'home', loss of rights over his or her body, and loss of political status. This triple loss is identical with absolute domination, natal alienation and social death (expulsion from humanity altogether). To be sure, as a political-juridical structure, the plantation is a space where the slave belongs to a master. [...] As an instrument of labour, the slave has a price. As a property, he or she has a value. His or her labour is needed and used. The slave is therefore kept alive but in a state of injury, in a phantom-like world of horrors and intense cruelty and profanity. [...] Slave life, in many ways, is a form of death-in-life. As Susan Buck Morss has suggested, the slave condition produces a contradiction between freedom of property and freedom of person. An unequal relationship is established along with the inequality of the power over life. This power over the life of another takes the form of commerce: a person's humanity is dissolved to the point where it becomes possible to say that the slave's life is possessed by the master.[3] Because the slave's life is like a 'thing', possessed by another person, the slave existence appears as a perfect figure of a shadow. In spite of the terror and the symbolic sealing off of the slave, he or she maintains alternative perspectives towards time, work and self. This is the second paradoxical element of the plantation world as a manifestation of the state of exception. Treated as if he or she no longer existed except as a mere tool and instrument of production, the slave nevertheless is able to draw almost any object, instrument, language or gesture into a performance and then stylize it. Breaking with uprootedness and the pure world of things of which he or she is but a fragment, the slave is able to demonstrate the protean capabilities of the human bond through music and the very body that was supposedly possessed by another.[4]

If the relations between life and death, the politics of cruelty and the symbolics of profanity are blurred in the plantation system, it is notably in the colony and under the apartheid regime that there comes into being a peculiar terror formation [...].The most original feature of this terror formation is its concatenation of biopower, the state of exception, and the state of siege. Crucial to this concatenation is [...] race. [...] The colonies are the location par excellence where the controls and guarantees of judicial order can be suspended – the zone where the violence of the state of exception is deemed to operate in the service of 'civilization'.

That colonies might be ruled over in absolute lawlessness stems from the racial denial of any common bond between the conqueror and the native. In the eyes of the conqueror, savage life is just another form of animal life, a horrifying experience, something alien beyond imagination or comprehension. In fact, according to Hannah Arendt, what makes the savages different from other human beings is less the colour of their skin than the fear that they behave like a part of nature, that they treat nature as their undisputed master. Nature thus remains, in all its majesty, an overwhelming reality compared to which they appear to be phantoms, unreal and ghostlike. The savages are, as it were, 'natural' human beings who lack the specifically human character, the specifically human reality, 'so that when European men massacred them they somehow were not aware that they had committed murder'.[5] [...]

The sovereign right to kill is not subject to any rule in the colonies. In the colonies, the sovereign might kill at any time or in any manner. Colonial warfare is not subject to legal and institutional rules. It is not a legally codified activity. Instead, colonial terror constantly intertwines with colonially generated fantasies of wilderness and death and fictions, to create the effect of the real. [...]

1   Michel Foucault, *Il faut défendre la société: Cours au Collège de France, 1975–1976* (Paris: Seuil, 1997) 213–34.

2   See Saidiya V. Hartman, *Scenes of Subjection: Terror, Slavery and Self-Making in Nineteenth-Century America* (Oxford: Oxford University Press, 1997); and Manuel Moreno Fraginals, *The Sugarmill: The Socioeconomic Complex of Sugar in Cuba, 1760–1860* (New York: Monthly Review Press, 1976).

3   Susan Buck-Morss, 'Hegel and Haiti', *Critical Inquiry*, no. 26 (2000) 821–66.

4   Roger D. Abrahams, *Singing the Master: The Emergence of African American Culture in the Plantation South* (New York: Pantheon, 1992).

5   Hannah Arendt, *The Origins of Totalitarianism* (New York: Harvest, 1966) 192.

Achille Mbembe, extracts from 'Necropolitics', *Public Culture*, vol. 15, no. 1 (2003) 11–40.

Hamza Walker
On Steve McQueen: *Gravesend*//2007

[...] The subject of *Gravesend*, a new short by British filmmaker Steve McQueen, is coltan, a mineral so valuable it is the new blood diamond. Short for colombite-tantalite, coltan is an ore rich in tantalum, a metal used in capacitors found in a host of computer driven electronics. As a result, coltan's price on the open market has surged some tenfold within the past decade. Eighty per cent of the world's supply comes from the eastern region of the Democratic Republic of Congo, many of whose mines are in the hands of Rwandan rebels. There is no incentive to end what for them is a lucrative conflict, as the demand for coltan continues unabated, and indeed, abetted by the craze for the latest model cell phone or gaming console. Cropping up in the headlines, the conflict, while in and of itself tragic, symbolizes a history far from healed, as our global economic order is unable to dissociate itself from a blood-soaked, imperialist predecessor.

Coltan's is a tall story to tell. Relative to a topic teeming with documentaries, McQueen's approach is unapologetically abstract. Compressed within 17 minutes is a meditation on empire and the fascinating portrait of an ore. Shot on 35mm film, and decidedly non-narrative, *Gravesend* is structured around a series of radical leaps in location, modes of thought and mood. Like a musical composition, it consists of movements varying in tempo. The mainstays of its footage are bouts of realism alternately broken by a fast-paced but lyrical, abstract animation, aerially tracking the Congo River, and a slow time-lapsed dissolve that is a somber reflection on empire.

Gravesend makes its most radical leap in the opening sequences, boldly juxtaposing images of coltan's other-worldly refinement with its all too earthly origins. These states of matter are worlds apart, and save for that which is strictly visual, *Gravesend* is resolutely purged of information illustrating any causal economic links in between. From a high-tech refinery more believable as something from a James Bond film, to a wild and fecund jungle interior, it is not only a question of where these scenes are occurring, but when. Between polar extremes, the net effect is a present moment understood as thoroughly heterogeneous, an uneven mixture of a pre-modern past of pickaxe and shovels, and a future ideal in which imperial power has effervesced into the 'invisible hand' of supply and demand. [...]

Gravesend takes its name from a town in Kent, England. Located on the south bank of the Thames, it was from *Gravesend* that Marlow, the protagonist of Joseph Conrad's *Heart of Darkness*, set sail for the Congo. The time-lapsed footage of the sun setting over a harbor skyline punctuated by smokestacks renders, as if verbatim, the foreboding melancholy established in the opening pages of *Heart of Darkness*:

A haze rested on the low shores that ran out to sea in vanishing flatness. The air was dark above Gravesend, and farther back still seemed condensed into a mournful gloom, brooding motionless over the biggest, and the greatest, town on earth. And at last, in its curved and imperceptible fall, the sun sank low, and from glowing white changed to a dull red without rays and without heat, as if about to go out suddenly, stricken to death by the touch of that gloom brooding over a crowd of men. Forthwith a change came over the waters, and the serenity became less brilliant but more profound. The old river in its broad reach rested unruffled at the decline of day, after ages of good service done to the race that peopled its banks, spread out in the tranquil dignity of a waterway leading to the uttermost ends of the earth.

For all of Conrad's eloquence, the phrase that more readily comes to mind is 'The sun never sets on the British empire.' McQueen's sunset, while graphically illustrating the historical twilight of empire's formal political structures, is also rhetorical, questioning the very pastness of the past. Did the sun set on the British empire? Did empire come to an end? McQueen's conspicuous lingering over a sunset makes this sequence an allegory unto itself. Preceded by an image of coltan prospecting in which the end of a shovel rhythmically emerges from a grave-sized pit that is anything but shallow, this rhetorical question begs reframing. Are we ready to bury empire? More to the point, does emphasizing empire's end obscure an exploitation that is historically uninterrupted, as the West, still dependent on its former colonies, perpetuates gross iniquity now accompanied by internecine conflict?

Over and above any socio-economic and political machinations, *Gravesend* favours discreet outward appearances. For McQueen, the facts of the matter are visual and visual alone as *Gravesend*'s stunning production values attest. He insists that *Gravesend* 'first and foremost is about looking', even at the expense of knowing what we are observing. Textual footholds are dismissed; no maps, no dialogue, no villains and no experts. There is nothing to indicate or verify the setting as the Congo, nor the nature of substances before the lens. Although precise and highly specific in bearing towards a subject better known through journalism, *Gravesend* steadfastly refuses to inform in that manner, opting instead to extract visually from its subject generalities that ultimately function allegorically. Unflinchingly direct, *Gravesend*'s camerawork is a brazen species of realism. A sequence featuring a close-up of severely weathered hands hammering at stones, picking out black morsels of coltan, is without doubt the direct descendant of Gustave Courbet's 1849 realist masterpiece *The Stone Breakers*, only now it is accompanied by the dull thud of striking pay dirt.

Gravesend does not trace the fate of a valuable ore from extraction to refinement. Nor do the worlds these states of matter represent collide. They are not only connected but interdependent, part of an equation that accommodates their profound incommensurability. While its unembellished footage brings it into a discursive relationship with documentary and other forms of reportage, *Gravesend* above all else is a poem, and an epic one at that. […]

Hamza Walker, extracts from 'The Grand Scheme of Things' (Chicago: The Renaissance Society at the University of Chicago, 2007). First published in exhibition poster for 'Steve McQueen: Gravesend', 2007.

Tehching Hsieh
In Conversation with Iona Whittaker//2015

Tehching Hsieh's major series of performance artworks commenced in 1978 with One Year Performance 1978–79 – *the 'cage piece' in which Hsieh spent a full year locked inside a wooden cage he built himself in his second floor studio at 111 Hudson Street.* 'Time Clock' *(as it is informally named) followed* (One Year Performance 1980–81), *for which he set himself the task of clocking in and photographing himself every hour for one year.* […]

Iona Whittaker You seem like a practical person.

Tehching Hsieh I don't write because I'm not a language person, I just do. (*laughs.*) I feel my work needs some sort of bridge; every conversation means I learn a different point of view. I have my way to approach things. Some people want you to be more political, but actually I am more like a cave man – primitive. I trust my intuition. Of course, I understand civilization; New York is civilized – very strong. I came to do my work in the city; I didn't go to the mountains to be a hermit because I knew that staying in the city to do this kind of work would be ironic, and that's what I wanted. I am more interested in philosophical thinking. But I leave my work open to different interpretations. For example, some people think of the time clock piece as industrial, as if it is about workers. […] But that is talking only about working. I'm also talking about life. It's not a 9 to 5 job: I lived in it, 24 hours a day for a year – it is life. Your heartbeat continues. Art and life become one. My work shows different perspectives of thinking about life. For me, life is a life sentence; life is passing time, life is free thinking. […]

Basically, I use time. Life is passing time; how to pass time is not my concern. It doesn't matter what kind of life one has – everybody makes their own schedule. I created my schedule for passing time. I don't do art any more, but to me doing life and doing art is all the same – doing time. The difference is that in art you have a form. […]

Whittaker When you did the time clock, you missed 133 punches, didn't you? […] Does this mean anything to you, or is it just how it is? There is always something you cannot control.

Hsieh For me, it's still natural: 94–95 per cent, I made it. (*energetically, he pulls out the record.*) You see here? December was the worst month. Then I thought, 'I mustn't get worse!' Up to that point it was natural, but after December I felt concerned about it. The way I understand it is, if I got 100 per cent right, it would feel too strict and not an understanding of human beings. This 94–95 per cent means that I'm not perfect, and that's human. If I got just 60 per cent, of course, the audience would think, 'You didn't do this job well.' But I would say that everybody is different; some people could do better than me, I'm sure. But nobody would want to waste time doing this without a reward. (*laughs*.)

Whittaker I think these performances would not work without a light heart. I imagine people ask you: 'Is this a fulfilling thing to do?'

Hsieh Well, it's not easy to complete the work, but the work is not about endurance. I pass time in an artform. I did work every hour, continuously, like breathing. It is one year, a cycle. It doesn't matter if you're creative or not, or if you are poor or rich. The quantity of one year of time is the same; that is universal. I just keep the work basic, keep my life simple. But you need complexity in order to be simple.

Tehching Hsieh and Iona Whittaker, extracts from 'Doing Time: Interview with Tehching Hsieh', *RanDian* (19 March 2015). (http://www.randian-online.com/np_feature/doing-time-interview-with-tehching-hsieh/)

Karl Marx
Grundrisse//1857–58

[…] The fact that in the development of the productive powers of labour the objective conditions of labour, objectified labour, must grow relative to living labour – this is actually a tautological statement, for what else does the growing productive power of labour mean than that less immediate labour is required to create a greater product, and that therefore social wealth expresses itself more and more in the conditions of labour created by labour itself? – this fact appears from the standpoint of capital not in such a way that one of the moments of social activity – objective labour – becomes the ever more powerful body of the other moment, of subjective, living labour, but rather – and this is important for wage labour – that the objective conditions of labour assume an ever more colossal independence, represented by its very extent, opposite living labour, and that social wealth confronts labour in more powerful portions as an alien and dominant power. The emphasis comes to be placed not on the state of being *objectified*, but on the state of being *alienated*, dispossessed, sold [*Der Ton wird gelegt nicht auf das Vergegenständlichtsein, sondern das Entfremdet-, Entäussert-, Veräussertsein*]; on the condition that the monstrous objective power which social labour itself erected opposite itself as one of its moments belongs not to the worker, but to the personified conditions of production, i.e. to capital. To the extent that, from the standpoint of capital and wage labour, the creation of the objective body of activity happens in antithesis to the immediate labour capacity – that this process of objectification in fact appears as a process of dispossession from the standpoint of labour or as appropriation of alien labour from the standpoint of capital – to that extent, this twisting and inversion [*Verdrehung und Verkehrung*] is a *real* [*phenomenon*], not a merely *supposed one* existing merely in the imagination of the workers and the capitalists. But obviously this process of inversion is a merely *historical* necessity, a necessity for the development of the forces of production solely from a specific historic point of departure, or basis, but in no way an *absolute* necessity of production; rather, a vanishing one, and the result and the inherent purpose of this process is to suspend this basis itself, together with this form of the process. The bourgeois economists are so much cooped up within the notions belonging to a specific historic stage of social development that the necessity of the *objectification* of the powers of social labour appears to them as inseparable from the necessity of their *alienation vis-à-vis* living labour. But with the suspension of the *immediate* character of living labour, as merely *individual*, or as general merely internally or merely externally, with the positing of the activity of individuals as immediately general or *social* activity, the objective moments of production are stripped of this form of alienation; they are thereby posited as property, as the organic social body within which the individuals reproduce themselves as individuals, but as social individuals. The conditions which allow them to exist in this way in the reproduction of their life, in their productive life's process, have been posited only by the historic economic process itself; both the objective and the subjective conditions, which are only the two distinct forms of the same conditions.

The worker's propertylessness, and the ownership of living labour by objectified labour, or the appropriation of alien labour by capital – both merely expressions of the same relation from opposite poles – are fundamental conditions of the bourgeois mode of production, in no way accidents irrelevant to it. These modes of distribution are the relations of production themselves, but *sub specie distributionis*. It is therefore highly absurd when e.g. John Stuart Mill says: 'The laws and conditions of the production of wealth partake of the character of physical truths … It is not so with the distribution of wealth. That is a matter of human institutions solely.' (*Principles of Political Economy*, 2nd edition, London, 1849, vol. I, 239, 240.) The 'laws and conditions' of the production of wealth and the laws of the 'distribution of wealth' are the same laws under different forms, and both change, undergo the same historic process; are as such only moments of a historic process. [...]

Karl Marx, extract from 'Grundrisse der Kritik der Politischen Ökonomie' (1857/58); first published in *Grundrisse der Kritik der Politischen Ökonomie* (Rohentwurf: Institut für Marxismus-Leninismus, 1939–41); trans. Martin Nicolaus, *Grundrisse: Outlines of the Critique of Political Economy* (Harmondsworth: Penguin Books, 1993) 831–2.

Alice Creischer
Primitive Accumulation as Exemplified in Potosí//2010

[...] 'As if the crown were never quite willing to accept the moral responsibility of forced labour' [in sixteenth-century Peru-Bolivia],[1] the *mita* [the Spanish colonial appropriation of *Mit'a*, mandatory public service in Inca society] was never officially endorsed by the Spanish Crown. Ultimately this was a continuation of the practice applied by the encomenderos, albeit state-sanctioned, and on a universal scale. On his five-year tour (*Visita General*) throughout the provinces, the viceroyal and great reformer of colonial government Francisco Toledo became the first actually to stipulate *mita* quotas. These ranged annually from roughly 5 to 8 per cent of the male population aged between eighteen and fifty. Peter Bakewell puts the initial number of *mita* workers to have reached Potosí in 1573 at around 9,500.[2] By the time of the next census, conducted in La Plata and La Paz just two years later, this figure had risen by between 34 and 35 per cent, buoyed by the steady demand for labour. Toledo divided up the *mita* day into one-third working time and two-thirds idle. In their rest period, the workers sold themselves as free labourers, since the *mita* wages only covered the minimum number of calories a person needed to survive,[3] but not clothing, accommodation, working materials or food for their families, who accompanied them to Potosí. The wages stipulated by Toledo (paid out in silver), of 2.7 to 3.5 reales per day, were maintained over the next twenty years, and were not adjusted to take account of inflation.

Toledo exploited the existing social hierarchical structures of Inca society to organize the *mita*. 'A ruling group of six leading principals ... from various points of the draft areas was appointed and given administrative authority … over all other *curacas* and Indians in the *Mita*. … Their duties were … to ensure that the due number of workers appeared; but then in general to oversee the administration of the draft in Potosí.'[4] These 'captains' were under pressure to ensure fulfilment of the quotas or pay cash in lieu of the absent workers. The communities also had to supply the mitayos with provisions for the journeys. All this led to growing indebtedness: 'The historiography of Africa has demonstrated the crucial role in colonial and neocolonial economies of temporary labour migrations, recruited with varying degrees of coercion. … The costs of the maintenance during idle periods and reproduction of labour power are relegated to the sphere of the indigenous communities, while the entrepreneur … pays only the costs of the immediate labour-power. Therefore, forced migratory labour is a means by which communities transfer value to the sphere of production in which their labour is applied. … It should be emphasized that the object of exploitation is not the individual migrant but the entire community.'[5] Toledo's threefold reform: the consolidation of the *Indios* into settlements, the tribute system, and the *mita*, clearly highlight this link: 'The *reducciones* regrouped the diminished indigenous population into villages, confirming land rights … the indigenous territory, relocated and reduced … became means for the reproduction of labour-power for Spanish enterprises. The concentration of the population facilitated both evangelization and collection of tribute.'[6]

Let us now compare the historical criteria underlying primitive accumulation which Karl Marx identified in England from the fifteenth to the seventeenth century, with the situation in the Peruvian viceroyalty during the same period: 'The primitive accumulation is a … separation of the labourers from all property in the means by which they realize their labour … when great masses of men are suddenly and forcibly torn from their means of subsistence, and hurled as free and "unattached" proletarians on the labour market. The expropriation of the agricultural producer, of the peasant from the soil, is the basis of this whole process.'[7] Enrique Tandeter writes: 'The Andes were traversed by massive human migrations and the abandonment of precisely those villages that were subject to the *Mita* recruitment.'[8] Bakewell stresses that 'the large movements of people to and from the town … cannot but have brought interruptions of agricultural cycles … the mere fact that the *Mita* shifted alone annually, according to Toledo's rules, between a sixth and a fifth of the tributaries from a large portion of the central Andean upland serves as an indicator of disruption. Since at least … *Mitayos* took wives with them and … children also, it is probably no exaggeration to suggest that the *Mita* drew to Potosí, along with the *Mitayos*, an equal number of dependents. So that the annual movement of population resulting from *Mita* may have reached in some years 25,000.'[9]

1   Peter Bakewell, *Miners of the Red Mountain: Indian Labor in Potosí, 1545–1650* (Albuquerque, 1984) 54.

2   Ibid., 47.

3   Ibid., 103.

4   Ibid., 70.

5   Enrique Tandeter, *Coercion and Market* (Albuquerque, 1992) 22.

6   Bakewell, op. cit., 123.

7   Karl Marx, *Capital*, vol. I (Moscow, n.d.) 479f; first English edition of 1887 ed. Friedrich Engels.

8   Tandeter, op. cit., 27.

9   Bakewell, op. cit., 110f.

Alice Creischer, extracts from 'Primitive Accumulation as Exemplified in Potosí', in *Das Potosí-Prinzip: Wie können wir das Lied des Herrn im fremden Land singen?*, ed. Alice Creischer, Max Jorge Hinderer, Andreas Siekmann (Berlin: Haus der Kulturen der Welt, et.al., 2010) 235–8.

Nick Dyer-Witheford
Toxic Work//2015

[…] We can distinguish in the basic industrial processes of computer manufacture 'core jobs' in semiconductor production, performed in 'clean rooms' by bunny-suited workers, and the 'peripheral jobs' of preparing printed circuit boards, printers and cables, performed in far less clinical settings – indeed, often in workers' own homes. In addition Silicon Valley featured service workers: janitors cleaning the offices of hacker geniuses, gardeners manicuring the lawns of high-tech campuses, food servers, parking lot attendants, security guards – all labour maintaining the fundamentals of mammalian existence in a world devoted to high-technology machines. Together these industrial and service jobs provided the computer revolution's proletarian manual labour.

In 2000 there were officially about 65,000 electronic assembly workers, 40,000 non-assembly manufacturing workers, and 200,000 service workers in Silicon Valley. These jobs were filled by a workforce shaped in Santa Clara's traditions of female, migrant agricultural labour. In electronics plants the majority of production workers were women from ethnic minorities, while the engineering and management staff were predominantly male and white. Migrants were drawn to production lines and service work in various waves. In the semiconductor industry Latino women were the largest single group in the

1980s, and continued to dominate service jobs, but by the 1990s women from Asia – Vietnam, the Philippines, Malaysia – had become the majority in industrial processing. Undocumented migrant workers, not included in official labour estimates but targeted in erratic sweeps by immigration authorities, were variously estimated to compose from 10 to 25 per cent of the workforce. [...]

Silicon Valley pioneered 'flexible' labour practices that would become hallmarks of cybernetic capital, sacrificing circadian rhythms and social life to the frenetic pace of technological innovation and entrepreneurial start-ups. This had a gendered aspect:

> For women, this really means working three Jobs – or 'Three Shifts' as some immigrants call it – one at a sweatshop in the formal economy, a second taking care of the family, and then a third working in the informal economy, taking in laundry or cleaning houses at the weekends.[1]

Temporary work, piece work and home work proliferated. Silicon Valley corporations outsourced not only cafeteria work, garbage removal and janitorial services, but also secretarial and clerical work, subcontracted to temp agencies. These were jobs for which employers assumed 'no responsibility for benefits, pensions or severance pay'; workers were 'hired when needed, dumped when demand slackens, and fired and blacklisted for any hint of opposition.'[2]

Flexible working conditions were particularly pernicious in the 'peripheral jobs' of electronic assembly. The Valley became the home of a new sort of enterprise which would eventually globalize its scope: electronics contract manufacturers. These took on workers as assembly contracts became available; work would in turn be contracted to second or third tier contractors, with pay and conditions deteriorating at each downward rung. This produced the true Silicon Valley sweatshops – assembly of electronic components by workers in their own homes, at piece rates that were only sustainable by mobilizing entire families, including children and the elderly. [...]

1   RW (Revolutionary Worker), 'Living on the Bottom of Silicon Valley: Proletarians in California's High Tech Zone', *Revolutionary Worker Online* (14 May 2000).
2   Ibid.

Nick Dyer-Witheford, extracts from *Cyber-Proletariat: Global Labour in the Digital Vortex* (London: Pluto Press, 2015) 66–8.

My show is a way of giving time back to the staff who work there. When they accept this offering, without their wages being suspended, the work will emerge

Maria Eichhorn, Statement on exhibition at Chisenhale Gallery, 2016

THE GOOD OF WORK

Jeremy Deller
On *The Battle of Orgreave*//2002

On 18 June 1984 I was watching the evening news and saw footage of a mass picket at the Orgreave coking plant in South Yorkshire, in which thousands of men were chased up a field by mounted police. The image of this pursuit stuck in my mind and for years I wanted to find out what exactly happened on that day, with a view to re-enacting or commemorating it in some way. It would not be an exaggeration to say that the strike, like a civil war, had a traumatically divisive effect at all levels of life in the UK. Families were torn apart because of divided loyalties, the union movement was split on its willingness to support the National Union of Mineworkers, the print media especially contributed to the polarization of the arguments to the point where there appeared to be little space for a middle ground. So in all but name it became an ideological and industrial battle between the two sections of British society.[1]

When I started to undertake research, the consequences of the confrontation took on a much larger historical perspective. It was a day that had been anticipated and planned for by the then government, even before it came to power [...]. After over a year of archive reading, listening and interviewing many of those involved the re-enactment finally did take place on, or as close to as possible, the original site, with over 800 participants. Many of these participants were former miners (and a few former policemen) who were reliving events from 1984 that they themselves took part in. The rest were members of battle re-enactment societies from all over the country.

I wanted to involve members of these societies for mainly two reasons: first of all, they are well trained in recreating combat and in obeying orders. More importantly, I wanted the re-enactment of the Battle of Orgreave to become part of the lineage of decisive battles in English History.

I was also interested in the term 'living history' that is frequently used in relation to re-enactments, and I thought it would be interesting for re-enactors to work alongside veterans of a recent confrontation, who are an embodiment of the term. Also as an artist I was interested in how far an idea could be taken, especially one that is on the face of it a contradiction in terms: a recreation of something that was essentially chaos.

I would never have undertaken the project if people locally felt it was unnecessary or in poor taste. As it was, we encountered support from the outset because there seemed to be an instinctive understanding of what the re-enactment was about. I was not interested in a nostalgic interpretation of the strike [...].

Over a thousand people were involved in the project, either through taking part, filming or helping with research. I would personally like to thank everyone who has shown faith in the project or was at least willing to give it a go.

1   I apologize for the fact that the title The Battle of Orgreave does not acknowledge the miners in Scotland and Wales who took part in the strike but it was a title that seemed to stick, even when I first thought of the re-enactment eight years ago.

Jeremy Deller, extract from foreword, in Jeremy Deller, *The English Civil War Part II: Personal Accounts of the 1984–85 Miner's Strike*, ed. Gerrie van Noord (London: Artangel, 2002) 7.

Mierle Laderman Ukeles
On *Touch Sanitation*//1980

On 24 July 1979, I started shaking hands with the first of all New York City's 8,500 sanitation men and officers, 'sanmen', the housekeepers of the whole City, workers in the largest of maintenance systems. I called the performance Touch Sanitation, a maintenance ritual act, celebrating daily survival. To each man I said, 'Thank you for keeping New York City alive.'

As an artist, I tried to burn an image into the public eye, by shaking, shaking, shaking hands, that this is a human system that keeps New York City alive, that when you throw something out, there's no 'out'. Rather there's a human being who has to lift it, haul it, get injured because of it (highest injury rate of any US occupation), dispose of it, 20,000 tons every day. Our garbage, not theirs.

As a woman artist injecting myself into a 'man's world', I represented the possibility of a healing vision: not a pretend sanman, not an official investigator, nor a media voyeur, not a social scientist; rather a 'sharer' in an ecological vision of the operating wholeness of urban society.

Over the next eleven months, through all four seasons, I followed in their footsteps, modelling my performance art-time on the sanman's eight-hour work shifts, starting at 6 a.m., or 4 p.m., or midnight. To reach all 59 sanitation districts in every part of New York City, I divided the performance into ten 'Sweeps', ten circles of the City, creating a citywide spiral tracking-form, hand to hand.

I did a round-robin, where you get called back to work with no choice after only 8 hours off, for several days running, until your eyeballs turn inside out and you don't know what time it is. I ate with sanmen, often on curbsides when restaurants wouldn't serve them. I talked with them on audiotape and shot video throughout. Mostly I stayed behind the hopper, as they do – where you can't escape the scare of the wind, sheets of rain, beating sun, stumbling in the snow, when you get soaked from sweat inside your rain-gear and drenched outside anyhow, facing the stink and ultimate jungle of juxtapositions that is garbage.

A world unfolded, work performed right in the public eye, where sanmen feel so isolated they could be working on the moon, a world most people have no idea about. I saw the hypocrisy of our society that demands complete eight-hour everyday 'productivity' (which sounds reasonable especially when New York City is in extremely dire fiscal straits), yet which, at the same time, presents that sanitation worker with utterly degrading work conditions and facilities, often one toilet for 120 men, no showers!, frozen pipes, Byzantine work shifts, improperly packaged garbage – overflowing, frozen to the ground, smeared curb to curb – the excessive glut of waste from our egregious consumerism. I developed a reflexive flinch from the common public attitude that merges the worker with the waste product that we, not they, make but which nevertheless stigmatizes them. They spoke of being thought of as part of the garbage, the lowest of the low.

'I hope you washed your hand,' people said to me all year, as if sanmen didn't wear gloves or remove them when they weren't handling the garbage, forgodssakes. Do they say that after you meet a surgeon?

I got depressed, I got enormously angry. Many sanmen, thousands, said, 'You're the only person in the world who gives a damn about us.' Is that ridiculous? Is that any way to run a society?

I got enlightened about the expertise of balance, twenty to thirty-year spans of strength, about camaraderie and life-death teamwork under such stress your hair could stand up on end, mostly about spirit even where there's zero morale and supreme endurance, dedication, keeping going no matter what comes at you.

I finished on 26 June 1980. But they didn't. Does the noise of the hopper's grinding away aggravate you? It means we've made it to another day.

Mierle Laderman Ukeles, statement on *Touch Sanitation* (1977–80), in *Issue: Social Strategies by Women Artists*, ed. Lucy R. Lippard (London: Institute of Contemporary Arts, 1980); reprinted in *Feminism – Art – Theory: An Anthology 1968–2000*, ed. Hilary Robinson (Oxford: Blackwell, 2006) 106–7.

Anne Teresa de Keersmaeker
In Conversation with Rudi Laermans//2012

Anne Teresa de Keersmaeker […] I've never had a problem with traditions or limits, I've always been fascinated by limits … There is no freedom in freedom, there is only freedom in structure. Freedom in itself doesn't exist, it is always proportional and it always defines itself in relation to something else. That's simply one of the basic rules of improvisation. No freedom without rules, without a relationship to something else.

Rudi Laermans Does that explain your commitment to the importance of craftsmanship or métier in dance, something you're also trying to teach young people at P.A.R.T.S. [Performing Arts Research and Training Studios]?

de Keersmaeker Yes, but don't get me wrong, I'm not a fanatic who believes that everything's a matter of construction and composition. I'm partial to them, but that partiality is supported by even deeper-set ideas about the more general laws that control our existence. In that context I do indeed appreciate craftsmanship, a certain savoir-faire, the ability to organize time and space with bodies pertaining, for instance, to sound – strategic or otherwise. That's also what I mean by composition as a line of thought. I'm rather Marxist that way: there is no practice without theory, and no theory without practice. I often find both the theoretical reflection on practice and the practices based on theory quite thin. So craftsmanship in itself is not enough, it has to be based on a thinking about it.

Laermans The difficulty is, I think, that there are no fixed rules about craftsmanship any more. There are no more formulas, which means that even if you apply a certain 'savoir-faire' you have to reinvent the rules repeatedly, while remaining loyal to ideas about proper dimensions and perspectives …

de Keersmaeker Yes … yes, that really occupies my mind. And the more you are interested in it, the less you are left with … Sometimes I'm a little afraid because everything happens only inside your head – while I prefer to work with people in the studio. […]

Laermans [It seems to me that] within concrete professional relationships, you do not regard the dancers as commodities to be squandered but give them time to develop their potential.

de Keersmaeker The dancers you work with in the studio are like clay, you really work with them. Or no, not clay, that's a wrong image, because it suggests that you can shape them at will. Whereas you do a lot of things together, and you also spend an incredible amount of time together … But I have learned that, though we engage with each other, I shouldn't get too attached to them. […] By now, I'm aware at the beginning of a new work relationship that it will end one day too. It's now, and maybe the next months, and maybe the next year … but it will also not be there. More than before I am now capable of committing myself with body and soul to a creative process and to subsequently think 'let it go' at the supreme moment. It's change, it will take another shape … It's just a phase, a moment … But I will commit myself to the moment. […]

Laermans What do you consider the basic values of P.A.R.T.S?

de Keersmaeker I see it as a place where people meet who know that they can give shape to matters that concern us all by using their bodies in the most individual way. As it is the most human of instruments, the body is the most suitable means of doing so. Our existential experience and our perception of the world lie embedded in our bodies. Each morning you rise and each night you go to bed within this very small space. […]

Anne Teresa de Keersmaeker and Rudi Laermans, extracts from 'Sharing Experience: An Interview with Anne Teresa de Keersmaeker', in *Being an Artist in Post-Fordist Times*, ed. Paul de Bruyne and Pascal Gielen (Rotterdam: NAi Publishers, 2012) 83–97.

Fischli & Weiss
How to Work Better//1991

1   DO ONE THING AT A TIME
2   KNOW THE PROBLEM
3   LEARN TO LISTEN
4   LEARN TO ASK QUESTIONS
5   DISTINGUISH SENSE FROM NONSENSE
6   ACCEPT CHANGE AS INEVITABLE
7   ADMIT MISTAKES
8   SAY IT SIMPLE

9   BE CALM

10 SMILE

Fischli & Weiss, *How To Work Better* (1991). The artists found this text used in a factory in Thailand and installed the phrases in large stencilled letters on the side of an office block in north Zurich, visible when approaching the city by train from the airport. Reproduced in *Work Ethic*, ed. Helen Molesworth (Baltimore: Baltimore Museum of Art, 2003) 6.

Michelangelo Pistoletto
In Conversation with Marie Josée Corsten, Pascal Gielen and Luigi Coppola//2009

If there is one artist who over the last decades has done almost everything possible to respond to social changes such as globalization, post-Fordism and neoliberalism, it is Michelangelo Pistoletto. In 1996 he founded the Cittadellarte organization that spawned more than just a political movement (Love Difference); it also involves an investigation into alternative economic systems and, pragmatically, collaboration with local industry in order to place art at the centre of what he calls 'a socially sound transformation'. [...]

The Italian philosopher Paolo Virno says that in a post-Fordist economy – the economy in which we are living now – art is dissolved in society just like a medicine dissolves in a glass of water. As a consequence, the autonomy of the artist and of art is shrinking. When we try to understand the work of your organization Cittadellarte it seems to us that you activate this process. You really want to place art at the centre of society, especially in the economic system. Cittadellarte artists deal directly with companies. What is the goal of this operation?

Michelangelo Pistoletto Managing a company requires deep involvement and vast responsibility. Here at Cittadellarte we are interested in touching the real structure of society. Cittadellarte itself can be considered a company. To be productive, and consequently make a company work, you have to take risks. To develop a productive concept, you have to believe firmly in a project, look at the socio-economic horizon, examine what the market currently offers, to understand what you can propose and if this proposal has to be completely new, or draw inspiration from the models tradition provides. It's a complex process that has to lead to results. This productive model, I think, can be adapted to describe the process of artistic creation. Being an artist means taking risks in coming up with ideas, images and models. To arrive at invention through adaptations, but also through provocation.

Another interesting parallel is with science. The method is the same. Artists and scientists make a series of trials, they experiment, until one day the 'revelation' comes; this is the moment at which a 'creative leap' takes place. I am interested in the dynamics of risk-taking to achieve results, be they a good marketable product, or an artistic, technological, scientific or economic invention. This is why I'm interested in art as much as in science and in the economy, but my first interest at the moment is spirituality. I mean spirituality as immanence, not as an escape from reality. Spirituality as the possibility to go far with the imagination and then return to the concreteness of the act, as an extension of the capacity of thought, as a combination of thought and action. Cittadellarte aims to create tools common to all fields of social action, precisely through this concept of spirituality, which becomes the common denominator of art, science, economics and politics. [...]

If you look at the concrete results right now, here in Cittadellarte, you can detect a typical kind of economy. The micro economy has less to do with mass production than with handcrafted products that are unique and are based on more labour-intensive production processes. The economy seems to be going back, in Western Europe, to this more exclusive production – even in hi-tech. The reasoning is that, now we have China for mass production, in Europe we can go back to more sustainable, exclusive products, which are restricted in volume and can also be very expensive. Most of the things we have seen here, at least, are produced in the local area. But isn't this a reactionary position?

Pistoletto [...] We were speaking earlier of post-Fordism; I think we have to go back to Fordism, but certainly in a completely different way with respect to the past. What was positive in the Fordist system was the direct relationship between production and consumption – the workers themselves bought the product. Fordism was based not on fairness, but on capitalization of profit. This search for capitalization led to a paroxysm, to the consumerist system, with its creation of increasingly numerous needs, needs financial speculation made its own. We need to balance consumption and production, bringing production closer to real needs. This is why, here at Cittadellarte, for instance, our restaurant, Cafeteria, uses the zero kilometre concept – keeping production on a short leash by offering food that comes from local producers, and only when it's in season. It's really necessary to enhance regional micro-production: this way we save energy and breathe life into the territory and the relation of proximity between production and consumption. And we create autonomy.

Michelangelo Pistoletto, Marie-Josée Corsten, Pascal Gielen and Luigi Coppola, extracts from 'L'astuzia della spiritualità – The Cleverness of Spirituality: An interview with Michelangelo Pistoletto', in *Being an Artist in Post-Fordist Times*, ed. Paul Bruyne and Pascal Gielen (Rotterdam: NAi Publishers, 2009) 55–67.

Liam Gillick
The Good of Work//2011

Art is a history of doing nothing and a long tale of useful action. It is always a fetishization of decision and indecision – with each mark, structure and engagement. What is the good of this work? The question contains a challenge to contemporary practitioners – or 'current artists', a term I will use, as contemporary art no longer accounts for what is being made – that is connected more to what we have all become than to what we might propose, represent, or fail to achieve. The challenge is the supposition that artists today – whether they like it or not – have fallen into a trap that is predetermined by their existence within a regime that is centred on a rampant capitalization of the mind.

The accusation inherent in the question is that artists are at best the ultimate freelance knowledge workers and at worst barely capable of distinguishing themselves from the consuming desire to work at all times, neurotic people who deploy a series of practices that coincide quite neatly with the requirements of the neoliberal, predatory, continually mutating capitalism of the every moment. Artists are people who behave, communicate and innovate in the same manner as those who spend their days trying to capitalize every moment and exchange of daily life. They offer no alternative to this. […]

It requires precise and close observation of the production processes involved in order to differentiate between knowledge workers and current artists. If the question 'Why work?' is the original question of current art, it is necessary, in order to counter the accusation that artists are in thrall to processes of capitalization beyond them, to look at a number of the key issues around control. And to address them in a fragmented way. […]

So what happened to the promise of leisure? Maybe this is what art can offer us now – a thing to use or reflect upon in a zone of permanent future leisure, as the 'arts' as instrumentalized deployment becomes a more refined and defined capitalized zone. This zone is never geared towards artists alone but instead directed towards the general population as a way of rationalizing and explaining away innovations within the workplace as being part of a matrix of doubt and difference. Modes of leisure have been adopted by artists as a way to openly counter notions of labour as sites of dignity and innovation and in order to critique, mock or parody the notion of an artistic life as role-play within the leisure zone. Yet the promise of leisure is not synchronized with artistic production. The withdrawal of labour and the establishment of structures in which intentions and results are uneven are markers that go beyond the promise of post-labour, which was always just the projection of a neurotic non-state.

So are we left with only the possibility of the good artist who fulfils the critical criteria? The artist who works – more or less permanently – and always finds a way to account for him or herself within a context demanding more and more interpretation? It is not leisure, but is it really work? Within this subset we have to engage in a careful process of categorization, meaning that we have to look at the methodological groupings that emerge within the art context rather than what is produced. […]

The two main trajectories of current art both attempt to clear us of the accusation: restructuring life (ways to work) and withdrawing from life (ways to free work). Categorizations of art in this case can superficially appear to mirror attitudes to work. It is quite appropriate for artists to co-opt working models and turn them to their own ends, from the factory to the bar and even to the notion of the artist's studio, as specific sites of production that used to either mimic established daily structures or deliberately avoid and deny them. Categorizations of art are not limited to what is produced but are connected more deeply to how things might be produced. It is necessary to focus on production rather than consumption (including the new formalism of responsible didactic criticism) if one is to unlock art's potential and permit a recasting of the accusation.

The notion of withdrawing or limiting production is the key to decoding the anxiety about work. One of the enduring powers of art, and one of the devices used by contemporary artists to consolidate specificity once they have attained a degree of recognition, is a withdrawal of labour or a limiting of supply. Doing the opposite – operating freely, openly and on demand – is viewed as a problem within the gallery structure and resists the simple commodification of art. This shift to production consciousness by current artists, away from reception consciousness by contemporary artists, is a form of active withdrawal.

This notion of withdrawal can be understood in relation to the following: are there answers or questions in the work? This is central to the defence against the accusation. A postmodern understanding is that the current artist asks questions of the viewer while standing beside them. It is this sense of art as something that asks questions of the viewer that is misunderstood in the knowledge-worker accusation. The shift of position from confrontation to proximity is in practice a shift in category. Within the realm of the knowledge worker, the new consumer is always activated and treated as a discriminating individual who can be marketed to directly – spoken to face to face. Documentary practice places the user and the producer alongside each other. The exhaustion created by the continual capitalization of the recent past and the near future has its source in the knowledge worker's attempt to account for every differentiation, whereas the artist is producing every differentiation alongside the recipient of the work. [...]

The assumption that there is a 'they' or 'them' is part of the problem involved in understanding how artists function within society. Artists are also 'they' or 'them' who have made a specific decision to operate within an exceptional zone that does not necessarily produce anything exceptional. For adherence to a high-cultural life is a negotiated concept within the current art context. This critical community is simultaneously subject and audience. Therefore we have a situation in which an artist will propose a problem and then position it just out of reach precisely in order to test the potential for an autonomy of practice.

Reporting the strange in the daily – that which cannot be accounted for is at the heart of artistic practices, yet not for purposes that can be described outside the work itself. And still, working less can result in producing more. The rate of idea-production within art is inconsistent, which is a deliberate result of the way art is produced and how it can become precise and *other* even while it flounders and then proudly reports back to us within the self-patrolled compound masquerading as a progressive think-tank.

Artists function in micro-communities of discourse that are logical and contingent within their own contexts, as well as (often) generationally related. Current artists are caught within generational boundaries. The notion that artists are a perfect analogue of the flexible entrepreneurial class is a generational concept that merely masks a lack of differentiation in observation of practice and the devastating fact that art is a permanent battle with what came just before. That is the good of work. Replacing the models of the recent past with better ones. [...]

Liam Gillick, extracts from 'The Good of Work', in *Are You Working Too Much? Post-Fordism, Precarity, and the Labour of Art*, ed. Julieta Aranda, Brian Kuan Wood, Anton Vidokle (Berlin: Sternberg Press, 2011) 60–73.

Jacques Rancière
Proletarian Nights//2012

The reader who discovers this book in the twelfth year of the twenty-first century may well ask what strange object she or he has in their hands. How can these stories about French locksmith, tailors, shoemakers and typographers from the nineteenth century interest anyone in the age of digital revolution, non-material production and the globalized market? They would certainly not be the first to ask such a question. It was already the case with the French readers who opened this book when it was first published thirty years ago. At that time, however, there was no talk yet of globalization, nor indeed of the end of the proletariat, history and utopias. [...]

Its author was a professional philosopher, whose work had begun in the 1960s, inspired by his participation in Louis Althusser's theoretical enterprise, which sought to give Marxist theory a new foundation. Yet instead of advancing philosophical theses, he was telling stories of French workers in the nineteenth century. And, as for Marxism, he offered no analysis of industrial production and capitalist exploitation, nor of social theories and the struggles of working-class parties and unions. His workers, moreover, were not 'real' workers; they were old-style artisans, dreamers who versified or invented philosophies, who met together in the evenings to set up short-lived magazines, enthused about socialist and communist utopias but generally did not get involved in putting these into practice. [...]

For the workers of the 1830s, the question was not to demand the impossible, but to realize it themselves, to take back the time that was refused them by educating their perceptions and their thought in order to free themselves in the very exercise of everyday work, or by winning from nightly rest the time to discuss, write, compose verses, or develop philosophies. These gains in time and freedom were not marginal phenomena or diversions in relation to the construction of the workers' movement and its great objectives. They were the revolution [...].

It is the need to explain this revolution that gives the present book its unusual structure. It introduces us directly into the speech of these workers, in all its forms, from personal confidence or the recital of daily experience through to philosophical speculations and programmes for the future, by way of the fictitious stories recorded in their journals. It does not accept any difference of status, any hierarchy between description, fiction or argument. This is not in the name of some fetishist passion for lived experience. That would be itself the alibi for a distribution of roles that gives the people speech in order to verify that they are indeed speaking the language of the people, and grants the poor the experience of reality and the flavour of daily life so as better to reserve for itself the privilege of the creative imagination and the explanatory word. But it is precisely this distribution of roles between the language of the people and literary language, reality and fiction, document and argument, that these 'popular' texts challenge. [...]

To account for the subversive power of their work I was forced to break with the habits of social science, for which these personal accounts, fictions or discourses are no more than the confused products of a process that social science alone is in a position to understand. These words had to be removed from their status as evidence or symptoms of a social reality to show them as writing and thinking at work on the construction of a different social world. That is why this book renounced any explanatory distance. It instead sought to create the sensitive fabric required to make this upturning of the order that keeps times and discourses in their place resound in our own present. That is why severe theorists and historians deemed it to be literature. My object was rather to reaffirm that the motivations of the philosopher and the scholar are cut from the same common cloth of language and thought as are the inventions of writers, and as are these proletarian tales.

It is in this sense that the untimeliness of this book should be understood. [...] Contemporary forms of work are bringing back into currency these phenomena of dividing time and participating in several worlds of experience that I described in *Proletarian Nights*: the oscillation between work and unemployment; the development of part-time work and temporary work of all kinds; the explosion of people dividing their time between study and wage-labour; the explosion, too, of men and women trained for one kind of work and doing another, working in one world and living in another – which is also what immigration means. In this world, the question is always to subvert the order of time prescribed by domination, to interrupt its continuities and transform the pauses it imposes into regained freedom. It is to unite what separates and to divide what it ties together by asserting, against the rationality imposed by its managers, their governments and experts, a capacity for thought and action that is common to all. This is what made for the resistant strength of the reveries of the proletarian night. It is also what makes them so hard for superior minds to tolerate, today just as yesterday. The equality of intelligences remains the most untimely of thoughts it is possible to nourish about the social order.

Jacques Rancière, extracts from author's preface to 2012 edition of *Proletarian Nights: The Workers' Dream in Nineteenth-Century France* (1981), trans. John Drury (London and New York: Verso, 2012), vii, ix, x, xi–xii.

Mary Kelly
A Brief History of the Women's Workshop of the Artists' Union//c. 1973

A group of women artists first met in London, in January 1972, at a studio in Southwark where two of the founding members worked, to discuss the possibility of joining the newly formed Artist's Union. We wanted to do this as an organized group, rather than individuals, in order to ensure that women's demands became an effective part of the Union's aims and programme of action.

The main activity of the Artist's Union is located within the workshops which are set up, by majority vote at regional meetings, to deal with the special areas affecting artists; for example, education, art patronage and exhibitions. Our women's group succeeded in establishing a special workshop on women and have been working actively in the Union on that basis ever since.

The Artist's Union formed with the aim of seeking affiliation to the Trades Union Congress, and with this in mind, the members ratified a constitution and elected officers in May 1972. The Women's Workshop made nominations for all positions, and as a result Mary Kelly was elected as Chairman, and Margaret Harrison and Carol Kenna to the Secretariat. We also demanded that the Union seek to establish parity on the Regional Council, which consists of all Union officers and workshop convenors, and in the entire Union membership as well.

With women actively engaged in running the Union, women's issues were brought to the foreground: 'To take action to end sexual and racial discrimination in the arts' was established by a majority vote as one of the Union's major aims, membership cards were altered to include 'Do you need crêche facilities at Branch meetings?', and resolutions were passed in support of the women workers occupation at Fakenham and the night cleaners campaign.

One of the aims of the Women's Workshop is to set up links with women's sections in other unions. In a regional report we stated: 'The Women's Workshop maintains that women in whatever sector they are employed are largely unorganized and consequently receive the lowest pay and work in the worst conditions; it is our intention to support our sisters in their struggle for unionization and also in the action they take as organized workers.'

As women artists working within a male-dominated culture we face the following contradiction: the notable absence of women in history as practising artists and their overwhelming presence as subject matter, portrayed in a way which often idealizes but nevertheless confirms their second-class social status. In order to make a start at changing our situation we proposed these actions:

To pressure local councils to provide studio space for women with children.

To ensure that public galleries and national museums include women artists in both retrospectives and contemporary surveys.

To demand that art colleges hire female staff in proportion to the number of female students (could be enforced through the anti-discrimination bill)

To examine the entrance requirements for art schools (especially proposed A-Levels) in relation to discrimination against women.

Mary Kelly, extract from 'A Brief History of the Women's Workshop of the Artists' Union 1972–1973' (c. 1973); in *Feminism – Art – Theory: An Anthology 1968–2000*, ed. Hilary Robinson (Oxford: Blackwell, 2001) 87–8.

Francis Alÿs
On *When Faith Moves Mountains*//2002

On 11 April 2002, five hundred volunteers were supplied with shovels and asked to form a single line at the foot of a giant sand dune in Ventanilla, an area outside Lima. This human comb pushed a certain quantity of sand a certain distance, thereby moving a 1600-foot-long sand dune about four inches from its original position.

Lima, a city of nine million people, is situated on a strip of land along the Pacific coast of Peru. The city is surrounded by enormous sand dunes on which shanty towns have sprung up, populated by economic immigrants and political refugees who escaped the civil war fought during the 1980s and 90s by the military and guerrilla groups like Shining Path. After a week of scouting, we chose the Ventanilla dunes, where more than 70,000 people live with no electricity or running water.

When Faith Moves Mountains is a project of linear geological displacement. It has been germinating ever since I first visited Lima, with Cuauhtémoc Medina, the Mexican curator and critic. We were there for the last Lima Bienal, in October 2000, about a year before the Fujimori dictatorship finally collapsed. The city was in turmoil. There were clashes on the street and the resistance movement strengthened. It was a desperate situation, and I felt that it called for an 'epic' response, a 'beau geste' at once futile and heroic, absurd and urgent. Insinuating a social allegory into those circumstances seemed to me more fitting than engaging in some sculptural exercise.

When Faith Moves Mountains attempts to translate social tensions into narratives that in turn intervene in the imaginal landscape of a place. The action is meant to infiltrate the local history and mythology of Peruvian society (including its art histories), to insert another rumor into its narratives. If the script meets the expectations and addresses the anxieties of that society at this time and place, it may become a *story* that survives the event itself. At that moment, it has the potential to become a fable or an urban myth. As Medina said while we were in Lima, 'Faith is a means by which one resigns oneself to the present in order to invest in the abstract promise of the future.' The dune moved: This wasn't a literary fiction; it really happened. It doesn't matter how far it moved, and in truth only an infinitesimal displacement occurred – but it would have taken the wind years to move an equivalent amount of sand. So it's a tiny miracle. The story starts there. The interpretations of it needn't be accurate, but must be free to shape themselves along the way.

This process can also operate on the narratives of art history, not to mention those of the art world. *Paradox of Praxis* (1997), a piece in which I pushed a large block of ice through the streets of Mexico City until it melted into a puddle of water, was a settling of accounts with Minimalist sculpture. Sometimes, to make something is really to make nothing; and paradoxically, sometimes to make nothing is to make something.

Similarly, *When Faith Moves Mountains* is my attempt to deromanticize Land art. When Richard Long made his walks in the Peruvian desert, he was pursuing a contemplative practice that distanced him from the immediate social context. When Robert Smithson built the *Spiral Jetty* on the Salt Lake in Utah, he was turning civil engineering into sculpture and vice versa. Here, we have attempted to create a kind of Land art for the landless, and, with the help of hundreds of people and shovels, we created a social allegory. This story is not validated by any physical trace or addition to the landscape. We shall now leave the care of our story to oral tradition, as Plato says in the *Republic*. Only in its repetition and transmission is the work actualized. In this respect, art can never free itself from myth. Indeed, in modern no less than premodern societies, art operates precisely within the space of myth.

In this sense, myth is not about the veneration of ideals – of pagan gods or political ideology – but rather an active interpretive practice performed by the audience, who must give the work its meaning and its social value. [...]

Francis Alÿs and Saul Anton, extract from 'A Thousand Words: Francis Alÿs Talks about "When Faith Moves Mountains"', *Artforum*, vol. 10, no. 40 (Summer 2002) 146–7.

Petra Lange-Berndt
Occupy, Migrate, Disintegrate ... Carolee Schneemann
and Annette Messager's Studio Abandonment//2010

Dirt and mess are among the traditional *topoi* of the workshop, and at the beginning of the 1970s the French artist Annette Messager focused on this aspect when she described her Paris studio as follows:

> I live in a fairly small and very cluttered apartment. It's all in a messy state, really higgledy-piggledy. [...] So one day I decided to divide my apartment in two, and to focus only on precisely defined activities that are in each case determined by the space I'm in. To do this I gave myself two different names corresponding to these activities. In my bedroom, where the 'housework' takes place, I go as Annette Messager Collector. In the 'studio', a completely normal living room where 'studio work' takes place, I call myself Annette Messager Artist.[1] [...]

In 1970/71 the French artist and theorist Daniel Buren wrote an essay about the crisis of the studio and came to the conclusion that the context of the workshop as a frame, envelope and place where the work originates was so important that it should be exhibited.[2] [...] Annette Messager too engages in a critique of the studio. However instead of adopting attitudes with historically masculine connotations and occupying spaces, she advocates a narrative space that plays more intensively with new roles, materials and places that arise from the immediate living environment. For example, her studio drawing is woven into a story that tells of her life, and most of all of a guesthouse where the artist keeps lots of birds. Accordingly it is mainly sparrows who occupy her atelier: *Le repos, L'ombre vivante attaquée par sa realité, La punition* and *La promenade* display animals in various states of taxidermy.

In her atelier 'The Artist' is also concerned with creation – but instead of an intellectual concept the focus was on craft-related production conditions of bodies made to look natural. Accordingly, the caption of the studio drawing lists 'skinning, flaying, mounting' [...] – specialist, technical terms in taxidermy. [...] To find out how the impression of a natural bird is created, [...] Messager dissects [...] the stuffed sparrows thoroughly. On closer inspection it is apparent that after this procedure the birds reveal irregularities in their taxidermy, such as legs that have been snapped off or missing eyes. These gruesome injuries prevent a successful duplication of natural scientific norms, highlighting instead the techniques, materials and spaces that have, in the first place, created the effect of nature preserved intact. [...] By contrast with the natural scientists of the eighteenth and nineteenth centuries, Messager was unable to acquire materials that reflect a clearly natural origin: Messager recreated these birds [...] from feathers sourced domestically from pillows or feather dusters, winding the material into messy balls which she then carefully crocheted together.

In her living room that she has converted into an atelier, Annette Messager is thus not working as an artist in the classic sense [...]. Rather, [...] she slips here into the operative role of both 'Collector' and 'practical housewife' – plus taxidermist. [She] conflates her living room with the taxidermists' laboratory, and through a careful knitting together, links the profession of taxidermist – with its historically male connotations – to the history of craft techniques. On one hand she is referring to Lucy Lippard's 'hobby art' of housewives.[3] On the other, in eighteenth- and nineteenth-century France it was primarily female feather-workers who created fashionable accessories out of feathers alongside birds' wings [...]. Indeed 'The Artist' slipped into the role of such craftswomen, but instead of working in the area of fashion, works in the domain of taxidermy. Contrary to her own statements on the matter, a repetition of existing structures was not enough, but she was also aware of the history of craft techniques [...] in order to valorize this process and its associated materials under cover of her two-room, live-in studio. Ultimately, she was able to use them as a critical instrument by creating and exhibiting an encyclopaedia of former media landscapes in her bedroom and, in the living room, her own natural history museum with alternative stuffed animals – a new kind of nature. [...] She [practised] an effective disintegration of the traditional construction (the workshop) whereby, in this case, according to Buren, alongside 'picture frame, niche, pedestal, palace, church, gallery, museum' *atelier* also explicitly means 'power, art history, economics' – that is, workplace, narrative space and social context.[4]

1   [footnote 2 in source] This quotation appears in a fictional diary that the artist wrote for an exhibition catalogue: 'A. Messager: Ein Tag aus dem Leben der Annette Messager Sammlerin – Ein Tag aus dem Leben der Annette Messager Künstlerin' in Annette Messager Sammlerin – Annette Messager Künstlerin (Munich: Städtische Galerie im Lenbachhaus, 1973) 8.

2   [3] Daniel Buren, The Function of the Studio (1970–71), trans. Thomas Repensek in October, vol. 10 (Fall 1979) 51. [...]

3   [6] Lucy R. Lippard, 'Making Something from Nothing (Toward a Definition of Women's "Hobby Art")', Heresies, vol. 1, no. 4 (Winter 1978) 62–5.

4   [8] Daniel Buren (1970–71), op. cit., 51.

Petra Lange-Berndt, extracts from 'Besetzen, abwandern, auflösen … Die Aufkündigung des Ateliers bei Carolee Schneemann und Annette Messager', in *Topos Atelier: Werkstatt und Wissensform*, ed. Michael Diers and Monika Wagner (Berlin: Akademie Verlag, 2010) 75–92. Translated by Philippa Hurd, 2017.

Mladen Stilinović
In Praise of Laziness//1998

As an artist, I learned from both the East (socialism) and West (capitalism). Of course, now when the borders and political systems have changed, such an experience will no be longer possible. But what I have learned from that dialogue stays with me. My observation and knowledge of Western art has lately led me to a conclusion that art cannot exist any more in the West. This is not to say that there isn't any. Why cannot art exist any more in the West? The answer is simple. Artists in the West are not lazy. Artists from the East are lazy; whether they will stay lazy now when they are no longer Eastern artists, remains to be seen.

Laziness is the absence of movement and thought, dumb time – total amnesia. It is also indifference, staring at nothing, non-activity, impotence. It is sheer stupidity, a time of pain, futile concentration. Those virtues of laziness are important factors in art. Knowing about laziness is not enough, it must be practised and perfected. Artists in the West are not lazy and therefore not artists but rather producers of something ... Their involvement with matters of no importance, such as production, promotion, the gallery system, museum system, competition system (who is first), their preoccupation with objects, all that drives them away form laziness, from art. Just as money is paper, so a gallery is a room.

Artists from the East were lazy and poor because the entire system of insignificant factors did not exist. Therefore they had time enough to concentrate on art and laziness. Even when they did produce art, they knew it was in vain, it was nothing.

Artists from the West could learn about laziness, but they didn't. Two major twentieth-century artists treated the question of laziness, in both practical and theoretical terms: Duchamp and Malevich.

Duchamp never really discussed laziness, but rather indifference and non-work. When asked by Pierre Cabanne what had brought him most pleasure in life, Duchamp said: 'First, having been lucky. Because basically I've never worked for a living. I consider working for a living slightly imbecilic from an economic point of view. I hope that some day we'll be able to live without being obliged to work. Thanks to my luck, I was able to manage without getting wet.'

Malevich wrote a text entitled 'Laziness – the real truth of mankind' (1921). In it he criticized capitalism because it enabled only a small number of capitalists to be lazy, but also socialism because the entire movement was based on work instead of laziness. To quote:

People are scared of laziness and persecute those who accept it, and it always happens because no one realizes laziness is the truth; it has been branded as the mother of all vices, but it is in fact the mother of life. Socialism brings liberation in the unconscious, it scorns laziness without realizing it was laziness that gave birth to it; in his folly, the son scorns his mother as a mother of all vices and would not remove the brand; in this brief note I want to remove the brand of shame from laziness and to pronounce it not the mother of all vices, but the mother of perfection.

Finally, to be lazy and conclude: there is no art without laziness.
Work is a disease – Karl Marx.
Work is a shame – Vlado Martek.

Mladen Stilinović, 'In Praise of Laziness', *Moscow Art Magazine*, no. 22 (1998). (www.guelman.ru)

Maria Eichhorn
Statement//2016

Research, experiences, and various kinds of reflection lead me to ideas. In this case, my engagement with time and the way it's defined in relation to labour led me to the creation of this piece. My show at the Chisenhale Gallery is a way of giving time back to the staff who work there. When they accept this offering, without their wages being suspended, the work will emerge. Jacques Derrida states in his book *Given Time: I. Counterfeit Money* (1991) that 'to give time, the day, or life is to give nothing, nothing determinate, even if it is to give the giving of any possible giving, even if it gives the condition of giving.' Proceeding from this thought experiment of Derrida's, I want to interrogate the possibility of suspending the capitalist logic surrounding the notion of exchange and try to make a space in life sans labour a reality, by returning time to those who lack it, or who need it.

The Maria Eichhorn Aktiengesellschaft (Maria Eichhorn Public Limited Company), 2002, which I established on the occasion of Documenta 11 and is still in existence, relates especially well to this current project. It is an entity that possesses its own stocks and belongs to no one – the money originally invested in it, a little over $56,000, is not allowed to accrue in value. My Chisenhale piece has been conceived in a similar spirit – again, underscoring that 'time' belongs to no one and should somehow be reevaluated, or even extricated from contemporary economies.

That the exhibition space and gallery offices are closed is just a spatial consequence of this gesture – these are, after all, the areas where the staff pursues its labour. The institution itself and the actual exhibition are not closed, but rather displaced into the public sphere and society. A sign will be affixed to the Chisenhale gate explaining all of this, and additional information will be made available on the gallery's website, its social media, an so on. An automatic e-mail reply written specifically for this exhibition will also include a message stating that all incoming e-mail will be automatically deleted and that said recipient cannot be reached until after the close of the exhibition. When the gallery's employees come back to work, there will not be a great deal of e-mails waiting to be dealt with, thankfully.

The first reaction to my proposal? Hearty laughter. Then the Chisenhale's director, Polly Staple, and I met one on one and discussed the project intensively for about three hours. After that, Katie Guggenheim, the curator of exhibitions and events, got involved. The three of us went back and forth for a long time, analysing and reanalysing every single facet of this work. I am entirely grateful to both of them for making this project possible.

Maria Eichhorn, 'Artist's Statement: Maria Eichhorn Talks About Her Solo Exhibition at Chisenhale Gallery (As told to Himali Singh Soin)', *Artforum* (14 April 2016). (artforum.com)

Francis Alÿs is a Belgian-born artist based in Mexico City.

Rasheed Araeen is a Pakistani-born British artist, writer and curator based in London.

Marwa Arsanios is an American-born artist based in Beirut.

Jonathan Beller is Professor of Humanities and Media Studies, the Pratt Institute, New York.

Walter Benjamin (1892–1940) was a German-Jewish critical theorist and writer associated with the Frankfurt School.

Franco 'Bifo' Berardi is an Italian media theorist and media activist.

Claire Bishop is Professor of Contemporary Art, The Graduate Center, City University of New York.

Luc Boltanski is a French sociologist and Director of Studies, L'École des hautes études en sciences sociales (EHESS), Paris.

Nicolas Bourriaud is a curator and critic, and Director, La Panacée/Centre de culture contemporaine, Montpellier.

Julia Bryan-Wilson is Associate Professor, Modern and Contemporary Art, University of California, Berkeley.

Sabeth Buchmann is Professor of Modern and Postmodern Art and Head of the Institute for Art Theory and Cultural Studies, Academy of Fine Arts Vienna.

Maria Chekhonadskih is a Russian curator, art critic and theorist.

Ève Chiapello is a French sociologist and Director of Studies, L'École des hautes études en scienes sociales (EHESS), Paris.

Chto Delat is a Russian collective of artists, critics, philosophers and writers working to merge political theory, art and activism.

Alice Creischer is a German artist and curator based in Berlin.

Clémentine Deliss is a British-born independent curator and publisher.

Jeremy Deller is a British artist based in London.

Nick Dyer-Witheford is Associate Professor in the Faculty of Information and Media Studies, University of Western Ontario.

Maria Eichhorn is a German artist based in Berlin.

Kodwo Eshun is a British-Ghanaian artist and theorist, and Lecturer in Visual Cultures, Goldsmiths, University of London.

Harun Farocki (1944–2014) was a German filmmaker and video artist.

Silvia Federici is an Italian-American activist and Professor Emerita, Hofstra University, New York.

Fischli & Weiss are Swiss artists Peter Fischli (b. 1952) and David Weiss (1946–2012).

Mark Fisher (1968–2017) was a British cultural theorist and Lecturer in Visual Cultures, Goldsmiths, University of London.

Claire Fontaine is a Paris-based artist collective.

Andrea Fraser is an American artist and Professor, Interdisciplinary Studio, UCLA, Los Angeles.

Liam Gillick is a British artist based in New York.

Melanie Gilligan is a Canadian-born artist based in New York.

María Teresa Gramuglio is Professor of Literature, University of Buenos Aires.

Isabelle Graw is Professor of Art Theory and Art History, Staatliche Hochschule für Bildende Künste (Städelschule), Frankfurt am Main, and editor of *Texte zur Kunst.*

Gulf Labor Coalition is a coalition of international artists and activists who aim to bring attention to migrant workers' rights in Abu Dhabi.

Haben und Brauchen is a Berlin-based informal platform advocating the recognition and preservation of self-organized artistic practice.

Tehching Hsieh is a Taiwanese performance artist based in Brooklyn.

The Invisible Committee is a collective and anonymous pen name.

Marisa Jahn is an American artist and lecturer at The New School, New York, and MIT.

Caroline A. Jones is Professor of Art History, Department of Architecture, MIT.

Lamia Joreige is a Lebanese artist and filmmaker based in Beirut.

Anne Teresa de Keersmaeker is a Belgian dance choreographer.

Mary Kelly is an American feminist artist based in Los Angeles.

Jihoon Kim is Assistant Professor of Cinema and Media Studies, Chung-Ang University, South Korea.

Kata Krasznahorkai is a curator and research fellow at the University of Zurich.

Petra Lange-Berndt is Professor and Head of the Department of Art History, University of Hamburg.

Maurizio Lazzarato is an Italian sociologist and philosopher based in Paris.

Anthony W. Lee is Idella Plimpton Kendall Professor of Art History, Mount Holyoke College, Massachusetts.

Sarah Lehrer-Graiwer is a curator and teacher at Otis College of Art and Design, Los Angeles.

Isabelle Lindermann is a researcher at the University of Hamburg.

Lucy R. Lippard is a writer, art critic and exhibition organizer based in New Mexico.

Goshka Macuga is a Polish-born artist based in London.

Paolo Magagnoli is an Honorary Associate in the Department of Art Histor, University of Sydney.

Karl Marx (1818–83) was a German philosopher, social scientist and co-author, with Friedrich Engels, of *The Manifesto of the Communist Party* in 1848.

Achille Mbembe is a Cameroonian philosopher, political theorist and teacher at the University of the Witwatersrand, Johannesburg.

Adrian Melis is a Cuban artist based in Athens.

Jasmina Metwaly is a Polish video artist based in Cairo.

Gustav Metzger (1926–2017) was a German-born artist based in London.

Paweł Mosćicki is a philosopher and lecturer at the Institute of Literary Research, Warsaw.

Antonio Negri is an Italian social and political theorist and philsopher.

Ahmet Öğüt is a Turkish-born conceptual artist based in Amsterdam and Berlin.

Michelangelo Pistoletto is an Italian artist based in Turin.

Precarias a la Deriva is a feminist collective based in Madrid concerned with highlighting the experiences of precarious workers in the current economy.

Jacques Rancière is Professor of Philosophy, The European Graduate School, Leuk-Stadt, Switzerland.

Raqs Media Collective are a collective of artists and curators based in New Delhi.

Gerald Raunig is a philosopher, art theorist and teacher at Zurich University of the Arts, and the European Institute for Progressive Cultural Policies, Vienna.

Philip Rizk is a Cypriot-born filmmaker and activist based in Cairo.

Irit Rogoff is Professor of Visual Cultures, Goldsmiths, University of London.

Nicolás Rosa (1938–2006) was an Argentinian essayist, literary critic and translator.

Martha Rosler is an American artist based in Brooklyn.

Dietmar Rübel is Chair of History and Theory of Art, University of Fine Arts, Munich.

Tino Sehgal is a British-German artist based in Berlin.

Santiago Sierra is a Spanish artist based in Madrid.

Robert Smithson (1938–73) was an American artist based in New York and New Jersey.

Nick Srnicek is Lecturer in International Political Economy at City, University of London.

Hito Steyerl is a German artist and filmmaker, and Professor of New Media Art, Berlin University of the Arts.

Mladen Stilinović (1947–2016) was a Croatian artist based in Zagreb.

Mierle Laderman Ukeles is an American artist based in New York.

Paolo Virno is Professor of Philosophy at the University of Rome.

Joseph Vogl is Professor of Literature and Cultural Theory, Humboldt-Universität Berlin and permanent Visiting Professor, Department of German, Princeton University.

W.A.G.E. is a non-profit organization based in New York concerned with the labour relationship between artists and institutions.

Anne Wagner is Professor Emerita, Modern and Contemporary Art, University of California, Berkeley.

Bibliography

This section comprises selected further reading and does not repeat the bibliographic references for writings included in the anthology. For these please see the citations at the end of each text.

Agamben, Giorgio, *Potentialities: Collected Essays in Philosophy*, ed. Werner Hamacher and David E. Wellbery (Stanford: Stanford University Press, 1999)

Agamben, Giorgio, *The Use of Bodies* (2014); trans. Adam Kotsko (Stanford: Stanford University Press, 2016)

*Arbeit**, ed. Silvia Eiblmayr and Katy Deepwell (Frankfurt am Main: Revolver, 2005)

Are You Working Too Much? Post-Fordism, Precarity and the Labour of Art, ed. Julieta Aranda, Brian Kuan Wood, Anton Vidokle (Berlin: Sternberg Press, 2011)

Arendt, Hannah, *The Human Condition* (Chicago: Chicago University Press, 2013)

Art Workers – Material Conditions and Labour Struggles in Contemporary Art Practice, ed. Minna Henriksson, Erik Krikortz, Airi Triisberg (2010) (www.art-workers.org/download/ArtWorkers.pdf)

Arvatov, Boris, *Art and Production* (London: Pluto Press, 2017)

Bagcioglu, Neylan, 'Artistic Labour: Seeking a Utopian Dimension', in *Cadernos de Arte e Antropologia*, vol. 5, no. 1 (2016) 117–33

Benjamin, Walter, 'The Author as Producer' (1934); trans. Anna Bostock, in *Understanding Brecht* (London and New York: Verso, 1998) 85–103

Berardi, Franco 'Bifo', *The Uprising: On Poetry and Finance* (Los Angeles: Semiotext(e), 2012)

Bin beschäftigt (Bremen: GAK Gesellschaft für Aktuelle Kunst, 2006)

Bishop, Claire, *Artificial Hells: Participatory Art and the Politics of Spectatorship* (London and New York: Verso Books, 2012)

Braidotti, Rosi, *The Posthuman* (Cambridge: Polity Press, 2013)

Brave New Work: A Reader on Harun Farocki's Film 'A New Product', ed. Nina Möntmann (Cologne: Verlag der Buchhandlung Walther König, 2014)

Bryan-Wilson, Julia, *Art Workers: Radical Practice in the Vietnam War Era* (Los Angeles: University of California Press, 2009)

Bryan-Wilson, Julia, 'Occupational Realism', *TDR/The Drama Review*, vol. 56, no. 4 (Winter 2012)

Bureau for Open Culture. A Manual for the Immaterial Worker (New York: Printed Matter, 2011)

Burgis, Tom, *The Looting Machine: Warlords, Tycoons, Smugglers and the Systematic Theft of Africa's Wealth* (London: William Collins, 2015)

Butler, Judith, *Precarious Life: The Powers of Mourning and Violence* (London and New York: Verso, 2004)

Caring Culture: Art, Architecture and the Politics of Public Health (Actors, Agents and Attendants series), ed. Marcus Miesen and Andrea Phillips (Berlin: Sternberg Press, 2011)

Castel, Robert, *From Manual Workers to Wage Labourers: Transformation of the Social Question* (Piscataway, New Jersey: Transaction Publishers, 2002)

Collectivism after Modernism: The Art of Social Imagination after 1945, ed. Blake Stimson and Gregory Sholette (Minneapolis: University of Minnesota Press, 2006)

Crary, Jonathan, *24/7: Late Capitalism and the Ends of Sleep* (London and New York: Verso, 2013)

Critique of Creativity: Precarity, Subjectivity and Resistance in the 'Creative Industries', ed. Gerald Raunig, Gene Ray and Ulf Wuggenig (London: MayFly Books, 2011)

Crossing Values/Valeurs croisées, Les Ateliers de Rennes, Biennale d'art contemporain (Dijon: Les Presses du Réel, 2009)

Cuenca, Alberto López, 'Artistic Labour, Enclosure and the New Economy', *Afterall*, no. 30 (Summer 2012) 4–13

Deleuze, Gilles, 'Postscript on the Societies of Control', *October*, vol. 59 (1992) 3–7

de Duve, Thierry, *Sewn in the Sweatshops of Marx: Beuys, Warhol, Klein, Duchamp* (Chicago: University of Chicago Press, 2012)

Deller, Jeremy, *All that is solid melts into air* (Hayward: Hayward Gallery, 2014)

The Deep of the Modern: A Subcyclopaedia, Manifesta 9: The European Biennial of Contemporary Art, ed. Cuauhtémoc Medina and Christopher Michael Fraga (Genk, Limburg: 2012)

Diederichsen, Diedrich, *On (Surplus) Value in Art: Reflections*, No. 1 (Berlin: Sternberg Press, 2008)

Dimitrakaki, Angela, *Gender, ArtWork and the Global Imperative: A Materialist Feminist Critique* (Manchester: Manchester University Press, 2013)

Economy: Art, Production and the Subject in the 21st Century, ed. Angela Dimitrakaki and Kirsten Lloyd (Liverpool: Liverpool University Press, 2015)

Egenhofer, Sebastian, *Towards an Aesthetics of Production* (Zürich: Diaphanes, 2017)

Engels, Friedrich, *The Condition of the Working Class in England* (New York: Penguin Books, 1987)

Eribon, Didier, *Returning to Reims* (Los Angeles: Semiotext(e), 2013)

Exhausting Immaterial Labour in Performance. Joint issue of *Le Journal des Laboratoires* and *TkH Journal for Performing Arts Theory*, no. 17 (October 2010)

The Fall of the Studio: Artists at Work, ed. Wouter Davidts and Kim Paice (Amsterdam: Valiz, 2009)

Flemming, Peter, *Resisting Work: The Corporatization of Life and its Discontents* (Philadelphia: Temple University Press, 2015)

Foucault, Michel, *The Birth of Biopolitics: Lectures at the College de France, 1978–1979* (2004); trans. Graham Burchell (New York: Palgrave MacMillan, 2008)

Gielen, Pascal, *The Murmuring of the Artistic Multitude: Global Art, Memory and PostFordism* (Amsterdam: Valiz, 2010)

Gill, Rosalind, and Andy Pratt, 'Precarity and Cultural Work in the Social Factory? Immaterial Labour, Precariousness and Cultural Work', *On Curating*, vol. 16 (2013) 26–40.

Godard, Jean-Luc, *Arbeit, Liebe, Kino: Rette sich wer kann (Das Leben)* (Berlin: Merve Verlag, 1981)

Gorz, André, *Reclaiming Work: Beyond the Wage-Based Society* (Cambridge: Polity Press, 1999)

Harvey, Sylvia, *May '68 and Film Culture* (London: British Film Institute, 1978)

Hatherley, Owen, *The Chaplin Machine: Slapstick, Fordism and the International Communist Avant-Garde* (London: Pluto Press, 2016)

Hochschild, Arlie, *The Managed Heart: Commercialization of Human Feeling* (Berkeley and Los Angeles: University of California Press, 2012)

Home, Stewart, *The Art Strike Papers* (Edinburgh: A.K. Press, 1991)

Horne, Victoria, 'The Art of Social Reproduction', *journal of visual culture*, vol. 15, no. 2 (2016) 179–202

It's the Political Economy, Stupid: The Global Financial Crisis in Art and Theory, ed. Gregory Sholette and Oliver Ressler (London: Pluto Press, 2013)

Jones, Caroline A., *Machine in the Studio: Constructing the Postwar American Artist* (Chicago: University of Chicago Press, 1996)

Kafka, Franz, 'A Visit to a Mine', *The Metamorphosis & Other Stories*, trans. Willa and Edwin Muir, (New York: Schocken Books, 1995) 155–8

Kiaer, Christina, '"Into Production!": The Socialist Objects of Russian Constructivism', in *Transversal Texts*, vol. 3 (2009) (http://eipcp.net/transversal/0910/kiaer/en)

Kunst, Bojana, *Artist at Work: Proximity of Art and Capitalism* (Washington: Zero Books, 2015)

Kris, Otto, and Ernst Kurz, *Legend, Myth and Magic in the Image of the Artist: A Historical Experiment* (New Haven and London: Yale University Press, 1979)

Labour and Wait, ed. Julie Joyce (Santa Barbara: Santa Barbara Museum of Art/Santa Monica: Ram Publications, 2013)

Lazzarato, Maurizio, *Marcel Duchamp and The Refusal of Work* (Los Angeles: Semiotext(e), 2014)

Living Labour, ed. Milena Hoegsberg and Cora Fisher (Oslo: Henie Onstad Kunstsenter, 2013)

Lorey, Isabell, *State of Insecurity: Government of the Precarious* (London and New York: Verso, 2015)

Mandel, Ernest, *Late Capitalism* (1972); trans. Joris de Bres (London and New York: Verso, 1999)

Marx, Karl, *Capital: A Critique of Political Economy, Vol. I (1867)*; trans. Ben Fowkes (London: Penguin, 2004)

Mastaii, Judith, *Social Process/Collaborative Action: Mary Kelly 1970–75* (Vancouver: Charles H. Scott Gallery, 1997)

McKee, Yates, *Strike Art: Contemporary Art and the Post-Occupy Condition* (London and New York: Verso, 2016).

McRobbie, Angela, *Be Creative: Making a Living in the New Culture Industries* (Hoboken, New Jersey: John Wiley & Sons, 2015)

Meltzer, Milton, *Slavery: A World History* (Boston: Da Capo Press, 1993)

Menger, Pierre-Michael, 'Artists as Workers: Theoretical and Methodological Challenges', *poetics*, vol. 28 (2001) 241–54

Mertes, Cara, 'There's No Place Like Home: Women and Domestic Labour', in Dirt & *Domesticity: Constructions of the Feminine* (New York: Whitney Museum of American Art, 1992) 58–73

Molesworth, Helen, 'House Work and Art Work', *October*, no. 92 (Spring 2000) 71–97

Negri, Antonio, and Michael Hardt, *Empire* (Cambridge, Massachusetts: Harvard University Press, 2000)

Osten, Marion von, 'Irene ist Viele! Or What We Call "Productive" Forces', *e-flux journal*, no. 8 (September 2009)

Oushakine, Serguei A., '"Against the Cult of Things:' On Soviet Productivism, Storage Economy and Commodities with No Destination', *The Russian Review*, vol. 73, no. 2 (2014) 198–236

Papadopoulos, Dimitris, and Vassilis Tsianos, 'The Autonomy of Migration: Animals of Undocumented Mobility' (http://translate.eipcp.net/strands/02/papadopoulostsianos-strands01en)

Pollock, Griselda, *Vision and Difference: Feminism, Femininity and Histories of Art* (London and New York: Routledge, 2003)

Post-Fordism and its Discontents, ed. Gal Kirn (Maastricht: Jan Van Eyck Academie, 2010)

Rahtz, Dominic, 'Indifference of Material in the Work of Carl Andre and Robert Smithson', *Oxford Art Journal*, vol. 35, No. 1 (2002) 33–51

Rancière, Jacques, *The Politics of Aesthetics* (London: Bloomsbury Academic, 2013)

Reckwitz, Andreas, *The Invention of Creativity: On the Aestheticisation of Society* (Cambridge: Polity Press, 2017)

Sekula, Allan, 'Reading an Archive: Photography between Labour and Capital', in *The Photography Reader*, ed. Liz Wells (London and New York: Routledge, 2004) 443–52.

Sennett, Richard, *The Corrosion of Character: The Personal Consequences of Work in the New Capitalism* (New York: W.W. Norton, 2000)

Simondon, Gilbert, *On the Mode of Existence of Technical Objects* (1958); trans. Cecile Malaspina (Minneapolis: Univocal Publishing, 2017)

Sohn-Rethel, Alfred, *Intellectual and Manual Labour: A Critique of Epistemology*; trans. Martin Sohn-Rethel (New York: Macmillan, 1978)

Spivak, Gayatri Chakravorty, 'Can the Subaltern Speak?', in *Marxism and the Interpretation of Culture*, ed. Cary Nelson and Lawrence Grossberg (London: Macmillan, 1988) 271–313

Stakemeier, Kerstin, and Marina Vishmidt, *Reproducing Autonomy: Work, Money, Crisis and Contemporary Art* (London: Mute Books, 2016)

Stiegler, Bernard, *Automatic Society: Volume 1, The Future of Work*, trans. Daniel Ross (Cambridge: Polity Press, 2016)

Tiqqun, *Theory of Bloom* (Berkeley: LBC Books, 2012)

Toscano, Alberto, 'The Maid and the Money-Form', *Meta Mute* (25 April 2014) (http://www.metamute. org/editorial/articles/maid-and-money-form)

Weeks, Kathi, *The Problem with Work: Feminism, Marxism, Antiwork Politics and Postwork Imaginaries* (Durham, North Carolina: Duke University Press, 2011)

What People Do for Money, Manifesta 11: The European Biennial of Contemporary Art (Zürich, 2016)

'Women's Work', *n.paradoxa: international feminist art journal*, vol. 27 (January 2011)

Work Ethic, ed. Helen Molesworth (University Park, Pennsylvania: Penn State University Press, 2003)

Work to do! Self-Organization in Precarious Working Conditions, ed. Sønke Gau and Katharina Schlieben (Zürich: Shedhalle, 2009)

Workers Leaving the Workplace (Łodzi: Muzeum Sztuki w Łodzi, 2010)

Work, Work, Work: A Reader on Art and Labour, ed. Jonatan Habib Engqvist, Annika Enqvist, Michele Masucci, Lisa Rosendahl, Cecilia Widenheim (Berlin: Sternberg Press, 2012)

ACKNOWLEDGEMENTS

Editor's acknowledgements
I am grateful to Iwona Blazwick and the Whitechapel Gallery for commissioning this volume. Ian Farr and Francesca Vinter deserve deep thanks for their editorial work, as does Philippa Hurd for her fluent translations. This book would not have been possible without the generosity of the authors: I am profoundly grateful to all those who gave permission to reproduce their writings, in particular Kata Krasznahorkai, Isabelle Lindermann and Adrian Melis, who wrote statements especially for this volume, and Julia Bryan-Wilson, whose exemplary research had great influence on this publication. I would also like to thank warmly my (very hard working) artist friends, most of all Nadja Kurz, Melanie Börner, Marten Schech, Johanna Rüggen and Max Kowalewski; the members of the post-graduate school 'Materiality and Production' at the Heinrich-Heine-Universität Düsseldorf, in particular Timo Skrandies, Daniel Blanga-Gubbay, Emanuele Coccia, Katharina Kelter, Louis Schreel and Julia Vomhof; as well as Kerstin Flasche, Ralf Gutjahr, John Malamatinas, Sarah Sigmund and Bettina Uppenkamp. My deepest gratitude goes to Dietmar Rübel, Petra Lange-Berndt, Daniel Herrmann and Isabelle Lindermann for their advice and support, and last but not least my parents and my late grandmother Rosa.

Publisher's acknowledgements
Whitechapel Gallery is grateful to all those who gave their generous permission to reproduce the listed material. Every effort has been made to secure all permissions and we apologize for any inadvertent errors or omissions. If notified, we will endeavour to correct these at the earliest opportunity. We would like to express our thanks to all who contributed to the making of this volume, especially: Saul Anton, Rasheed Araeen, Marwa Arsanios, Jonathan Beller, Claire Bishop, Nicolas Bourriaud, Julia Bryan-Wilson, Sabeth Buchmann, Maria Chekhonadskih, Alice Creischer, Chto Delat, Jeremy Deller, Maria Eichhorn, Fischli and Weiss, Claire Fontaine, Liam Gillick, Gulf Labor Coalition, Haben und Brauchen (Julia Lazarus), Philippa Hurd, Marisa Jahn, Caroline A. Jones, Lamia Joreige, Jihoon Kim, Kata Krasznahorkai, Mierle Laderman Ukeles, Petra Lange-Berndt, Anthony W. Lee, Isabelle Lindermann, Lucy Lippard, Achille Mbembe, Paolo Magagnoli, Adrian Melis, Pawel Mosćicki, Ahmet Öğüt, Precarias a la deriva, Raqs Media Collective, Irit Rogoff, Dietmar Rübel, Joanna Sokołowska,

Hito Steyerl, Mladen Stilinović, W.A.G.E., Hamza Walker, Iona Whittaker. We also gratefully acknowledge the cooperation of: *Artforum*, *Bomb*, University of Chicago Press, e-flux, Duke University Press, I.B. Tauris, University of Minnesota Press, The MIT Press, MIT Press Journals, *Mousse*, NAi Publishers, Peter Lang, Pluto Press, The Renaissance Society, Ronald Feldman Gallery (Megan Paetzhold), Semiotext(e), Verso.

Whitechapel Gallery is supported by

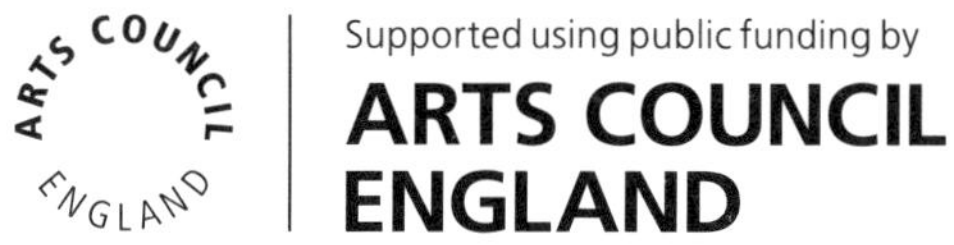